Degrees in Violence

Degrees in Violence

Robert Mugabe and the struggle for power
in Zimbabwe

DAVID BLAIR

continuum
LONDON • NEW YORK

CONTINUUM
The Tower Building, 11 York Road, London SE1 7NX
370 Lexington Avenue, New York NY 10017-6503

www.continuumbooks.com

First published 2002
Reprinted 2002

British Library Cataloguing-in-Publication Data
A catalogue record for this book is available from the British Library.

ISBN: 0-8264-5974-9 (hardback)
     0-8264-6239-1 (paperback)

Typeset by Kenneth Burnley, Wirral, Cheshire
Printed and bound in Great Britain by Creative Print and Design Wales, Ebbw Vale

Contents

To my parents

Introduction

Shiva Naipaul used the opening page of *North of South,* his bleakly compelling account of an African journey, to describe a book's introduction as a 'self justifying exercise, a kind of special pleading on behalf of a book whose nature and purpose might so easily be misunderstood'. Let me vindicate Naipaul's words to the full. What follows is not a biography of Robert Mugabe, nor is it a comprehensive history of Zimbabwe since the achievement of independence in 1980.

Instead, the heart of this book is found in the tumultuous period when I was privileged to be a spectator of events. From the moment that Mugabe lost a referendum in February 2000, a remarkable political drama began unfolding. One of the few serving African presidents to have led the struggle against colonial rule – the last standard-bearer of a famous generation – began fighting like a tiger to hold power against an opposition born from the spiralling economic collapse of his country. This is an account of that vicious struggle for power, as it appeared to a journalist who observed it. The mind and personality of Mugabe dominate the narrative and so this book delves into his life story and provides a survey of events from 1980 onwards. Yet the election rallies, farm invasions, food riots, fuel queues and officially inspired terror of 2000–2001 lie at its core.

This story is not over, for no one yet knows the outcome of the struggle. I have not had access to official sources in Zimbabwe; indeed, my access to the country itself was abruptly curtailed, and so my analysis of the decisions and motives of the ruling élite is necessarily fallible. What follows is a snapshot of an extraordinary, beautiful, multiracial country moving through a climactic period of its history.

DAVID BLAIR
Cape Town
December 2001

Acknowledgements

I am indebted to the hundreds of Zimbabweans from all walks of life who entrusted me with their stories, often at considerable risk to themselves. For their protection, many of the names in this book have been changed.

I owe an immense amount to my colleagues on the *Daily Telegraph*. Alec Russell was a guiding light from my first tentative days trying to earn a living as a journalist. Without his unfailing kindness and wise advice, I would certainly have gone home in failure. Stephen Robinson sent me to Harare in the first place, allowed me generous space on his foreign pages and offered constant support. Anton La Guardia was a brilliant and considerate colleague during his visits to Zimbabwe; indeed, I was probably the first stringer in history who genuinely welcomed the arrival of his bureau chief. Charles Moore was good enough to allow me time off to write this book. On the foreign desk, I received nothing but support and kindness from Paul Hill, Francis Harris, Patsy Dryden, Sebastien Berger, Robin Gedye and Theresa Jeffrey.

This book owes much to my fellow journalists in Harare. They were always generous with information and advice, while their company enlivened many long days on the road. I offer my grateful thanks to: Jan Raath, Angus Shaw, Grant Ferrett, Basildon Peta, Andy Meldrum, Cris Chinaka, Firle Davies, Iden Wetherell, Mduduzi Mathuthu, Howard Burditt, Joe Winter, Stella Mapenzauswa, Rob Cooper, Mike Hartnack, Conrad Nyamutata, Luke Tamborinyoka, Geoff Nyarota, Edwina Spicer, Susan Njanji, Paul Cadenhead, Martin Rushmere, Mercedes Sayagues, Chengetai Zvauya, Brian Hungwe, Sandra Nyaira, Lloyd Mudiwa and Energy Bara. Nine of these friends and colleagues were assaulted, arrested or deported during the events covered by this book.

However bad the news, my life in Harare was made enjoyable by many people. I am especially grateful to Robert Adams and Nicky Harford, with whom I stayed immediately after arriving in Zimbabwe. For touring the country with me, watching bad movies, consuming long lunches, organizing my birthday party or simply keeping me in good cheer, I offer my thanks to: Sarah Michael, Lisette Ramcharan, Vanessa Burditt, Richard Lindsay, Mike Jack, Diana Mitchell, and Lyzzie and Rory O'Donoghue.

For granting me interviews in London, I am grateful to Lord Carrington, Peter Longworth CMG and Christina Longworth. Others working in the confines of Whitehall, who would not wish to be named, also helped. You know who you are, and I am grateful. Needless to say, responsibility for any errors in the pages that follow is entirely mine.

Lastly, for ensuring my departure from Harare and thus giving me the chance to write this book, I must thank Jonathan Moyo.

DAVID BLAIR

Acronyms and Expressions

Acronyms

ANC	African National Congress
CFU	Commercial Farmers' Union
CIO	Central Intelligence Organisation
MDC	Movement for Democratic Change
NCA	National Constitutional Assembly
NDP	National Democratic Party
RF	Rhodesian Front
UANC	United African National Council
Zanla	Zimbabwe African National Liberation Army
Zanu-PF	Zimbabwe African National Union – Patriotic Front
Zapu	Zimbabwe African People's Union
ZCTU	Zimbabwe Congress of Trade Unions
ZD	Zimbabwe Dollar
Zexcom	Zimbabwe Ex-Combatants' Foundation
Zipra	Zimbabwe People's Revolutionary Army

Shona expressions

Chinja Maitiro	Change your ways (MDC slogan, meaning more than the literal translation)
Gukurahundi	The wind that sweeps away the chaff before the rains (popular term for the Matabeleland atrocities)
Hondo	War
Mabhunu	Derogatory term for white man
Murungu	White man
Mangwanani	Good morning
Pamberi ne	Forward with
Pasi ne	Down with
Pungwe	Political meeting

Prologue

If the white farmers do not give us what we want, they will bury themselves down six feet. (Chenjerai Hitler Hunzvi, leader of Zimbabwe's War Veterans' Association, 15 July 2000)

A sea of fists rose and fell while hoarse, ear-splitting chants echoed around the courtyard. At the base of a 14-storey tower block, a large crowd had gathered. Old men dressed in ragged trousers, torn shirts and multicoloured flip-flops bellowed with rage. Haggard women with blankets wrapped around their waists cradled wailing babies. Barefoot, emaciated street children, dressed only in tattered shorts, danced and sang excitedly. Standing at the front of the crowd was a cluster of smart figures wearing suits and dark glasses, with mobile phones held to their ears. They seemed calm, composed and self-satisfied as they led the chants of their followers.

Shouting loudest was the dominant element of the mob – teenage boys dressed in what had become their uniform. Each wore a white T-shirt emblazoned with the inscrutable, bespectacled face of President Robert Mugabe, above the words 'Vote Zanu-PF'. As they roared their anger, chants mingled with the wails of babies and excited screeches of street urchins to create a crescendo of fury and fear. Over 2,000 of Mugabe's fanatical supporters, the shock troops of Zimbabwe's regime, had massed for another rally. Once again, the headquarters of his Zanu-PF party (Zimbabwe African National Union – Patriotic Front) in central Harare rang with their cries.

Outside the entrance to the courtyard, 100 yards from the boiling mass of the crowd, the subdued objects of much of their anger huddled together. We were a small, quiet group on that day. About six journalists from the international media and Zimbabwe's beleaguered independent press had arrived to cover the rally. Together, we represented the global conspiracy that Mugabe claimed was bent on toppling his regime and wrecking his country.

Judging by the cries from the crowd, they all believed him. To the mob before us, we were devils incarnate, the living, breathing embodiments of Mugabe's enemies. Two thousand fists rose and 2,000 voices roared their hatred of – well – us actually. By now, I was quite familiar with the chants heard at all Zanu-PF rallies. They open with the phrase *'pasi ne'*, which in Shona, Zimbabwe's main language, means 'down with'. Words like *'murungu'*, meaning 'white man', often feature. The mob went through their customary routine with gusto.

'Pasi ne British!' shouted a man at the front of the crowd. Hundreds of clenched fists punched the air. *'Pasi!'* roared the mob.

'Pasi ne murungu!'

'Pasi!', came the reply.

'Pasi ne British imperialism!'

'Pasi!'

We talked together, feigning unconcern. All of us had covered Zanu-PF rallies before, yet this one seemed more menacing than usual; indeed, none of us could quite summon the courage to enter the courtyard and approach the crowd. We all hid our nerves with self-consciously casual conversation. I chatted to Cris Chinaka, the Harare bureau chief of Reuters, Firle Davies from the BBC, Andy Meldrum from *The Guardian* and Howard Burditt, a Reuters photographer.

Suddenly a dozen women turned their attention on us. They waved and shouted in Shona, while others on the fringe of the crowd glared with open hostility. Amid the high-pitched shrieks, I caught some words. *'Tino kuurayayi'* they yelled. *'Ibeai pano kana.'*

I turned to Cris Chinaka, the only Shona speaker present. 'What are they saying, Cris?'

'They're shouting "Go away from here, or we will kill you",' he replied simply.

At that moment, the knot of women broke away from the crowd and ran towards us, waving, stabbing their fingers and screaming. Two were dressed in colourful outfits, the rest ragged, drawn, impoverished and wearing Mugabe T-shirts. All their faces were contorted, their eyes wild with hatred. As they drew near they broke into English.

'Go, get away from here.'

'You write lies, you are all liars, get away from here.'

'We don't want to see you here, you whites.'

'Go, white liars, just go.'

The next moment, we were surrounded, while a group of men armed with clubs hovered on the edge of the crowd, staring in our direction. I was suddenly reminded of numerous interviews with the bleeding victims of Zanu-PF mobs. Many had recounted how women sparked a mood of hysteria before thugs moved in for the assault.

A plump woman wearing an expensive, flowing dress stabbed her finger at me. 'You must get away from here right now you white pig, or we will kill you,' she said. It was difficult to think of a suitable reply. None immediately occurred to me. I developed a sudden interest in the tree beside me and studied it with keen attention. About 20 men had moved away from the crowd and were shouting 'Go, just go.'

'What do you think?' I asked Howard, as three women screamed in his face. He smiled thinly.

'A tactical retreat might be in order.'

We were models of diplomacy, tact and decorum. 'Of course we will go,' we told the women. 'We're sorry to have upset you.' We moved away from the shrieking mass as casually as we could. We turned our backs on Zanu-PF headquarters and walked towards the Sheraton hotel, a safe haven about 200 yards away. It seemed like miles. With every step we fought back an impulse to break into a run. But apparently satisfied with their handiwork, our tormentors allowed us to retreat unmolested.

Once inside the car park of the Sheraton, we huddled together once again. The rally was being organized by veterans of the guerrilla war against white rule of the 1970s. Chenjerai Hitler Hunzvi, the notorious leader of the War Veterans' Assocation, would be addressing the crowd. While his hatred for journalists was legendary, he liked nothing more than being mentioned in the newspapers and getting his face on television. If we could speak to him, or one of his cronies, our safe passage into the rally would be guaranteed.

I rang Andrew Ndlovu, one of Hunzvi's henchmen. In Zimbabwe, you never quite know what reception you will get. I had met Ndlovu a couple of times and, while making it perfectly clear that he considered me a misguided agent of the wicked forces of British imperialism, he had always been friendly. He answered his mobile phone while standing in the midst of the rally. I could hear the chants in the background. 'David, my friend, how are you?' he asked.

'Andrew, we've been trying to cover your rally but some of your friends, erm, didn't seem too pleased to see us. They chased us away in fact. Do you think you could give us an escort so we can enter safely?'

'Oh, of course, of course, we welcome the press,' he replied. 'I will send someone to get you immediately.'

A few minutes later, a smiling figure arrived at the entrance of the Sheraton car park. Instead of a Mugabe T-shirt, he wore flowing, green robes and a white cap. 'Are you the journalists please?' he asked. 'My name is Godwin.' He shook hands with each of us in turn, reversing the grip with every shake in the African fashion. 'You follow me and everything will be OK.' We retraced our steps and headed towards the crowd, one smiling man with six nervous journalists in tow.

Ahead was the Zanu-PF headquarters building, a familiar Harare landmark found, appropriately enough, on Rotten Row. An enormous cockerel – the symbol of Zanu-PF – surmounts the modern office block, making it unmistakable. A gift from the Chinese Communist party, the building did not simply accommodate the most powerful men in Zimbabwe. Members of Mugabe's politburo occupied the offices on its upper floors, while the lower reaches of the building had been turned into a vast dormitory for Zanu-PF's shock troops. The gangs who waged a brutal onslaught against the party's opponents lived, ate and slept in this sinister construction. For that reason, most people in Harare gave it a wide berth.

We walked through its gates and entered the courtyard. We stayed close to Godwin as he led us through the crowd, towards the entrance of the building, where Hunzvi and his henchmen sat, shaded from the African sun. At first we encountered nothing more than hostile stares. One face after another, young and old, male and female, twisted with hatred.

We pushed through the crowd, sweating bodies pressing against us. Then the insults began. '*Mabhunu, mabhunu,*' people hissed, the abusive term for whites roughly equivalent to '*kaffir*'. A youth wearing a Zanu-PF T-shirt thrust his face within inches of mine. His eyes were yellow, inflamed by drugs, his breath reeked of alcohol. 'You white dog,' he rasped. In front of me, a woman grabbed Firle Davies by the arm. 'White bitch,' she screeched.

As we moved towards the front of the crowd and became visible to everyone, a steady murmur of anger began. It rose steadily. Within seconds, it had become a roar. '*Mabhunu, mabhunu, pasi ne mabhunu!*' Two thousand voices shouted their hatred. I saw Hunzvi sitting back in his chair, a broad grin spreading across his face. He was clearly enjoying himself. Our safety depended solely on him and he was savouring this demonstration of power. Without Hunzvi's protection, the mob appeared quite willing to tear us limb from limb. In a brief moment of panic, I thought that was exactly what they had in mind. Bring in the journalists and spear them to death. But then we were led to the steps at the building's entrance. We sat at the feet of Hunzvi and his henchmen, hemmed in by the mob on three sides.

I found myself pressed against a plump woman wearing a red outfit covered with pictures of Mugabe. The President's face was emblazoned across the enormous, heaving prow of her bosom. Spread before me was a sea of hostile faces. I turned to my neighbour and offered the Shona greeting: '*Mangwanani*'. She burst out laughing and then, with a rapid jerk of her head, spat on my shoulder. Globules of white saliva ran down my sleeve. The woman's friends roared with laughter.

On my right sat Chengetai Zvauya, a reporter from *The Standard*, an independent newspaper fiercely critical of the regime. He was clearly known to the crowd. Suddenly dozens of fingers were pointing and volleys of abuse were hurled towards him. 'Sell-out, sell-out,' came the cry. 'Traitor, traitor.' While my pieces for the *Daily Telegraph* passed largely unnoticed in Harare, his were read on every street corner, and now the crowd was determined that he would pay the price. A man in a dark cap and leather jacket seized Chengetai by the arm and dragged him to his feet.

Chengetai was wild eyed with terror. He spoke in rapid-fire Shona, pleading his innocence, defending himself with a desperate fervour. The storm of abuse continued. To our shame, none of Chengetai's colleagues intervened. We were all rooted to the spot with fear, convinced that if we raised our voices, worse would follow. Then he was bundled away by two men. Together with the other journalists, I had the impression that Chengetai was merely ejected from the rally. Only later did we learn that he was dragged inside the headquarters building, held for two hours and severely beaten.

I am sorry to say that once Chengetai had been hauled away, something I had done nothing to prevent, I concentrated solely on doing my job. I had to cover Hunzvi's speech and then escape in one piece. The jostling and abuse, the hostile glares and hysteria all faded from consciousness. I remember feeling a great surge of relief as Hunzvi finally got to his feet. He wore blue jeans and a black leather jacket, with a Mugabe T-shirt underneath. His sweating, bald pate glinted in the sunlight as he waved his fist and led the mob in chants of obedience to their master. This time, the cries began with '*Pamberi ne*', meaning 'forward with'.

'*Pamberi ne* Zanu-PF!', shouted Hunzvi.

'*Pamberi!*' came the answering shout.

'*Pamberi ne* Comrade President R. G. Mugabe!' a mass of hands punched the air in unison.

'*Pamberi!*' they roared.

When Hunzvi had finished his roll-call of chants, he ranted at the crowd in his high-pitched, childish voice. At that moment, the followers of this faintly ridiculous figure had been placed above the law. With Mugabe's full support, they were occupying over 1,000 white-owned farms and were blamed for the murders of five landowners and an unknown number of their black workers. For the benefit of the journalists present, Hunzvi spoke in broken English. I made a verbatim note of his words and they went as follows: 'The land must be taken from the whites. There can be no compromise. This is our land. If the white farmers carry on offering what they are offering, they will be offered six feet under. We are saying, we have been patient enough. If the white farmers do not give us what we want, they will bury themselves down six feet. The British say they will be evacuating their citizens. Let me tell you, when we start, they will not be able to evacuate them.'

This was Saturday, 15 July 2000. As Hunzvi rose to address his followers in the winter sunshine, farms across Zimbabwe were being raided, looted and, in some cases, burned to the ground. His 'war veterans' were fakes and most had never served in the bush. Yet this motley collection of thugs and murderers had become the shock troops of Mugabe's regime. The first phase of their campaign had been the violent invasion of white–owned farms. Mugabe had reawakened deep grievances from the colonial era and vowed to dispossess the 4,000 remaining white farmers. Their property would be handed over to poor blacks, thereby reversing the central injustice of the past, which had left millions of acres of prime land in the hands of a tiny minority. The poor blacks would, incidentally, be expected to support Mugabe in perpetuity in return for his largesse.

The next stage of the campaign was a brutal onslaught against the Movement for Democratic Change, the main opposition party. As Hunzvi spoke, his mobs were rampaging through remote villages and heaving, impoverished townships, hunting down suspected supporters of the MDC. Operating from a network of base camps, usually Zanu-PF offices through-out the country, they had forced the opposition underground in vast areas of Zimbabwe. By that morning, Hunzvi's men had murdered over 37 sus-pected MDC supporters and thousands more had been assaulted, raped, abducted, burned alive or tortured.

All this had unfolded against a background of economic disaster. Zimbabwe was once among the most developed countries in Africa. On that Saturday, it was the fastest-shrinking economy on the continent. Inflation ran at 57 per cent, the petrol stations were empty and queuing for fuel had become a national pastime. When we had fled into the car park of the Sheraton, nobody inside the hotel had noticed for the simple reason that the building was virtually empty. Tourism had been wiped out, unemployment exceeded 50 per cent and whole industries were closing. Every street corner was awash with beggars and abandoned children.

To Hunzvi and Mugabe, all this was the fault of the tiny white minority, at that time numbering no more than 70,000, about 0.6 per cent of the pop-ulation. Behind them were the British, scheming to re-colonize Africa. The Western media was lying about Zimbabwe and demonizing Mugabe. All the paranoia and vindictiveness of a ruthless regime struggling to hold power had surged to the surface. A country of 12 million people was being torn apart in the process.

As Hunzvi's speech went on and on, I decided to leave. Together with my colleagues, I ran the gauntlet of the crowd once more. This time, I blanked out the hostility; I ignored the stares and the shouted abuse washed over me. But when I reached the back row of the mob, a burly man kicked me on the leg. Then he laughed.

Prologue

Above me fluttered the green, red, gold and black stripes of the Zimbabwean flag, flying beside the headquarters of the party that had fought for the country's independence and once clung to the ideal of racial reconciliation. At that moment, it was impossible to imagine the hope and optimism that had greeted Zimbabwe's birth as a free nation barely 20 years before. It seemed inconceivable that Mugabe had once spoken the words of a passionate peacemaker, filled with zeal for unity and forgiveness.

Chapter 1

Our Country, All of Us, Together

1980 and before

Zimbabwe cannot just be a country of blacks. It is and should remain our country, all of us, together. (Zanu-PF election manifesto, February 1980)

You have given me the jewel of Africa. (Robert Mugabe to Ian Smith, 3 March 1980)

To roars of approval from the packed terraces of the football stadium, 100 soldiers marched past, side by side. As the khaki-clad troops presented arms, blazing floodlights illuminated their sweating faces – black and white, drilling together with absolute precision. Barely four months earlier, these men had been killing one another.

For the euphoric crowd witnessing the ceremony marking the birth of independent Zimbabwe, it seemed almost too good to be true. Soldiers from three opposing armies formed the ranks of the guard of honour. Now they marched as one – winners and losers, in perfect step. The victors had served in two black guerrilla forces and the leader of the largest was at the centre of attention on this joyous night.

Robert Mugabe was about to be sworn in as Zimbabwe's first Prime Minister and his nerves showed. As he took the oath of office, shortly before midnight on 17 April 1980, his hands shook. He played with his glasses, appeared unsure of what to do with their heavy frames, and finally snapped them off as he read: 'I, Robert Gabriel Mugabe, do solemnly swear that I will faithfully serve Zimbabwe in the office of Prime Minister of the government.' His words were drowned in cheers from the crowd and staid applause from the dignitaries beside him on the platform – Prince Charles, representing the Queen, Lord Soames, the last Governor of Rhodesia, and Lord Carrington, the British Foreign Secretary.

At midnight, the Union Flag slid down the pole, followed by a blue

9

spotlight, while the band struck up 'God Save the Queen' and the audience clapped politely. Then the new flag of Zimbabwe was raised, and the terraces exploded with the ear-splitting sound of euphoria. Some of the whites in the VIP enclosure wept openly, but it turned out that they had been tear-gassed by mistake. So delirious were the 40,000 massed in the grandstand that the police fired a volley of tear-gas canisters to keep control. Rufaro stadium in the capital, Salisbury (about to be re-named Harare), would never witness a moment of such innocent, intoxicating euphoria again.

Mugabe took power over a country with a history of bitter racial conflict stretching back to the arrival of the white 'pioneer column' in 1890. Zimbabwe was the last of 15 British colonies in Africa to achieve independence and few were burdened with such a convoluted, troubled history. The colony had been founded in 1893 by Cecil Rhodes, the buccaneering diamond magnate and imperialist ideologue, and named Southern Rhodesia in his honour. Attracted by its lush farming land and generous deposits of gold, white settlers had flocked across the Limpopo river to set up home in Queen Victoria's new domain.

Britain allowed them almost complete freedom to govern its colony and they duly transformed Rhodesia into an apartheid state in all but name. Everything, absolutely everything, was designed to guarantee their privilege. Cruelly ingenious electoral laws ensured their political dominance. Of the 65 seats in parliament, blacks could hold a maximum of 15, and even that concession, made as late as 1961, had been hotly disputed. Schools, hospitals and housing were racially segregated and in the sweeping plains of Rhodesia, most of the fertile land was reserved for white farmers.

Ian Smith became Prime Minister in 1964 at the head of the Rhodesian Front, a party that shamelessly played on the worst fears and prejudices of the 228,000 whites living among 4.8 million blacks. Unable to persuade Britain to grant independence to Rhodesia as a white-dominated state, Smith promptly made a Unilateral Declaration of Independence on 11 November 1965. It was illegal, treasonable and the first rebellion by white settlers since the Boston Tea Party of 1776. But Smith had ensured that Britain would be unable to impose black majority rule on Rhodesia and most whites enthusiastically supported this unlikely rebel, a former Spitfire pilot in the Royal Air Force who had served with distinction in the Second World War.

At first, the black population was almost eerily quiescent. Yet the white rebellion against Britain soon prompted a black rebellion against Rhodesia. By 1972, African guerrillas had launched a brutal war against Smith's regime. At least 30,000 were killed, with the whites suffering proportionately greater losses than any other ethnic group. Smith was vilified across the world as a 'racist tyrant' and the war was fought to a standstill. He was finally compelled to attend the Lancaster House conference in London in 1979, where an agreement emerged for black majority rule and Rhodesia's formal independence as the new nation, Zimbabwe, named after the Great Zimbabwe Ruins that had once been the capital of an ancient African empire. All that remained was an election, supervised by Britain, to choose the new nation's first leader.

One of the few points of agreement between white Rhodesians and the British government was that victory for Mugabe was a terrifying prospect. In the words of Lord Carrington: 'I viewed it with the greatest possible horror. One felt he was a Marxist and one wondered how awful he was going to be.'[1] Mugabe's hardline reputation had been created by countless inflammatory speeches delivered since he achieved dominance over his movement in 1976. In a typical radio address, broadcast in 1978, Mugabe urged his guerrillas to intensify their war against the white man: 'Let us hammer him to defeat. Let us blow up his citadel. Let us give him no time to rest. Let us chase him in every corner. Let us rid our home of this settler vermin.'[2] Language of this kind led whites to fear for their lives if he ever came to power. Mugabe seemed pre-ordained to inflame the brutal tradition of racial conflict.

His main opponent in the election could not have been more different. Joshua Nkomo, the leader of the Zimbabwe African People's Union (Zapu) was, from Smith's viewpoint, the least worst choice. Nkomo was pragmatic, portly, ebullient, lazy and moderate. He could justly claim to be the founder of the black nationalist movement and had alternated as firebrand orator, political prisoner and guerrilla leader since the 1950s. But through all this he remained a natural deal-maker, a conciliator, someone the whites could do business with. His relationship with Mugabe was one of mutual distrust and loathing, which also endeared him to the whites.

Nkomo's relaxed approach to life was best demonstrated by his habit of accepting guns from the Soviet Union and cash from Lonrho, the British mining company, at the same time. His crippling handicap was that he came from Matabeleland, the home of the minority Ndebele people, meaning that he could never hope to be a national leader. Nonetheless, when the votes were counted on 3 March 1980, many whites hoped that Nkomo would emerge as the leading force in their new government.

As for who would become Prime Minister, they trusted that no change would be required. Under international pressure, Smith had made a deal with black moderates in 1978 that allowed a nominal transition to majority rule while keeping the real power in the hands of whites. Abel Muzorewa had become Prime Minister in May 1979 and was destined to play a bit part in his country's history. 'Useless' is the word most commonly associated with this Gucci shoes-wearing Methodist bishop. Muzorewa was an amiable nonentity, a convenient puppet for Smith and a cover for the continuation of white power. Whites poured money into his United African National Council (UANC) and hoped that their puppet would be allowed to continue his performance.

Yet for all their foreboding about Mugabe, the realists believed he was going to win. Smith and Carrington had developed a keen mutual loathing, but on this point they were agreed. As Carrington put it: 'Once you accepted black majority rule, Mugabe was the black who would rule. I felt he was bound to win.'[3] The cruel logic of African elections usually divided parties along tribal lines and awarded victory to whichever represented the largest ethnic group. Mugabe was from the majority Shona people, comprising about 70 per cent of the population, whereas Nkomo's constituency among the Ndebele was barely 20 per cent. The numbers were on Mugabe's side, and that alone led Smith and Carrington to predict a Zanu-PF victory.

At 9 a.m. on Tuesday, 4 March 1980, the election results were announced on television. A white newsreader, visibly nervous, introduced the Registrar General, who read out the tally of parliamentary seats in flat, dispassionate tones. Muzorewa's UANC had won three. Nkomo's Zapu had taken 20. Mugabe's Zanu-PF had swept 57.

In the chaos that followed, the streets of the capital were filled with cheering crowds of blacks, singing, dancing and roaring their delight. Cries of '*Pamberi ne* Zanu-PF' echoed around the genteel department stores and hotels of central Salisbury. Among those celebrating Mugabe's victory was a 28-year-old miner and Zanu-PF 'political commissar' called Morgan Tsvangirai. Later to become Mugabe's most prominent opponent, Tsvangirai spent this euphoric day toasting his leader's triumph with friends at the mine and lustily singing every one of Zanu-PF's songs.

It was a remarkable victory, exceeding the expectations of everybody, with the possible exception of Mugabe himself. Even taking into account the 20 seats reserved for whites, all of which had earlier been won by Smith's followers, Mugabe had achieved an absolute majority of the 100-member parliament. Zanu-PF had enough to seats to govern alone and he could exclude all other parties from his cabinet.

The white community was shaken to its foundations. By 12 noon, three hours after the result was announced, hundreds of homes had been placed on the market, travel agents swamped with queues, white-owned shops locked up and closed and children taken out of school, while a handful of families packed everything they owned and headed for the South African border. White soldiers from the Rhodesian Light Infantry were ordered to maintain a reassuring presence on street corners and tearful people pleaded with these uniformed figures to somehow derail Mugabe's victory and rescue them at the eleventh hour. Some of the soldiers, hardened veterans of the bush war, broke down and wept.[4]

Yet Mugabe had done something remarkable. At 7 p.m. on the previous day, when the votes were still being counted and all the signs pointed to a Zanu-PF victory, Smith's phone rang. A polite voice asked whether he would be willing to meet Mugabe. Slightly bewildered, Smith accepted and left his home in the Salisbury suburb of Avondale. He drove to the spacious house that his enemy had recently acquired – 27 Quorn Avenue in Mount Pleasant, little more than a five-minute journey. Once the preserve of white Rhodesians, Mugabe had chosen one of the smartest addresses in the capital.

He greeted Smith at the door and ushered his visitor into the lounge, where the two men sat in armchairs, facing one another. It was an incongruous meeting. The racist tyrant, talking with the Communist terrorist. Smith usually referred to Mugabe as 'satan's apostle' and had authorized several bids to assassinate him. The guerrilla leader had returned the compliment by promising to shoot Smith the moment he came to power. Mugabe had accused the Rhodesian of 'crimes against the people' that would 'make him hang a thousand times over'. In a 1977 radio address, Mugabe said of Smith: 'The only valid kind of negotiations we are willing to allow this hard core criminal is with our firing squad.'[5]

Now the two men talked easily, even warmly. Mugabe could not have been more charming. Smith had expected a humourless fanatic. He met an engaging man, with a self-deprecating chuckle. Years later, Smith told me of his surprise:

> Mugabe could not have been more courteous and polite. He shook my hand, he patted my arm, he laughed. I couldn't get over this bloke's reasonableness, the breadth of his vision and particularly his desire for reconciliation and keeping the white people, accepting the need for them. He said 'We've got to have you.'[6]

Mugabe told Smith that he wanted to reassure the 200,000 whites, outnumbered by almost seven million blacks. They would not be victimized; on the contrary, he wanted them to stay in Zimbabwe and help rebuild the country. He was realistic enough to know that Zimbabwe's economy needed their crucial skills and capital. Mugabe wanted the white farmers to carry on producing food for the country. Only the land they were not using would be handed over to poor blacks. He stressed how fortunate he was to inherit a country with a skilled workforce, served by roads and railways that were among the best in Africa. With mounting surprise, Smith recalls Mugabe saying: 'You have given me the jewel of Africa.'[7]

On the night of his election victory, Mugabe broadcast to a nation divided between euphoria and despair. A nervous white woman introduced him as the 'Prime Minister elect, Comrade Robert Mugabe'. The message he delivered, in a quiet monotone, was aimed at the section of the nation that feared and loathed him. Dressed in a sober suit and the wide-rimmed glasses that had become his hallmark, Mugabe repeated the assurances he had given to Smith. There would be no retribution, no revenge. Zimbabwe would follow a policy of racial reconciliation. He concluded with the words:

> We will ensure there is a place for everyone in this country. We want to ensure a sense of security for both the winners and the losers . . . I urge you, whether you are black or white, to join me in a new pledge to forget our grim past, forgive others and forget, join hands in a new amity and together, as Zimbabweans, trample upon racism.[8]

The national mood changed instantly. The country had woken with its bitter racial divisions on full display. Blacks danced in the streets while whites cowered in their homes. After Mugabe's broadcast, the mood among the white community turned full circle. Despair became relief and then hope. Perhaps things might not be so bad after all. Perhaps Mugabe was not quite the ogre they had feared.

A few hours before, Rufaro stadium overflowed for the tumultuous Independence ceremony, Mugabe delivered a televised address and passionately repeated his message of reconciliation. His extraordinary words made a deep, almost indelible impression:

> The wrongs of the past must now stand forgiven and forgotten . . . If yesterday I fought you as an enemy, today you have become a friend. If yesterday you hated me, today you cannot avoid the love that binds you to me and me to you. Is it not folly therefore that in these circumstances anyone should seek to revive the wounds and grievances of the past?[9]

With these words, Mugabe became a symbol of racial reconciliation. Nelson Mandela would not be released from prison for another decade and when he took up the task of burying divisions between black and white, he followed in Mugabe's footsteps.

By this time, the new leader had already formed a government of national unity. Zanu-PF held enough seats to govern alone, but Mugabe went out of his way to include his rivals. Nkomo became Home Affairs Minister and three more Zapu figures joined the cabinet. The whites were not forgotten. David Smith, who had served as Finance Minister in the Rhodesian regime, took over the Industry and Commerce portfolio. Most remarkably of all,

Mugabe approached Denis Norman, the leader of the Commercial Farmers' Union, representing white landowners, and made him Zimbabwe's first Agriculture Minister. No clearer reassurance could have been offered to the white farming community.

To drive the message home, Mugabe addressed a meeting of 300 white farmers in the capital on 19 May. According to *The Times*:

> Mr Mugabe told the farmers that they had a guaranteed future. He addressed them at their request amid fears that their land would be seized without compensation . . . One farmer said, after hearing Mr Mugabe speak, 'I was thinking of quitting the country, but, after hearing Mr Mugabe, I and many like me will stay and see how things work out. Mr Mugabe was very reasonable, very sensitive to our problems and very genuine in his assurances'.[10]

The Prime Minister went still further. Whites were kept at the helm of the security apparatus of the state. General Peter Walls had commanded the Rhodesian army. Mugabe asked him to stay on and lead the new Zimbabwean armed forces. Ken Flower had presided over the Central Intelligence Organisation since 1964 and served three prime ministers. Mugabe rang the Rhodesian spy chief, who had masterminded countless dirty tricks against black guerrillas, and asked him to stay in his job.

When Mugabe met Flower, the two men joked about their various attempts to kill one another. In his memoirs, Flower described a relaxed, good-humoured leader: 'He laughed when I showed readiness to confirm some of our attempts to kill him. "Yes, but they all failed, otherwise we would not be here together," he remarked. "And do not expect me to applaud your failures".[11] Flower was effusive about his new master and described him as 'conciliation personified'.[12]

The world applauded and Mugabe was showered with praise. Few leaders have taken power on such a tide of goodwill. Lord Soames, whose main task as transitional Governor had been the supervision of the election, gave his seal of approval to the new Prime Minister. In his valedictory address on 14 April, he spoke of his 'admiration and respect' for Mugabe and the 'spirit of reconciliation which has formed the Prime Minister's words and actions and his obvious determination to sustain the unity of the nation'.[13] For Soames, the birth of Zimbabwe was 'nothing less than a series of miracles'.[14]

Mugabe would later claim that British newspapers were always his bitter critics, willing Zimbabwe to fail. Nothing could be further from the truth – during his early period in power, Mugabe received the sort of coverage that leaders would kill for. Flick through copies of, say, *The Times* from 1980 and you will not find a word of criticism. On the contrary, immediately after Mugabe's election victory, *The Times* praised his 'considerable, if perhaps calculated generosity' and said:

> He takes power with complete authority . . . his majority must be held to reflect the will of the electorate by and large . . . Mr Mugabe has started with fair and wise words. For the present, he should be given every incentive to carry out his stated policy of reconciliation and nation building.[15]

On 6 March, *The Times* devoted an entire leader to dismissing fears that Mugabe was a doctrinaire Marxist. Instead, the paper argued, he was a 'clever and well-informed man'.[16]

Nicholas Ashford, a British correspondent, met Mugabe and wrote that he:

> found it hard to believe that this was a man whose name had struck so much fear and hatred into the hearts of the country's white community . . . Mr Mugabe is a quietly spoken, neatly-dressed man who is intellectually head and shoulders above his black nationalist rivals. He is an ascetic figure who does not drink or smoke and smiles only rarely.[17]

John Humphrys interviewed him for the BBC and later described Mugabe as: 'Polite and diffident, an austere intellectual, as quietly spoken and measured as an ageing don and as conciliatory as an Anglican vicar at a meeting of the Mothers' Union.'[18] These two accounts may stand as typical of Mugabe's portrayal in the British media in 1980, and the popular image of a studiously impressive man would survive for many years to come.

Perhaps the most unlikely praise came from Ian Smith. He summoned the world's press on 7 March and announced that Mugabe was a man he could work with. He was 'forthright and responsible', said Smith, and *The Times* carried the headline: 'Mr Smith ready to join the man he denounced as Satan's Apostle.'[19] By his treatment of Smith, Mugabe sought to demonstrate beyond doubt his claim to the moral high ground. His old enemy, whose misjudgements had arguably done more than anything else to plunge the country into war, was allowed to stay in parliament and keep his farm. Later, Mugabe permitted him to enjoy a quiet retirement. As I write in December 2001, Smith still lives in Harare, loses no opportunity to attack Mugabe and seems curiously immune from persecution.

In the space of a few weeks, Mugabe had pulled off an extraordinary feat. Countless people who had thought him a ruthless fanatic became convinced of his goodwill. And it was not merely a matter of presentation. As we shall see, Mugabe had intense personal reasons for feeling bitterness and hatred, yet he showed genuine magnanimity and moral courage. After suffering at the hands of white Rhodesia, he apparently found the will to forgive. Yet to most of those who praised him, and even some of his closest allies, he remained an enigma.

★ ★ ★

Robert Gabriel Mugabe was born in Kutama on 21 February 1924. Unlike many African leaders, he has never sought to craft a mythology around his origins – there are no tales about Mugabe killing lions or winning boyhood wrestling matches. If he has consciously sought to create any impression about his background, it is one of mystery.

The outlines of the story are familiar. A brilliant, if lonely schoolboy became a teacher and was then caught up in the black nationalist movement. After imprisonment, exile and war he achieved his lifetime's ambition. Yet any examination of Mugabe's life reveals another side to the story – his character flaws were glaring, and from adolescence onwards, they constantly lurked beneath the surface.

The young Robert Mugabe grew up in Kutama, a Jesuit mission station, consisting of nothing more than a cluster of mud huts, a red-brick church and a primary school, ringed by an expanse of bush and elephant grass. The mission was barely 50 miles west of the capital, but it was such a small, isolated world that the distance might as well have been 500.

Kutama was situated in a 'Native Reserve' called Zvimba, where the laws of Rhodesia allowed blacks to farm the land. Mugabe's mother, Bona, was a devout woman who wanted her son to become a priest. His father, Gabriel, was a very different character. Although he worked as the mission carpenter, Gabriel Mugabe held firm views about the Jesuits, and a stubborn, rebellious streak was to have profound consequences for his family.

Robert was the third of six children and the simple life of his family revolved around the mission. When he was born, it was under the sway of Father Jean-Baptiste Loubiere, a Frenchman, who in the words of one account, ruled Kutama 'like a medieval fiefdom'.[20] Mass was compulsory for everyone at 6 a.m. and evening prayers ended the day at 7 p.m. Meanwhile, Father Loubiere stamped out the African way of life by banishing the spirit mediums, whose communication with the ancestors played an essential part in traditional culture, and forcing women to wear Victorian-style ankle-length dresses.

The stern discipline clearly rankled with Gabriel Mugabe. In about 1930 he had an angry confrontation with the Jesuit. The cause of this argument is unrecorded, but its consequence was severe. Father Loubiere banished the

Mugabe family from Kutama. They were forced to move to another village about seven miles away, although the children were allowed to stay in the mission primary school. They lived with relatives in Kutama during term time and every weekend they walked along the dusty track to their parents' home.

At about this time, Raphael, Robert's elder brother, died of an easily preventable childhood ailment, probably diarrhoea. The loss made Robert particularly close to Michael, his eldest brother, and the boys would walk to their parents' village together. But after one journey in early 1934, at the height of the African summer, Michael collapsed from exhaustion. Fearing the wrath of Father Loubiere, his father did not dare take the boy to Kutama's tiny clinic. Michael died the following day. Distraught, Gabriel Mugabe left the village and abandoned his family, who would hear nothing from him for another decade. Before his tenth birthday, Robert had lost two brothers and his father.

Shortly afterwards, Father Loubiere died and was succeeded by Father Jerome O'Hea, a kindly Irishman who took a very different view of his responsibilities. Father O'Hea brought the Mugabe family back to Kutama and took Robert under his wing. Under this tutelage, the quiet, diligent boy flourished. He excelled at school, easily outpacing his classmates. But Robert was a natural loner, usually to be found with his books. David Garwe, a contemporary, described a boy who 'kept a little apart from everyone . . . he always seemed to enjoy his own company'.[21] While he never sought companionship, Robert made a deep impression upon Father O'Hea. Years later, the Jesuit described a boy with 'unusual gravitas' and an 'exceptional mind and an exceptional heart'.[22]

When he finished primary school, Robert decided to become a teacher and Father O'Hea helped with a scholarship that allowed him to qualify in 1941. The 17-year-old Mugabe began teaching at his old school and supported his mother and siblings from a salary of £2 per month. His father returned in 1944, desperately ill and with three small children in tow. After leaving the family, Gabriel Mugabe had travelled almost 300 miles to Bulawayo, Rhodesia's second city, and taken another wife. According to some accounts, he ventured south to Johannesburg and worked in the gold mines of the Rand. He died within weeks of his return and Mugabe became responsible for six children.

In his spare hours, he would also read obsessively. Mugabe adopted a rigorous routine that he would stick to in later life, rising at 4.30 each morning, studying for several hours before school began, helping in the fields once classes were over, and continuing his reading after nightfall. All accounts describe him in the same words: diligent, quiet, studious, introverted. Above all, he was alone. Guy Clutton-Brock, a white Rhodesian whose tireless efforts to promote racial harmony would make him a national hero of Zimbabwe, knew Mugabe well and later described him as 'a bit of a cold fish'.[23] When he left Kutama in 1944, Mugabe was devoid of friends.

He led the peripatetic existence of a loner, moving restlessly from school to school, never teaching anywhere for more than a few terms. There is no evidence of any political involvement. In 1948 black workers brought Rhodesia to a halt with a general strike, but Mugabe did not participate. Then in 1949 he won a scholarship to attend Fort Hare University in South Africa. He arrived in a hotbed of African nationalism, one of the few places where black students could get a university education. Nelson Mandela had been expelled nine years earlier for leading a student strike, and one of Mugabe's contemporaries was Mangosuthu Buthelezi, the South African Zulu leader.

Once again, Mugabe excelled academically and made no lasting friends. He would later say that his 'hatred and revulsion for the system started at Fort Hare . . . I decided I would fight to overthrow it'.[24] Yet after taking a BA in history and English literature, Mugabe returned to Rhodesia in 1952 and took up teaching once again, with no apparent qualms about being on the payroll of the colonial government. Not until 1960, at the age of 36, would he become actively involved in nationalist politics.

The prospect of earning more money for the family led him to Ghana in 1958, where he joined the staff of St Mary's Teacher Training College in Takoradi. This period in West Africa was, perhaps, the crucial turning point in Mugabe's life. Before then, he could well have stayed in teaching and ended his days as headmaster of a secondary school. But in Ghana, he saw the first African nation to have achieved independence from Britain. For the first time in his life Mugabe lived in a country ruled by a black government, and Kwame Nkrumah, Ghana's President, was a living symbol of the struggle against colonialism. Mugabe was inspired by what he encountered.

Yet he was still an awkward, lonely figure. A picture taken of a group of teachers at St Mary's shows Mugabe sitting in the middle of a dozen of his peers. He stands out a mile – all the other teachers are smiling, relaxed and wearing flowing African robes, while Mugabe sits in a dark suit, sombre, unsmiling, with his hair neatly parted on one side, in the Western fashion. This solitary, almost monastic lifestyle began to change at last when he met a 25-year-old Ghanaian teacher called Sally Hayfron and, at the age of 34, set out to make a friend for possibly the first time in his life.

Their courtship seems to have been singularly embarrassing. If the official account is to be believed, romance blossomed when Mugabe interrupted one of Sally's lessons and chose to correct her, before rows of giggling children, on a 'minor aspect of central African geography'. Their love grew when he tried cooking a traditional Ghanaian dish for Sally – and spilt hot oil over himself. Sally's biographers tell us that Mugabe's cooking was usually 'disastrous' and his future parents-in-law insisted on calling him 'Bob', but nonetheless, by the time he returned to Rhodesia in 1960, the couple had 'an emotional commitment'.[25]

Mugabe dropped teaching and plunged into nationalist politics soon after his homecoming. He joined the executive of the National Democratic Party, then the main vehicle for black dissent. But he was a latecomer to a movement already dominated by others. Joshua Nkomo led the NDP and towered over the struggle. His chief rival was Ndabaningi Sithole, author of *African Nationalism*, the founding text of the cause.

Yet Mugabe's dedication and capacity for sheer hard work were quickly recognized. James Chikerema, another nationalist, had known Mugabe since childhood and later became a bitter critic. However, he recalled: 'The moment he joined us in the struggle, I knew he was going to go right up because, by nature, he was a very brilliant young man.'[26]

Mugabe married Sally in April 1961 at St Peter's Catholic church in Salisbury. Thanks to the Jesuits, his Catholicism was, and remains, deeply ingrained and Sally converted shortly before their marriage. Mugabe's friends have no doubt that Sally influenced him for the better. Naturally vivacious and gregarious, she drew him out of his shell, while also being a wise, restraining voice. But politics ensured that their married life could not have been more turbulent.

The Rhodesians banned the NDP in 1961 and Zapu was founded as a replacement. In turn, Zapu was banned in 1962 and the pressure grew the following year. Mugabe and his wife were forced to flee Rhodesia in 1963 by walking through the bush for three days and fording the Shashe river into Botswana. It was a traumatic journey, especially for Sally, who was four months pregnant and had previously suffered a miscarriage. The couple eventually arrived in Dar-es-Salaam, the Tanzanian capital, in time for the most crucial period of the struggle's brief history.

A schism rocked the movement and led to the creation of the breakaway Zimbabwe African National Union (Zanu), under the leadership of Sithole. The issues were complex, but in essence, black nationalists were now forced to choose between Zapu, largely Ndebele, and led by the pragmatic Nkomo; and Zanu, largely Shona and dominated by the supposedly radical figure of Sithole. Mugabe naturally chose Zanu and became the movement's Secretary-General.

Immediately after the schism, Zanu's leadership returned to Rhodesia, but without Mugabe. He stayed in Dar-es-Salaam for the birth of his son, Nhamodzenyika, which in Shona means 'My country is in trouble.' He stayed with Sally and the baby for three months. He would never see his son again.

When Mugabe returned to Rhodesia in December 1963, he knew that he would be arrested on arrival. The split in the movement had sparked major unrest in Salisbury's black townships and the government was handed a perfect excuse to jail the black leaders under the draconian Law and Order (Maintenance) Act. By the time Mugabe returned home, most of his colleagues were already in prison and he was duly arrested at the airport.

Unlike Mandela, he was never accused of terrorism – Rhodesia's guerrilla war had not even begun. Moreover, Mugabe was never given the benefit of due process. He was imprisoned under repressive laws that gave the government sweeping powers to jail anyone it didn't like. Mugabe would have received a detention order signed by Desmond Lardner-Burke, the Justice Minister, reading:

Greetings. Whereas under the terms of Section 50 of the Law and Order (Maintenance) Act certain powers are vested in me and whereas certain information has been placed before me and whereas due to confidential information which I cannot reveal, I am satisfied you are likely to commit acts of violence throughout Rhodesia. Now, therefore, I hereby direct that you be detained in Salisbury Maximum Security Prison until this order is revoked or otherwise varied by me. God save the Queen.

And so Mugabe was consigned to Salisbury Maximum Security Prison, where he joined five other men in a dark, squalid cell, with a bucket for a toilet. There were not enough beds and the prisoners took turns to sleep on the floor. Mugabe was constantly moved: after a few months in Salisbury, he was dispatched to Wha Wha detention centre and then to Sikombela camp in Midlands province.

Petty humiliations were added to the rigour of prison life. Just before Smith's declaration of UDI, Mugabe and his fellow political prisoners were herded together and forced to strip naked in front of scores of Rhodesian soldiers. After this demeaning ordeal, they listened to Smith's announcement of UDI. Any chance of a negotiated transition to black majority rule had disappeared. Rhodesia was now a rebel, breakaway state where Britain would be unable to restrain the wilder impulses of the Smith regime.

More devastating news soon arrived. In December 1966, a letter from Sally told Mugabe that their son was dead. Nhamodzenyika had died of cerebral malaria in Ghana just after his third birthday. Mugabe had last seen his son as a three-month-old baby. Eddison Zvobgo, a senior Zanu figure, was with him in the cell when he learnt the news and, years later, described a scene of despair. 'He was in tears . . . he just sat in the corner quietly. I watched him sob.'[27] Mugabe asked for parole to be allowed to bury his son.

21

The prison governor supported his request and urged the authorities to show compassion. Smith made an extraordinary personal intervention and ensured that Mugabe stayed behind bars. Nhamodzenyika was buried in a simple grave in Accra, the Ghanaian capital. His father was not among the mourners.

After this, Mugabe became even more of a loner and threw himself into study. Before his imprisonment he had completed a BSc in economics and a BEd, both by correspondence. Now he buried his grief by enrolling on London University correspondence courses and acquiring another four degrees – an MSc in economics, a Bachelor of Administration and two law degrees – bringing his total to seven.

The prison authorities made his studies as difficult as possible. In the middle of the postgraduate law course, they abruptly halted the flow of books. Mugabe overcame this obstacle with the help of his wife. Sally was living in exile in London and she spent her days copying out entire volumes by hand in the Legal Library in Russell Square. Her painstaking notes were posted to her husband as letters, and by this method, Mugabe added to his list of academic achievements.

The endless, obsessive study and the tragic death of Nhamodzenyika are the aspects of Mugabe's prison life that all official accounts choose to high-light. But they overlook the dominant theme. What consumed Mugabe's restless, ambitious mind as much as anything else was his own political advancement. The leadership of Zanu was behind bars and the future of the movement decided during these crucial years. Above all, Mugabe wanted to displace Sithole and seize the leadership for himself. Erratic, delusional and possessed by a cosmic vanity, Sithole was an easy opponent to finish off. He hanged himself in Zanu's eyes by renouncing an armed struggle against Rhodesia in 1969 and, from then on, Mugabe moved steadily against him.

Senior Zanu figures passed a motion of no confidence in Sithole in 1974 and named Mugabe as his successor. Almost simultaneously, Smith was placed under pressure by apartheid South Africa to release the black leaders from prison and negotiate a deal. The South Africans sought détente with moderate black governments in Zambia and Tanzania and needed to demonstrate their goodwill by moderating Smith's behaviour. To this unlikely pressure the Zanu and Zapu leaders owed their freedom.

Mugabe was released in November 1974 after almost 11 years in jail. Commonwealth leaders from Kenyatta to Kaunda and Nehru to Banda would often glory in calling themselves 'Prison Graduates'. With the sole exception of Nelson Mandela, none spent longer behind bars than Mugabe. When he walked out of Salisbury Prison and joined his sister, Sabina, in their modest home in the township of Highfield, the pattern of conflict in Rhodesia was determined.

From 1972 onwards, a guerrilla war was being waged to overthrow Smith, known to the nationalists as the Second *Chimurenga* (meaning 'revolution').[28] Zanu had established a military wing – the Zimbabwe African National Liberation Army (Zanla) based in neighbouring Mozambique – and drew most of its support from the Shona people. China was providing the arms and cash. Nkomo's Zapu was based in Zambia, backed mainly by the Ndebele, and the Soviet Union was supplying its guerrilla wing – the Zimbabwe People's Revolutionary Army (Zipra).

Mugabe needed to secure his dominance by assuming command of Zanla and winning over Samora Machel, who was about to become President of Mozambique. Only by escaping Rhodesia and reaching Mozambique could he achieve these tasks. In April 1975, he left for the border, seeking to flee his homeland for the second time and evade the surveillance of the Rhodesian Special Branch. By a cunning use of decoy cars, Mugabe was driven unnoticed to Nyafaru village in the foothills of the Nyanga mountains, near the rugged frontier. He stayed with Chief Rekai Tangwena, whose people had earlier been deported from their ancestral lands by the Smith regime. According to the official account, a spirit medium warned Mugabe that the army was on his trail and he left for the border hours before the village was searched. We also learn that 'Comrade Mugabe had brought with him a great many books and was forced to leave some of these behind.'[29] The habits of prison study were clearly difficult to shake off, even during a dangerous escape.

Mugabe scaled the Nyanga ranges, evading Rhodesian patrols and eventually arrived in Mozambique. Yet Machel did not make him welcome. Like other African leaders, Machel was bemused by the sudden removal of Sithole and knew nothing of his self-proclaimed successor. 'You've had a coup? A coup in Smith's prison? Whose coup is that?' Machel is said to have asked the erstwhile guerrilla leader. Mugabe was kept under house arrest for over three months, and almost a year passed before Machel recognized him as Zanu leader.

This is not the place to explore the tangled web of infighting that dogged the black liberation movement. Suffice to say that by mid-1976 Mugabe had achieved dominance over Zanu and emerged as the most prominent black guerrilla leader fighting the Smith regime. The military commanders backed him and Machel had, at first reluctantly, been won over.

By 1977, thousands of Zanla guerrillas had infiltrated Rhodesia from bases in Mozambique and they launched a wave of attacks on white-owned farms. Yet Mugabe remained aloof from the day-to-day military operations, leaving them to Josiah Tongogara, his commander in the field. Instead, he concentrated on the propaganda war, delivering scores of radio broadcasts and speeches.

The most cursory glance at these blood-curdling diatribes shows why white Rhodesians hated and feared Mugabe so much. Whites were branded variously as 'blood-sucking exploiters', 'hard-core racists' and 'sadistic killers'. When they were overthrown by Zanla's 'ever victorious, ever advancing forces', Mugabe vowed to impose a Marxist-Leninist society. A typical speech delivered in 1978 referred to Lenin as 'the brain and hero behind the application of Marxist-Leninist principles', spoke warmly of Stalin and called Fidel Castro a 'valiant fighter'.[30]

Mugabe's collected writings amount to nothing more than crude Marxism, couched in the ponderous English of the mission school, complete with sub-headings like 'antagonistic contradictions' and 'the matrix of con-tradictions'. The banality is staggering. Mugabe is capable of such sentences as: 'Our war must thus remain hot. It must grow hotter, nay hottest.'[31] Reading his 'revolutionary' works, one searches in vain for something resembling an original idea. While Mugabe's keen intelligence is undoubted, he is clearly no intellectual. He cannot claim authorship over anything new. His political credo was borrowed from Karl Marx and Frantz Fanon, with a strong dash of Mao Tse-tung – command economics in a peasant society, mixed with anti-colonial nationalism. In other words, he held the same opinions as almost every other African guerrilla leader. Mugabe may have had seven degrees, but what passed for his political thought was indistin-guishable from that of any illiterate rebel.

His period as a guerrilla leader contained other warning signs for the future. Few people were close to him and almost all of Zanla's top comman-ders fell under his suspicion at some stage. Many paid a bitter price for defiance, real or imagined. Wilfred Mhanda, second in command of Zanla from 1975 to 1976, was suspected of disloyalty and flung into jail by Mugabe in 1977, alongside 68 others. He described his leader as: 'Arrogant, paranoid, secretive and only interested in power'.[32]

The quiet, studious figure was chronically insecure and liable to lash out at anyone who appeared to pose a threat. Tongogara himself died in a mysterious car crash in 1979, which his leader may not have been entirely unconnected with. When Mugabe emerged from the bush in 1980 and made such an extraordinary impression on the world, he succeeded in sup-pressing the flaws that were all too apparent to those around him.

★   ★   ★

What are the threads running through Mugabe's life? He waged a brutal guerrilla war and survived over a decade behind bars. Ruthlessness and resilience must surely be his prime characteristics. From childhood onwards, or perhaps from the deaths of two brothers onwards, he was a loner, almost without friends. Until he married at the age of 37, no one was close to him. His self-discipline, intelligence and appetite for hard work were remarkable. But above all, he was a man who sought power, almost for its own sake. While ideology was important, holding the reins of authority took precedence over everything else. All Mugabe's ruthlessness and guile was used to this one end.

Lord Carrington dealt with Mugabe almost every day for three months during the Lancaster House conference. He described his former interlocutor as: 'A very forceful personality and a formidable intellect. He had an intellect which the others didn't have. He's a very formidable man, although I think rather sinister.'[33] Carrington respected Mugabe's abilities but was never able to like him.

Others talk of his charm and Mugabe's ability to make the right impression in private. Peter Longworth was British High Commissioner in Harare from 1998 until 2001, a period when Zimbabwe's relations with London collapsed irretrievably. Nonetheless, he recalled: 'Visitors would emerge after an hour with Mugabe saying "What a nice bloke", because he's very charming and very articulate and he's not devoid of humour. It's very difficult to relate the man you meet with the man ranting on television.'[34]

Far from resembling an African despot, Mugabe looks like the primary schoolteacher he once was. He is small, not much over 5 feet 7 inches tall, with curious, effeminate mannerisms. Always immaculately dressed, usually in a three-piece suit, he clearly goes to immense trouble over his appearance. Not a speck of grey hair is ever visible on the head of this septuagenarian, and a tiny moustache, which prompts unfortunate comparisons with Hitler, is always neatly trimmed. The personal life of this Jesuit-educated Catholic has not been without incident. From the late 1980s onwards, Mugabe conducted an affair with Grace Marufu, a secretary at State House almost 40 years his junior. By the time Sally died in 1992, Grace had already borne him two children and a third followed their marriage in 1996. The death of Sally robbed Mugabe of a crucial balancing influence and may help to explain his subsequent behaviour.

Perhaps the most curious side of Mugabe is how anglicized he appears. His English is impeccable and slightly nineteenth century ('We could not say them nay' is a favourite phrase). At some stage in his life, perhaps influenced by Father O'Hea, Mugabe clearly tried to adopt an English accent. Words like 'demand' or 'command' are pronounced in the well-modulated tones of a BBC newsreader. Until 1999 Mugabe made three or four private visits to London each year and, famously, was a regular guest at Claridges and devotee of Harrods. He follows cricket closely, once making the remarkable statement: 'Cricket civilizes people and creates good gentlemen. I want everyone to play cricket in Zimbabwe. I want ours to be a nation of gentlemen.'[35] Wilfred Mhanda believes that Mugabe has always 'wanted to be an English gentleman'.[36] While Mhanda exaggerates the point, it is obvious that this self-styled hammer of imperialism has a far more complicated attitude to Britain than his rhetoric would suggest. Respect, possibly even admiration, mixes with resentment and loathing.

But all the insecurity of the natural outsider lurks behind this appearance. Where does that come from? Perhaps from the scars inflicted by a singularly tragic childhood. Perhaps from the countless bruises left by the years of war, exile and imprisonment. Perhaps there is a more obscure explanation. Mugabe is from the Zezuru clan, one of the smallest branches of the Shona tribe, making him vulnerable to a minority complex. But it seems unreasonable to expect a well-balanced human being to emerge from his range of experiences.

Colin Legum, the veteran Africa correspondent of the *Observer*, who once knew Mugabe, describes him as a 'paranoidal personality'. This is someone who, while not being clinically paranoid, behaves in a paranoiac fashion when subjected to severe, sustained pressure.[37] This seems to explain the link between Mugabe's behaviour and his experiences. All those hard knocks pushed him to behave in a paranoiac fashion and drew out the insecurity and vindictiveness within him. That was, and remains, the central trait – and crucial flaw – of his exceptionally complex personality.

How would a leader with this array of characteristics react to the situation that Mugabe encountered in 1980? At the outset, it is important to pay tribute to his magnanimity. Those words of reconciliation on Independence Day and that friendly meeting with Smith cannot be swept aside. They required extraordinary moral courage from Mugabe. But having made that acknowledgement, were there any other explanations for his behaviour? Remembering Mugabe's overriding desire to hold power at all costs, was not reconciliation good politics as well? Would not a paranoidal personality have seen that more clearly than anyone else?

Mugabe had won a sweeping election victory, true enough, but appearances can be deceptive. When he took the reins of power, he clearly believed that an array of forces was poised to overthrow him. Most dangerous of these was Nkomo, his old rival and leader of the Ndebele. Moreover, in the shape of Zipra, he had a guerrilla army. An alert observer at the Independence ceremony might have spotted a warning sign for the future – Nkomo was not allowed into the VIP enclosure at Rufaro, he was consigned to an obscure corner of the terraces and, as he later wrote: 'Hidden away like something to be scared of.'[38] Mugabe was 'scared' of him, and of the whites, Zimbabwe's other discontented minority. Unreconstructed Rhodesians could move against him and apartheid South Africa would be only too willing to fuel a rebellion.

However exaggerated this assessment – and the evidence suggests that it was wildly exaggerated – Mugabe saw the situation of 1980 in these terms. He responded like an astute politician. He sought to use the euphoria of independence to his advantage by drawing his opponents in and winning them over with the language of reconciliation and unity. But it soon became clear that this was only the first stage. There was a second barrel to Mugabe's strategy and it was here that the traits of a paranoidal personality came into play. In 1980 he neutralized Nkomo, his most dangerous opponent. But that was not good enough for his suspicious, insecure mind. So Mugabe moved to destroy Nkomo and all his followers.

NOTES AND REFERENCES

1 Interview with the author, 11 December 2001.
2 Robert Mugabe, *Our War of Liberation*, Mambo Press, Gweru, 1983, p. 18.
3 Interview with the author, 11 December 2001.
4 See Barbara Cole, *The Elite*, Three Knights, Johannesburg, 1984, pp. 419–20.
5 Mugabe, *op. cit.*, p. 13.
6 Interview with the author, 8 December 1999.
7 *Ibid*.
8 Address to the nation, 4 March 1980.
9 Address to the nation, 17 April 1980.
10 *The Times,* 20 May 1980.
11 Ken Flower, *Serving Secretly*, John Murray, London, 1987, p. 2.
12 *Ibid.*, p. 273.
13 *The Times,* 15 April 1980.
14 *Time* magazine, 28 April 1980.
15 *The Times,* 5 March 1980.
16 *Ibid.*, 6 March 1980.
17 *Ibid.*, 5 March 1980.
18 *Sunday Times*, 25 February 2001.
19 *The Times*, 8 March 1980.
20 Nathan Shamuyarira *et al.*, *Sally Mugabe – A Woman With a Mission*, Ministry of Information, Harare, 1994, p. 5.
21 Quoted in David Smith and Colin Simpson, *Mugabe*, Sphere, London, 1981, p. 14.
22 *Ibid.*, p. 12.
23 *Ibid.*, p. 19.
24 Shamuyarira *et al.*, *op. cit.*, p. 7.
25 *Ibid.*, pp. 8–9.
26 Interview on BBC TV, *Rebellion*.
27 *Ibid*.
28 An uprising in 1896, ruthlessly crushed, had been the First *Chimurenga*.

29 Nathan Shamuyarira and Charles Utete, writing in *Our War of Liberation*, Mambo Press, Gweru, 1983, p. 13.
30 Mugabe, *op. cit.*, pp. 82–3.
31 *Ibid.*, p. 101.
32 Interview with Helen Suzman Foundation, December 2000.
33 Interview with the author, 11 December 2001.
34 Interview with the author, 31 August 2001.
35 *Sunday Times*, 2 February 1984.
36 Interview with Helen Suzman Foundation, December 2000.
37 See Legum's fascinating profile of Mugabe in *New Statesman*, 27 August 2001.
38 Joshua Nkomo, *Story of My Life*, Methuen, London, 1984, p. 215.

Note: throughout this book, the following are Harare newspapers: *The Herald*, *Sunday Mail*, *Daily News* and *Financial Gazette*. Other newspapers are British, with the exception of *The Dispatch* and *Guardian*, which are both South African.

Chapter 2

Cobras in the House

1981–99

Zapu and its leader Dr Joshua Nkomo are like a cobra in the house. The only way to deal effectively with a snake is to strike and destroy its head. (Robert Mugabe, 1983)[1]

Shortly before dawn on 8 March 1983, the former Home Affairs Minister of Zimbabwe and the founding father of the liberation struggle stumbled across a dry river bed and fled his country. Joshua Nkomo was a hunted fugitive, forced to abandon Zimbabwe in fear of his life, escaping first to neighbouring Botswana and then into exile in Britain. During the bush war, Nkomo had been imprisoned, hounded and vilified by the Rhodesians. But as he later wrote: 'Nothing in my life had prepared me for persecution at the hands of a government led by black Africans . . . Never before had I wished that I were dead, but I wished it then. It was the bitterest moment of my life.'[2] At the age of 66 he became a refugee from the country he had helped liberate.

Dressing your ambitions in convenient ideological garb is one of the oldest tricks in politics, and Mugabe proved a master. He was determined to make Zimbabwe a one-party state and liked to argue that this arrangement was uniquely suited to Africa. 'The one-party state is more in keeping with African tradition,' he said in 1984. 'It makes for greater unity for the people. It puts all opinions under one umbrella, whether these opinions are radical or reactionary.'[3]

Naturally the one party in question would be his party, Zanu-PF. However you dressed up the argument, the one-party state meant that Mugabe would rule supreme and unchallenged. Remorseless political logic dictated that Nkomo and Zapu must be swept away and their stronghold in Matabeleland, the home of the Ndebele, subdued.

From late 1980 onwards, Nkomo's job as Home Affairs Minister was steadily made impossible. His presence in the cabinet became purely symbolic and his decisions were ignored or quietly countermanded. In Nkomo's own words, he became nothing more than a 'china ornament sitting in the showcase'.[4] When former guerrillas from Zipra and Zanla fought each other in the Bulawayo suburb of Entumbane in November 1980, he was isolated still further.

Zimbabwe's new army was supposedly a merger of the Rhodesian forces and the two rebel groups. In fact, 'ex-Zipras', as they were known, were treated with deep suspicion and their contribution to the liberation war was constantly denigrated by Zanu-PF. Tribal antagonism between the two movements, one largely Shona, the other Ndebele, lived on. In protest, perhaps 4,000 'ex-Zipras' deserted from the army and in February 1981 another round of clashes between the rival ex-guerrillas rocked Entumbane, killing 300.

Nkomo was abruptly demoted in January 1981 and given the meaningless job of Minister without Portfolio. In August, Mugabe quietly admitted 106 military advisers from North Korea, a country he greatly admired. They began training a new unit, the Fifth Brigade, that would be placed under his personal control, outside of the army command structure. Its soldiers were drawn from the largely Shona ranks of Mugabe's old guerrilla force, Zanla. Step by step, he was carefully preparing an onslaught. Later, Nkomo would ruefully refer to Fifth Brigade as 'Mugabe's North Korean trained private army.'[5]

Then, on 17 February 1982, Nkomo was summarily sacked from the government and accused of plotting to overthrow Mugabe. All of Nkomo's Zapu allies in the cabinet were also dismissed. Arms caches had been discovered on four farms occupied by former Zipra fighters. Enough rifles, machine guns, mortars, rocket-propelled grenades and cases of ammunition to fill 50 railway wagons were found. Yet the government had known about these arms dumps for months and there was no evidence linking them to Nkomo. These facts were conveniently forgotten and Zapu was accused of planning rebellion.

Bandits, made up of former Zipra fighters, began operating in Matabeleland. They were quickly branded 'dissidents' and blamed for a series of outrages, notably the murder of six tourists in July 1982 and an attack on the prime minister's official residence the previous month. Mugabe seized on these incidents as his excuse. What followed haunts Zimbabwe to this day.

The Fifth Brigade was deployed in the dry, rugged bush of Matabeleland in January 1983, ostensibly to fight the dissidents. In fact, it waged a brutal war against the local people, with the aim of crushing Zapu and enforcing support for Zanu-PF. Within days, atrocities began. Entire families were burnt to death in huts, villages razed to the ground, their inhabitants shot, beaten and tortured. A remarkable report, *Breaking the Silence – Building True*

Peace, later documented the atrocities with meticulous accuracy and fairness. It is in the raw, verbatim testimony of the victims that the true horror of Fifth Brigade's murderous campaign is exposed. One woman recounted:

> They accused my husband of having a gun, which he did not have. They shot at him. The first two times they missed, but the third time they shot him in the stomach and killed him. They then beat me very hard, even though I was pregnant. I told them I was pregnant and they told me I should not have children for the whole of Zimbabwe. My mother-in-law tried to plead with them, but they shouted insults at her. They hit me in the stomach with the butt of the gun. The unborn child broke in pieces in my stomach. The baby boy died inside. It was God's desire that I did not die too. The child was born afterwards, piece by piece. A head alone, then a leg, an arm, the body – piece by piece.[6]

On any street corner in Bulawayo, or in any of the tiny, impoverished villages of Matabeleland, victims of the atrocities can be found. The era of the massacres is known as *Gukurahundi* – a Shona word meaning the 'wind that sweeps away the chaff before the rains'. Say that word to anyone you meet and they will often recount, in calm and quiet tones, a harrowing experience.

Beside a dirt track, in the shadow of the rocky Matopos hills, I met Joel Dube, who still shuddered to recall his encounter with Fifth Brigade in 1985, when he was a boy of eight. The soldiers came to his primary school and gathered all the children under a tree. They were made to chant the familiar slogans of Zanu-PF: '*Pamberi ne* Mugabe, *Pamberi ne* Zanu-PF.' But the children, aged between five and eleven, did not shout loud enough for the soldiers. 'They started beating us,' said Dube. 'They lined up the whole school and beat us one by one. They used the butts of their rifles and whips.' A teacher pleaded for the soldiers to show mercy to the screaming children. He was shot dead in front of his pupils. Dube spoke of Mugabe with controlled fury. 'His behaviour makes us hate him. He has been killing us,' he said.

In one of Bulawayo's heaving townships, I met Gideon Nyathi. His village was raided by Fifth Brigade in 1984:

> They came to the village and accused my father of keeping the dissidents. They took him to a house and shot him in the leg. He died of bleeding. They took a man of 21 and hanged him upside down from a tree. They beat him on the head with sticks and clubs until he died. They gathered all the people and then took a young man. They

crushed his head with stones in front of everybody. They said we were dissidents, but we had never seen a dissident. It was just a trick by the regime to kill the people.

The people had to be killed because they supported Zapu. It was as simple as that. By terrorizing Matabeleland, Fifth Brigade sought to crush Zapu and impose the dominance of Zanu-PF. The campaign amounted to nothing more than the military enforcement of a one-party state. The massacres are sometimes given the misleading label 'genocide'. But Mugabe never sought to eliminate the Ndebele as a people – he used terror and violence to break their allegiance to his opponents.

Perhaps inadvertently, Mugabe gave the game away. He denied any atrocities but candidly summarized Fifth Brigade's objective. In May 1984 Mugabe told the BBC: 'The situation is one which requires a change on the part of the people of Matabeleland. They must be reoriented.'[7] Mass murder was the chosen method of 'reorientation'. The 261 pages of *Breaking the Silence – Building True Peace* record atrocities of mind-numbing horror.

Five children, aged between seven and twelve, were shot dead by soldiers in March 1983, as they sat eating maize outside their home in the village of Nseze. A group of 22 terrified villagers, including women and children, were herded inside a hut in Solonkwe in July 1983. Soldiers set the hut alight and all inside were burnt to death. Troops lined up 62 villagers, including teenage girls, on the banks of the Cewale river in March 1983 and mowed them down with machine guns. Seven were critically wounded but survived by pretending to be dead; all the rest were killed. The tribal nature of the campaign was betrayed by the encouragement given to soldiers to rape Ndebele women. This would create 'Shona babies'.

Mugabe sought to starve his opponents into submission by imposing a food embargo on Matabeleland South province in January 1984. After three years of drought, the 400,000 people in the area were dependent on emergency supplies and all aid was halted for four terrible months. How many starved to death is unknown. We do know that 'people had to resort to eating insects and grass seeds to try to survive'.[8]

In all, tens of thousands were tortured, beaten, raped or imprisoned. The massacres have an enduring legacy. Amani Trust, a charity that helps the survivors, estimated in 1999 that 70 per cent of the adults in Matabeleland were living with memories of torture, either experienced or witnessed.[9] As for the death toll, no one will ever know. The number of confirmed murders by Fifth Brigade is 3,750, but the true figure could well be twice that.

Mugabe was fully aware of the atrocities. As early as November 1982 he was given a report by the Catholic Commission for Justice and Peace that documented a series of outrages committed by soldiers during the first operations in Matabeleland. He met a delegation of Catholic bishops on 16 March 1983 and was given 'damning evidence of 5 Brigade atrocities'.[10] A commission of inquiry appointed by the government heard scores of witnesses describe 'mass shootings, burning to death of people in huts, mass beatings, mass detentions, involving various methods of torture and general psychological harassment'.[11] After the commission had finished gathering evidence in January 1984, its report was suppressed by the government and has never been revealed.

Despite this wealth of evidence, Mugabe and his ministers chose a strategy of brazen denial. On 6 April 1983, three weeks after meeting the bishops, Mugabe said that reports of atrocities came from 'a band of Jeremiahs which included reactionary foreign journalists . . . and sanctimonious prelates'.[12] Yet in the same month he made an inflammatory speech that appeared to sanction the murder of villagers. 'Where men and women provide food for dissidents, when we get there, we eradicate them,' Mugabe said. 'We don't differentiate when we fight because we can't tell who is a dissident and who is not.'[13]

Mugabe angrily denied the existence of any mass graves. Interviewed in 1985, he said: 'Wherever you have operations, you are bound to have one or two untoward incidents, but not the mass graves. Where are they? You travel the whole length and breadth of Matabeleland and you won't find a single mass grave.'[14] Hundreds of mass graves have been found all over Matabeleland. There is barely a village without one.

As the massacres continued, Mugabe maintained relentless pressure on Zapu. Armed men attacked Nkomo's house in Bulawayo on 5 March 1983. By chance, he was away, so they killed his driver and two domestic servants and made clear that any member of the Nkomo family would suffer the same fate. At this point, he sought safety in Britain. Nkomo had no doubt that Mugabe wanted him dead and later wrote: 'Robert Mugabe had decided to have me out of the way and he evidently did not care what method was used.'[15]

Mugabe had earlier described Zapu and Nkomo as 'a cobra in the house' and said: 'The only way to deal effectively with a snake is to strike and destroy its head.'[16] Mugabe's verbal attacks on Zapu were unrestrained. At Zanu-PF rallies supporters waved banners reading 'Nkomo must be killed' and 'Nkomo must be hanged', while Mugabe denounced Zapu as 'evil' and vowed: 'The dissident party and its dissident father are both destined not only for rejection but for utter destruction as well.'[17]

He was absolutely right. Although Zapu held all 15 seats in Matabeleland in the 1985 parliamentary election, Nkomo was cracking under the strain. After returning to Zimbabwe in August 1983, he watched the murder and disappearance of his supporters and the inexorable destruction of his party.

His moral outrage seems to have been mixed with bewilderment, even disbelief of what was happening. In 1983, Nkomo said: 'I have done everything to support our independence, right from the beginning to this day, and I get this now from Prime Minister Mugabe, sending young men to come and kill me and my family.'[18]

Finally, Nkomo began secret talks with Zanu-PF. The price that Mugabe demanded for an end to the onslaught was the dissolution of Zapu, the incorporation of its leading figures into Zanu-PF and the advent of a one-party state. When the talks broke down in April 1987, Mugabe responded by effectively banning Zapu. Its offices were raided and surviving officials jailed.

Nkomo surrendered wearily. On 22 December 1987 he signed a 'Unity Accord' with Mugabe and the two men appeared together in a show of friendship. To save Nkomo's face, the agreement was officially described as a voluntary merger between Zapu and Zanu-PF, leading to the creation of an entirely new party that happened to be called Zanu-PF, led by Robert Mugabe. After almost five years of ruthless repression, Mugabe had achieved his goal. Nkomo rejoined the government as a largely powerless 'Minister in the Prime Minister's Office', Zapu was dissolved and Zimbabwe became a *de facto* one-party state. It was game, set and match to Mugabe. In 1988 he issued an amnesty protecting Fifth Brigade's soldiers from prosecution. As I write, not one has faced justice for any crime.

Mugabe won a notable victory abroad as well as at home. The official terror campaign in Matabeleland did no damage whatever to his international reputation. In September 1983, when Fifth Brigade's massacres were at their height, President Ronald Reagan received him at the White House and heard Mugabe assure America that 'peace is a cornerstone of my government's policy'. He also told Reagan that any Fifth Brigade soldier found guilty of 'excesses' would 'be brought to book'.[19] One week later, he arrived in Dublin for a banquet in his honour hosted by Garret Fitzgerald, the Irish Prime Minister. When Mugabe attended a summit of Commonwealth leaders in New Delhi in October 1983, he faced no questions about atrocities at home. Instead, he called Margaret Thatcher 'an ally of apartheid'[20] because of her opposition to sanctions against South Africa.

He continued his tours of the world and was garlanded with various accolades for his leadership of Zimbabwe's freedom struggle. Edinburgh University awarded Mugabe an honorary doctorate in 1984, just as Fifth Brigade was enforcing his murderous starvation policy on the people of Matabeleland South. Four years after this ruthless use of food as a political weapon, Mugabe was awarded the Africa Prize for his contribution to a 'sustainable end to hunger'.

There were two reasons for this extraordinary propaganda success.

Against the background of the Cold War, Mugabe had endeared himself to the West by repeatedly snubbing the Soviet Union. As we have seen, China had supplied his forces during the guerrilla war, while Moscow backed Nkomo. For that reason Mugabe treated the Soviet Union with deep suspicion and Moscow was not permitted to open an embassy in Zimbabwe until 1981. Like Mobutu in Zaire and Moi in Kenya, Mugabe became an African leader whom the West was anxious not to alienate with awkward questions about human rights. Throughout the massacres, Britain kept a 100-strong military training team in Zimbabwe. Remarkably, when Fifth Brigade was finally withdrawn from Matabeleland in 1986, its soldiers, by then notorious, were immediately given the benefit of a course run by British instructors.[21] Their hated unit was then disbanded and its British-trained troops dispersed to other formations.

Yet Mugabe's success went deeper. His government had carefully crafted a propaganda line about the Matabeleland massacres. Nkomo was said to be in command of a 'dissident army' that was conniving with apartheid South Africa to overthrow Mugabe. Perhaps Fifth Brigade committed the odd massacre, Mugabe's spokesmen argued, but the atrocities had been exaggerated by 'Jeremiahs' and were an inevitable, if regrettable part of a large-scale counter-insurgency campaign.

Armed dissidents certainly operated in Matabeleland and they were responsible for outrages. But according to the government's own estimate, they never numbered more than 400 and at no stage posed the slightest threat to Mugabe's grip on power. Moreover, there is no evidence linking them to Nkomo. The Zapu leader was not as innocent as he liked to sound. In the aftermath of his defeat in the 1980 election, Nkomo did consider all options, probably including the overthrow of Mugabe. A former commander of the Rhodesian Special Air Service once told me that he met senior Zapu figures in the early 1980s and discussed toppling Mugabe. But there is nothing to suggest that this ever went beyond bar-room talk. There was no conspiracy.

But an astonishing number of experienced observers fell for this propaganda. In his survey of the continent, *The Africans,* David Lamb buys the line that Nkomo had 'an army from the Ndebele speaking minority' which Fifth Brigade was deployed to deal with. Describing a rag-tag force of under 400 as an 'army' seems an exaggeration and assuming Nkomo's command over it goes well beyond the evidence. Lamb admits that Fifth Brigade 'undertook its assignment with enthusiasm' and murdered 'several hundred', but he goes on to vindicate its commander's handling of the situation: 'Mugabe, however, did not overreact as most African Presidents do in times of crisis and personal challenge.'[22] Writing as the massacres continued in 1984, Lamb called Mugabe 'scholarly, disciplined' and 'perhaps the most capable leader in black Africa'.[23]

This image of a studious, ascetic leader who had guided his country to freedom survived the inferno of Matabeleland. Mugabe still basked in the glory of 1980 and those who had praised him to the skies were reluctant to change their view. He may well have become convinced that he could get away with anything.

*   *   *

By the end of 1987, Mugabe had moved with consummate guile and ruthlessness to consolidate his power. A series of constitutional amendments was rushed through parliament that transformed the way Zimbabwe was governed. The original constitution, agreed at Lancaster House, had provided for a Westminster-style parliamentary democracy. Mugabe now broke out of that straitjacket.

The office of Prime Minister was abolished and replaced by an Executive Presidency, with sweeping powers. Mugabe was sworn in as President on 31 December 1987. Under Lancaster House, 20 of the 100 seats in parliament had been reserved for the whites. Mugabe ensured the removal of this clause and whites lost their last entrenched hold on power.

This step was overdue and fully justified. But the practical effect was the obliteration of the parliamentary opposition. In the 1985 election, 15 Zapu MPs and 20 white members had been returned, alongside one MP from the tiny Zanu-Ndonga party, creating an opposition block of 36. Once the Unity Accord swallowed the Zapu members and merged them with Zanu-PF, and the whites lost their quota of seats, the opposition was reduced at a stroke to one MP out of 100.

Zimbabwe's one-party state had become a reality. This was crucial for Mugabe. All the constraints of 1980 – the government of national unity, the presence of opposing parties in parliament – had been stripped away. Nkomo was politically dead and from 1990 served as a largely ceremonial Vice-President until his death on 1 July 1999. Mugabe did not go so far as to proscribe opposition parties and the one-party state was never enshrined in law. He did not need to. Instead, he just heaped unbearable pressure on his opponents and waited for them to surrender.

When parliamentary and presidential elections were held in 1990, Mugabe had already done enough to guarantee his dominance. Edgar Tekere, a former ally, challenged for the presidency and managed only 17 per cent of the vote, after a campaign in which intimidation prevented him from campaigning in large areas of Zimbabwe. Mugabe had a few more aces up his sleeve. At the 1990 election parliament was suddenly enlarged to 150 members, with 120 elected and the remaining 30 appointed by the President. So Zanu-PF started the contest with 30 seats in the bag. The election itself went exactly as Mugabe would have wished – Zanu-PF won all but three seats.

From Mugabe's point of view, these were model elections. Now that the opposition had been crippled once and for all, he felt secure enough to lift the state of emergency in July 1990, which had been in force ever since UDI in 1965. Then he hosted a summit of Commonwealth leaders in October 1991 and signed up to the Harare Declaration of democratic principles, committing Zimbabwe to the full range of political freedoms.

But if Mugabe displayed remarkable ruthlessness and cunning, his economic management was consistently disastrous. All the restrictions of a command economy – price controls, dividend controls, exchange controls – ensured that foreign investment was minimal. Meanwhile, the government ran a budget deficit year on year that averaged 10 per cent of gross national product. It printed money to cover the gap and the inevitable result was inflation and stagnant growth. For Mugabe's first decade in power, the economy grew by an average of 2.7 per cent each year. By the standards of his later performance, this was miraculous. But with annual population growth of 3 per cent each year, real incomes were actually declining. Unemployment grew every year and reached 26 per cent in 1990.

Remarkable improvements were achieved. Zimbabwe's massive expansion of education and health services was hailed as a model for other African countries. In 1980 Zimbabwe had just 177 secondary schools serving 66,000 pupils. By the year 2000 this had grown more than tenfold to 1,548 schools and 700,000 pupils. Over the same period, literacy rose from 62 per cent to 82 per cent of the adult population, one of the best records in Africa. Improved primary health care led to a rise in child immunization rates from 25 per cent to 92 per cent. But all of these real achievements were undermined by the mismanagement of the economy. Better educated, healthier Zimbabweans were becoming poorer.

After his election victory, Mugabe announced a radical change of course. He accepted a Structural Adjustment Programme prescribed by the International Monetary Fund in 1991 and pledged himself to the free market. He did not do so out of conviction. By now, his penchant for borrowing money meant that no one had any confidence in Zimbabwe government bonds. The only way of covering his budget deficit was to seek the support of the IMF. In return, Mugabe solemnly agreed an ambitious package of economic reforms. The Zimbabwe Dollar would be floated, import tariffs reduced, state industries privatized and the panoply of controls lifted.

He would later invent a myth that this marked the onset of Zimbabwe's economic decline and that the crisis was, therefore, all the fault of the IMF. In fact, Mugabe ignored most of the free market reform package and it was never implemented in full. Corrupt, loss-making, state industries remained in the public sector, most of the controls stayed in place and the economy continued its downward slide. However dominant Zanu-PF appeared, the disastrous decline of the economy, taking place silently behind the scenes, was storing up trouble for the future.

Mugabe's decision to throw in his lot with the IMF caused the first stirring of opposition since the crushing of Zapu. Now that parliament was supine, the critics emerged from the Zimbabwe Congress of Trade Unions, led by Morgan Tsvangirai. The relaxation of import controls, as demanded by the IMF, led employers to cut wages and Tsvangirai accused the government of using workers as a 'sacrificial lamb' for its economic reforms. He became an increasingly vociferous critic of Mugabe and was detained for five weeks in 1991 on trumped-up charges of being a South African spy.

★   ★   ★

None of this worried Mugabe. His supremacy was unchallenged and the elections of 1990 may be seen as the high-water mark of his fortunes. Repression of the most brutal kind guaranteed his dominance, but it would be wrong to imply that he lacked genuine popularity. As Tsvangirai told me, the Mugabe of 1980 had 'enormous popular support, he was a national hero. In fact, at that stage, I think I would have died for the man.'[24] Mugabe won his first election with 63 per cent of the vote, buoyed by his standing as the man who had led Zimbabwe's freedom struggle. Intimidation accounted for some of this, but there seems little doubt that he was the people's choice in 1980. This stronghold encompassed the largely Shona areas of Zimbabwe; in other words, everywhere except Matabeleland and Bulawayo. In Mugabe's heartlands – the provinces of Mashonaland, Manicaland and Masvingo – that support endured well into the 1990s.

In 1995, another round of parliamentary elections produced a 150-member House with 147 Zanu-PF MPs. As for the presidential contest that followed in 1996, Mugabe was challenged by two erratic, exhausted dinosaurs from the past – Abel Muzorewa and Ndabaningi Sithole. Both realized that the whole business was a waste of time and tried to pull out at the last minute. They were barred from doing so in order to create the façade of a genuine contest and Mugabe duly won 92.7 per cent of the vote. Most of the electorate retreated into apathy. The national turnout was a pitiful 31.7 per cent and in Bulawayo, Ndebele resentment ensured that it was just 16 per cent.

Yet if Mugabe had been nationally unpopular in 1996, surely a more credible candidate would have been found to challenge him. In retrospect, it is clear that the electorate divided into three portions – Mugabe supporters, Mugabe opponents and the completely apathetic. For as long as the first and the last groups overwhelmed the second, the leader was safe.

But quietly and inexorably, forces were at work that threatened to wreck this equilibrium. As we have seen, year after year, hundreds of thousands of teenagers were leaving school and facing lives of poverty, thanks to the steady decline of Zimbabwe's economy. By 1998 unemployment was approaching 50 per cent, economic growth was negligible and living standards were falling month by month. The number of hopeless, impoverished people was growing, almost by the day.

Other, more subtle changes were also at play. By the late 1990s a new generation had emerged with no memory of the liberation struggle. Mugabe had no special claim on their affections – unlike people of Tsvangirai's age, they had never called him a national hero. Zimbabwe, of course, has a very young population, and at the close of the 1990s more than half of its people could not remember the colonial era. For Mugabe, the most dangerous people in Zimbabwe were jobless, hopeless people who had known no leader except himself. Before the turn of the millennium, they were the majority of the population.

To make matters worse, the outside world had been transformed beyond recognition. The global collapse of Communism and the unchallenged dominance of America were shattering developments for a Marxist of 1960s vintage like Mugabe. Zimbabwe was notionally a Marxist-Leninist state where ministers called each other 'comrade' and the most powerful body in the land was the Politburo. With bewildering speed, Mugabe found himself in a changed Zimbabwe, where he no longer had an automatic claim on his people's loyalty, and a changed world, where his ideology had been routed.

From 1997 onwards these twin forces began undermining the foundations of Mugabe's regime and his fortunes underwent a dramatic reversal. First he came under pressure from his most ardent allies – the veterans of the guerrilla war, who still referred to him as 'our commander'. Under the leadership of Chenjerai Hitler Hunzvi, they demanded payments for their role in liberating Zimbabwe and putting Mugabe in power. With a burning sense of grievance, they pointed out that former soldiers in the Rhodesian army were paid pensions from government funds, while ex-guerrillas got nothing.

Perhaps realizing that he would need these allies to withstand the challenges ahead, Mugabe agreed to their demands in August 1997 and an extraordinary financial package was put in place. Each war veteran would be given a lump sum of ZD 50,000 (then worth about £3,000) together with monthly payments of ZD 2,000 (about £125). The total cost of the deal was a staggering ZD 4,2 billion (over £260 million). About 50,000 people were given the cash, even though fewer than 30,000 war veterans had been demobilized when the war ended in 1979.

Inevitably, fake war veterans with the right political connections took the opportunity to claim their share of a bonanza. Much of the money was invested in a company established by Hunzvi and his cronies called Zexcom (Zimbabwe ex-Combatants' Foundation). Few investors in Zexcom received any dividend – except, of course, friends of Hunzvi. A fund was established to compensate those who had been disabled or maimed in the war. It was shamelessly looted by senior figures in Zanu-PF, who claimed non-existent injuries and then awarded themselves compensation. Hunzvi maintained he was 117 per cent disabled and compensated himself with ZD 400,000 (then worth £25,000).

An entirely predictable sequence of events unfolded. This festival of corruption and looting was clearly unaffordable for a tiny economy already in crisis. The Zimbabwe Dollar nose-dived and the economy sank into even deeper recession. Mugabe tried to impose a range of new taxes to cover the cost of the payments, but these provoked a general strike in December 1997. This brought what might perhaps be called the two Zimbabwes eyeball to eyeball. One Zimbabwe was middle aged, rural, uneducated and steeped in the folklore of the liberation struggle. The other was young, urban, educated and unable to understand why their hardships must be worsened for the sake of people calling themselves 'war veterans'.

Tsvangirai's trade unionists symbolized the latter group and closed down the country, although the man himself paid the traditional price of defiance – a group of thugs burst into his office, beat him almost senseless and tried to throw him out of his tenth-floor window. The burly ex-miner fought back long enough for his security guards to rescue him. Even Zanu-PF's annual Congress protested about the new taxes and that clamour forced them to be withdrawn. With them went any notion of orderly accounting; instead, the Reserve Bank simply printed the money for the war veterans.

Simmering discontent in the black townships of Harare boiled over into food riots in January 1998. Police lost control and the army was deployed and ordered to shoot on sight. At least ten people were killed and hundreds injured as Zimbabwe's capital experienced 48 hours of anarchy. This was the first sign of open revolt by the new, disaffected generation of Mugabe opponents.

How did he respond to this challenge? Looking at his past, his counter-moves were, I suggest, entirely predictable. If the people no longer remembered the liberation struggle, he would remind them. Its rallying cries would be revived and used to unite the nation behind Mugabe once more.

So in November 1997 he suddenly listed 1,471 white-owned farms for compulsory seizure. Successive Rhodesian governments had ensured that white farmers owned most of the best land, while millions of blacks were confined to barren, overcrowded areas. This injustice was at the heart of the liberation war. Mugabe's guerrillas had been trained to 'politicize the masses' and when they held late-night meetings in remote villages, the promise they made was: 'We will give you the white man's land.' In his own idiom, this message had kept 'the masses' on his side in the 1970s, so Mugabe hoped it would do the same in the 1990s.

Unfortunately, the constitution agreed at Lancaster House guaranteed farmers the right to full compensation and Zimbabwe had no money to pay them. So Mugabe made the gesture, published the list, accompanied this with stern rhetoric, but nothing actually happened and no land was seized. Yet it showed the way his mind was working. He would ride back to popularity by resurrecting the battle-cries of the past.

He would also remind his people that he was still a military leader. When civil war erupted in the Democratic Republic of Congo in August 1998, Mugabe decided that Zimbabwe must intervene. The parlous state of his treasury meant that no money was available. Nonetheless, he ended up sending 11,000 troops, about one-third of his army, to prop up the regime in Kinshasa, then led by President Laurent Kabila. Zimbabwe's national interest in becoming embroiled in a ruinous war hundreds of miles from its borders was never explained. The conflict was so unpopular in Zimbabwe that a news blackout was imposed, while reports that the war cost £20 million per month were furiously denied. As I write, Zimbabwe's soldiers have entered their fourth year in Congo, with no indication of when they might be withdrawn. What this episode betrayed was a proud, stubborn man, seeking to find a role in a changed world by doing what he once did best – commanding soldiers in a war.

But there was, of course, a second strand to Mugabe's reaction to these pressures: they drove him back to those heights of paranoia. He had to find some way of explaining what was happening, why his people were criticizing him, and he fell back on the old list of culprits. The British and the whites were behind everything. An ambitious range of conspiracy theories came into play.

When the editor and chief reporter of *The Standard,* an independent weekly, published a story about an alleged plot to launch a military coup in January 1999, they were immediately arrested and tortured by the army. Mark Chavunduka and Ray Choto disappeared for almost a week and were electrocuted, beaten and half-drowned. The High Court ordered their release on three occasions and was simply ignored.

What did Mugabe do? He appeared on television and claimed that a vast plot was at work, seeking his overthrow. The British were, of course, the first suspects. With obvious fury, Mugabe talked of 'British agents planted in our midst, intent on overthrowing the state'[25] and then expanded the list of subversives to include all white Zimbabweans.

From that moment onwards, the pattern of events was clear. Day by day, the collapse of the economy was undermining Mugabe's grip on power. He would respond by taking land from the whites and reverting to the language of the liberation war, while blaming the whites and the British for every problem. A titanic struggle for power was beginning.

★ ★ ★

But when I arrived in May 1999, the first impression I had of Zimbabwe was absolute calm and peace. Having previously lived in the chaotic, pot-holed shambles of Kampala, the Ugandan capital, I was astonished by how prosperous Harare appeared. Supermarkets sold everything, cinemas showed the latest films and you could drive to spacious houses in leafy suburbs along immaculate roads with – a rarity in Africa – functioning traffic lights.

Mugabe had begun blaming the British for everything, but I had no difficulty in getting permission to work as a journalist. A helpful official at the Information Ministry was pleased to provide the necessary paperwork and I was granted accreditation for three years. Meanwhile, the small independent press in Harare criticized Mugabe with apparent impunity and foreign correspondents enjoyed unrestricted access to Zimbabwe.

Soon after my arrival, I went to see George Charamba, then Director of Information in the President's Office. He was welcoming, polite and friendly, but this encounter was, for me, the first real sign of what was unfolding behind the scenes. Charamba gave me the full story. Land would be taken from the white farmers – 'there can be no compromise on that' as he put it – and everything that was going wrong was the fault of the old enemies. The British and white Zimbabweans were responsible for every sparrow that fell.

I was flattered to learn that I too had my part in the global conspiracy. 'The British press is concerned about one thing and one thing only – furthering the British national interest,' Charamba told me. 'In a way, you have to admire it. I sometimes wish that all our journalists here in Zimbabwe had the same focus.'

According to Charamba, Britain's national interests dictated that the 4,000 white farmers should continue tilling the soil of Zimbabwe. So London was trying to oust the man who threatened them. It was as straightforward as that. 'Why are we so concerned about these white farmers?' I asked him. Charamba chuckled knowingly. 'Because you think that after the farms, we will move on to the mines and then on to all the other commercial enterprises you have here. And then you fear every other African country will do the same and you'll finally lose everything. After all, 70 per cent of your economy comes from Africa.' Charamba appeared absolutely certain of this. Britain was entirely dependent on its economic stake in Africa. Those 4,000 farmers were 4,000 fingers in the dyke. If they were removed, the whole edifice would crumble.

So the conspiracy moved to its next stage. In order to remove Mugabe, the British had to turn his people against him. So they were funding the opposition Movement for Democratic Change as a front organization. According to Charamba, the independent newspapers that criticized Mugabe were all funded by the British ('so-called independent newspapers' was Charamba's description of them). The black journalists who worked for them were 'sell-outs'. The opposition amounted to nothing more than a hired gang of black traitors who were working under British supervision to protect white economic interests.

White Zimbabweans, especially the farmers, were the fifth column within the country, controlling the opposition, setting up the outspoken newspapers and sabotaging the economy. The conspiracy was so wide and all-embracing that absolutely anything could be fitted into it. But there was another twist. Charamba was convinced that 'many very powerful figures in Britain own farms in Zimbabwe'. This mysterious circle apparently wielded enormous influence over Tony Blair's government. Its Africa policy was geared towards nothing more than protecting their interests.

I asked Charamba to name these 'powerful figures'. He was a bit stumped by this question. He pulled some files off the shelves and made an ostentatious show of leafing through them, before saying: 'There are ten members of the House of Lords who have farms here.' Asked to name them, he looked uncertain, hesitated, consulted the bulging files and finally said: 'Kenneth Clarke.' The former Conservative Chancellor has never been a member of the House of Lords and it is hard to imagine him working a farm in Zimbabwe. It is even harder to imagine Tony Blair basing his entire approach to Africa on the need to serve Kenneth Clarke's financial interests. It is impossible to imagine anyone in the House of Lords having influence over anything important. 'Any more members of the House of Lords with farms here?' I asked Charamba. He thought deeply, his brow furrowed. After long reflection, he was unable to offer any names at all.[26]

Time and again I heard Mugabe's ministers repeat this line that powerful Britons doubled as landowners in Zimbabwe. A name mentioned by Mugabe himself was 'Lord Rifkind', presumably a reference to Sir Malcolm Rifkind, the former Conservative Foreign Secretary, who has also never sat in the House of Lords (and has not even been in the House of Commons since 1997).[27]

But the Zimbabwean élite actually believed all this, in blissful disregard of the facts. That Africa barely registers on the world's economic map and if Zimbabwe disappeared tomorrow, the British economy would not even hiccup, was conveniently overlooked. That all but a handful of white farmers were Zimbabwean citizens, not Britons, was ignored. That Britain is no longer a global super-power, capable of toppling regimes at will, was also forgotten. But this was how Mugabe and his minions thought. It provided the mental template they used to analyse every new challenge.

★ ★ ★

As the sun blazed down on a sea of smiling faces, the noisy terraces of Rufaro stadium were, I imagined, as euphoric as they had been on Independence Day 19 years earlier. Admittedly, the grandstand was only half full, but what the crowd lacked in numbers it made up for in enthusiasm. The 15,000 people were particularly ardent in their chants of 'Mugabe must go.'

This was 11 September 1999 and I was witnessing the launch of the Movement for Democratic Change (MDC). All around me were the natural supporters of the opposition – impoverished, urban youths and they roared the slogan coined by the MDC, '*Chinja maitiro*' (literally 'Change your ways' but encompassing much more than that). Morgan Tsvangirai had earned the hero worship of this crowd with his leadership of the Zimbabwe Congress of Trade Unions (ZCTU) during the general strikes of 1997 and 1998. Now the ZCTU had given birth to an opposition party and Tsvangirai would ride all these forces to become the most formidable opponent Mugabe had ever faced. In retrospect, the day he stood before the cheering audience in Rufaro was a crucial turning point in Zimbabwean history.

Tsvangirai spoke with a confidence never displayed by any previous opposition leader. 'In 1980, we came here to lower the Union Jack. Now we have come here to lower the flag of Zanu-PF,' he said. 'We have not come here to launch an opposition party. We have come to ensure that the MDC is the next government of Zimbabwe.'[28] Earlier, Tsvangirai told me that the MDC had an historic opportunity. 'We have a groundswell of support. The idea that Zanu-PF have any strongholds left in this country is a fallacy. In the rural areas, the discontent is as great as in the cities. We are going to seize this chance.'[29]

Tsvangirai looked like the trade unionist he was: a powerfully built, gregarious, down-to-earth man, with an easy smile. He was born in 1952 and after leaving school at 16, worked down a mine and in a textile factory. At the Bindura nickel mine, he was an ardent supporter of Zanu-PF and served as 'political commissar' for the workers. Tsvangirai stayed loyal to Mugabe well into the 1980s, and even now his attitude towards the old man is complicated by a deeply ingrained sense of respect.

As an energetic, popular operator, Tsvangirai rose up the Zimbabwe Miners Workers' Union and became its Vice-President in 1985. Later that year he was sent to Britain to study for a Diploma in Productivity at Cresta College near Nottingham. As fate would have it, the nine-month course coincided with the death-throes of the longest and bitterest industrial dispute in British history – the miners' strike led by Arthur Scargill. Tsvangirai witnessed it at first hand. He saw the battles on the picket lines and was deeply moved by the struggle. 'Naturally our sympathies were with the miners,' he told me years later. 'They were good people, and those picket lines, Jesus, they were terrible.' As a Zimbabwean trade unionist, Tsvangirai was invited to meet Scargill himself and was shocked by the man he found. 'He was completely oblivious of reality, completely oblivious,' Tsvangirai said. 'In fact, he almost reminded me of Mugabe.'[30]

After returning to Zimbabwe, Tsvangirai became Secretary-General of the ZCTU in 1988 and transformed organized labour from being a pliant arm of the government into its only effective opposition. Those general strikes had demonstrated his strength. Now the future of the opposition depended on Tsvangirai's performance.

He had a clear target to aim for. Parliamentary elections were due by June 2000 and they would provide the first opportunity for the new generation of Zimbabweans, the 'born frees' as they sometimes called themselves, to make their presence felt. This baseball cap- and T-shirt-wearing leader found himself at the head of a burgeoning movement.

What was the government's attitude to the MDC? As my talk with Charamba had indicated, their first response was to find a conspiracy to explain it, involving the usual cast of enemies. According to Mugabe and his minions, the MDC was not a legitimate opposition party: on the contrary, it was a dangerous front for white interests. The British had established the MDC as a central part of their thrust to re-colonize Zimbabwe. Whites controlled the party and Tsvangirai was nothing more than their puppet.

Soon after the MDC was formed, I spoke to Didymus Mutasa, one of the politburo's hardliners and a close ally of Mugabe. Short, affable, softly spoken and polite, Mutasa always treated me with great friendliness. At one stage he began calling me 'Comrade Blair'. In the genial tones of a kindly headmaster, he would expound the most peculiar theories.

'The MDC is not an opposition in its own right,' Mutasa told me. 'It is a puppet of the British government and of the ex-Rhodesians. They are not a legitimate movement, they are an anti-democratic movement and we cannot tolerate them.'

'Will you allow peaceful demonstrations by the MDC?' I asked.

'The answer is no. We will not tolerate them. I will fight them whenever I see them. They are coming in sheep's clothing when they are wolves and we are not going to tolerate them.' No one could accuse Mutasa of evading the question. To explain his point, he added: 'The MDC is seeking to reverse everything that Zanu-PF has done for this country since 1980. We cannot tolerate that. They want to restore the land to the white farmers and make us a colony again. We who fought for this country and took part in the liberation struggle cannot accept this.'[31]

For Mugabe and his followers, the MDC leaders were not political opponents. They were traitors, bent on handing Zimbabwe back to the whites. The MDC did not come from within Zimbabwe, it was the creation of sinister outsiders, with the wicked British wielding the whip hand. The party consisted of nothing more than white imperialists and black puppets. Its rank and file supporters were no better than accomplices to treason.

The convenient logic of this position was that any methods could be used to combat this menace. If the MDC consisted of a bunch of traitors, they deserved everything they got. Violence and murder were justified.

★   ★   ★

By the close of 1999 the stage was set for a violent confrontation. The approaching parliamentary election would pit the MDC, representing the ever-growing number of casualties of economic failure, against Zanu-PF, a party already convinced that its critics were intent on wrecking Zimbabwe and reversing its independence.

The most cursory examination of Mugabe's record up to 1999 should have made several points glaringly apparent. His brutal suppression of Zapu showed how far he would go to keep his grip on power. It also demonstrated that the magnanimous Mugabe of 1980 was emphatically not the real Mugabe. In retrospect, his conciliatory phase can be precisely dated and was extremely short. It lasted from 4 March 1980, when he won his first election, to 17 February 1982, when he sacked Nkomo. Taken alongside his behaviour before and afterwards, this was surely an aberration.

From 1982 onwards, his rule was dominated by a ruthless quest to crush his opponents and remain in office at whatever cost. In 2000 he would suffer his first electoral defeat and encounter the most serious threat ever to his grip on power. Looking at Mugabe's past, his reaction to this challenge should not have surprised anyone.

NOTES AND REFERENCES

1 Quoted in Joshua Nkomo, *Story of My Life*, Methuen, London, 1984, p. 2.
2 *Ibid.*, pp. 2–3.
3 Quoted in Lorraine Eide, *Robert Mugabe*, Chelsea House, New York, 1989, p. 84.
4 Quoted in David Smith and Colin Simpson, *Mugabe*, Sphere, London, 1981, p. 213.
5 Nkomo, *op. cit.*, p. 243.
6 Catholic Commission for Justice and Peace and Legal Resources Foundation, *Breaking the Silence – Building True Peace*, Harare, 1997, p. 52.

7 Archive footage shown in *Never the Same Again,* Edwina Spicer Productions, 2000.

8 Catholic Commission for Justice and Peace and Legal Resources Foundation, *op. cit.,* p. 57.

9 Interview with Shari Eppel, dir Amani Matabeleland, 28 October 1999.

10 Catholic Commission for Justice and Peace and Legal Resources Foundation, *op. cit.,* p. 53.

11 *Ibid.,* p. 61.

12 *Ibid.,* pp. 53–4.

13 *Ibid.,* p. 44.

14 Archive footage shown on BBC TV, *Rebellion.*

15 Nkomo, *op. cit.,* p. 3.

16 Quoted in *ibid.,* p. 2.

17 Shown on BBC TV, *Rebellion.*

18 Archive footage shown in *Never the Same Again,* Edwina Spicer Productions, 2000.

19 Quoted in Nathan Shamuyarira, *Mugabe's Reflections,* Har-Anand, New Delhi, 1994, pp. 35–6.

20 Quoted in Hugo Young, *One of Us,* Pan, London, 1990, p. 487.

21 Catholic Commission for Justice and Peace and Legal Resources Foundation, *op. cit.,* p. 57.

22 David Lamb, *The Africans,* Methuen, London, 1985, p. 336.

23 *Ibid.,* p. 103 & p. 334.

24 Interview with the author, 20 November 2001.

25 ZBC broadcast, 2 February 1999.

26 Interview with the author, 6 December 1999.

27 See Mugabe's interview with ABC TV, *Like it Is,* 10 September 2000, in which he said: 'The Actons and Rifkinds will lose their farms. They are in the House of Lords.'

28 Speech, 11 September 1999.

29 Interview with the author, 11 September 1999.

30 Interview with the author, 20 November 2001.

31 Interviews with the author, 13 September 1999 and 3 April 2000.

Chapter 3

Defeat

January–February 2000

The role of the Rhodesians, neo-colonialists and other retrogressive forces was and is stronger than Zanu-PF thought. (Chen Chimutengwende, Information minister, 18 February 2000)[1]

Honey Bear Lane is the most prosperous corner of Zimbabwe. Behind screens of slender poplar and pine trees hide the gilded mansions of Harare's élite. Drive along the quiet road and you catch glimpses of sparkling swimming pools and luxuriant gardens, complete with crimson bougainvillaea and tropical creepers. So verdant do the gardens appear that you might think a visitor reaches the front door by hacking a path through the greenery with a machete. Honey Bear Lane is Beverly Hills in the African bush. Even driving down it seems an act of unforgivable vulgarity. It's the sort of road that you purr along in a chauffeur-driven Mercedes, if you venture on to its tar at all.

In February 2000 I chugged along Honey Bear Lane looking for a petrol station. Or rather, I was looking for the queue of hundreds of cars that would, in time, wend its way through the streets and swamp a petrol station. It took some finding and my fuel gauge was showing empty, but eventually, after turning left into Stonechat Lane and then into a sidestreet, I encountered the stationary column of multicoloured vehicles. Somewhere, about one mile away through the winding streets, past the mansions, satellite dishes and multiple garages of Harare's élite, was the forecourt. Many hours would pass before I saw it.

In early 2000 queuing for petrol became a compulsory hobby for the few in Zimbabwe lucky enough to own a car. The entire country all but ran dry. Endless attempts were made by the official media to explain away the crisis, which crippled the economy, but the facts were very simple. Noczim, the state oil company, had a monopoly over the purchase of fuel for Zimbabwe. To no one's surprise, it was a corrupt, bankrupt wreck, sinking under debts

of around £200 million. The officials running Noczim had stolen everything that wasn't nailed down – and quite a bit that was. No fuel company
would supply it with a drop unless paid in hard currency, preferably well in
advance. But Zimbabwe had no foreign exchange reserves left. In
December 1999 the IMF had finally lost patience with Harare and ended all
support. Mugabe usually referred to the IMF as a 'monstrous institution'[2]
and treated its suggestions for economic reform with open contempt. So it
stopped giving him money. Zimbabwe's international credit-rating
promptly went through the floor, no one would lend Mugabe a penny and
therefore there was no cash to buy any fuel.

Hence I found myself devoting more and more time to the simple task of
staying mobile. Filling your tank in Harare came to demand the patience
and planning of a military operation. Above all, accurate intelligence was
essential. That morning my landlady had passed on a crucial piece of news.
Her informant, a senior figure in the shadowy world of forecourt attendants,
had let slip that our local Total station in the suburb of Helensvale was about
to receive a delivery of petrol, the first for a fortnight. By the time I set off,
scores of cars had already formed a queue in anticipation of the great event.
When I joined the line, the drivers ahead of me seemed lifeless, inert. About
six cars stretched in front of my humble Mazda 323, and then the queue
disappeared around a corner.

After ten minutes of silence, an excited figure appeared. He wore the blue
overalls of a Total forecourt attendant and stopped at each car in turn,
speaking to the driver with a broad smile on his face. When he reached me,
he said: 'The petrol is here. Congratulations, you are in queue position 137.'
He handed me a raffle ticket with my number on it. Apparently this meant
that I was guaranteed petrol if I waited long enough, hence the congratulations. Any car after the 150th had no chance – the precious liquid would all
be gone by the time it reached the forecourt. It was 2 p.m. and I settled
down for the long wait.

A fortnight earlier, the top brass of Noczim and the Transport Ministry
had called a press conference to explain themselves. Those journalists who
were still mobile gathered at the ministry's headquarters. We found a grim
office block, surrounded by an endless fuel queue that was grid-locking a
large portion of central Harare. Christian Katsande, the Permanent Secretary, who doubled as Chairman of Noczim, appeared to believe that the fuel
shortage was entirely the fault of consumers who, for unfathomable reasons,
insisted on buying the stuff in large quantities. He appealed to all of us to
'show restraint'. He ticked off journalists for 'exaggerating' the situation and
failing to 'create confidence in Noczim'. As Katsande talked, the sound of
hooting rose from the streets below. The window behind him afforded a
vantage point over Fourth Street, where a BP petrol station was swamped by

queues. Columns of vehicles approached it from every direction, some had formed interlocking circles stretching around the block. Others had tried to jump the queue and drivers hooted their rage.

A few storeys above them, Katsande told us everything was under control. He was a smooth talker, polished, fluent and persuasive. To bolster the message of reassurance, he had roped in Tom Walter, the American Managing Director of Mobil Zimbabwe. 'We will all cope with this problem together,' said Walter brightly, as if addressing keen college interns at a brain-storming session. 'Our colleagues at Noczim have outstanding teamwork.' This was certainly true. The long process of reducing a monopoly supplier of an essential product to a bankrupt hulk had certainly demonstrated outstanding teamwork. The individuals concerned had doubtless profited handsomely from their teamwork. But Katsande was particularly indignant about reports in the local press suggesting that Zimbabwe was about to run dry. 'We are not going to allow stocks to run dry. I can stake my credibility on that,' he said.[3] Zimbabwe ran dry a week later.

I had plenty of time to mull over all this as I sat in the queue. As the sun went down and the shadows lengthened, the line of vehicles edged forward. With glacial slowness, my car turned one corner, then another, then a third and emerged on to Crowhill Road. Suddenly the petrol station was visible. It was like a mirage on the horizon, a great red and white object, with a row of cars leading on to its forecourt. When queuing for fuel, the moment that you can actually see the petrol station marks a crucial psychological turning point. From then on, it seems like a downhill ride.

I chatted to my fellow drivers in the line. They were smiling and stoical about having to waste their days in queues. Many had taken time off work or abandoned their businesses for the afternoon. John Maponga was making his third bid to fill up. The previous day he had waited in two queues but the petrol had run out before he reached the head of the line. Now he mainly wanted to talk about those he blamed for the mess. 'Better to change the bloody government,' he said. 'Look what these ones are doing in Zimbabwe. I'm fed up. I think I will go to Zambia. At least they have petrol there.' Fuel queues often became social occasions and drivers would pass the time by talking in huddles. Venting anger about those who had created the mess was a good way of letting off steam.

Mugabe gave every sign of being bewildered by the fuel crisis. When the first petrol queues appeared, he instantly jumped on Western oil companies and accused them of deliberately failing to sell the stuff. 'Now our enemies are combining against us again. There has been a play on shortages of fuel so that our people will turn against their government,' he told the Zanu-PF Congress.[4] A few weeks later, Mugabe abruptly changed tack. His government had bought all the fuel Zimbabwe needed (so the Western companies had delivered after all?) and those evil white farmers had engineered the shortage. 'Look at what these whites do now,' he said. 'We know we bought adequate supplies of fuel, but they bought all of it in large drums and hid them on their farms.'[5] They must have been very large drums. If Mugabe was right, every field in every farm must have been crammed with millions of litres of flammable liquid. It was a wonder that thousands of acres of Mashonaland were not exploding every day.

When not blaming this scheming array of enemies, Mugabe lapsed into bemused incomprehension. In the middle of one endless petrol queue, I opened *The Herald,* an earnest, state-owned propaganda daily, and read: 'Along with most Zimbabweans, Comrade Mugabe cannot understand why the country does not have at least minimum reserves of essential fuels. He noted over the weekend that it was ridiculous that the country should face serious shortages.'[6] Apparently, Comrade Mugabe could not understand how severing relations with the IMF could in any way have contributed to the fuel crisis.

It was, however, contributing to ruining my day. By 5.30 p.m., after over three hours in the queue, there were still about 20 cars ahead of me. Then, at 6 p.m., as dusk fell, I made it to fourth place, clutching my raffle ticket with anticipation. But something was going wrong. The lights on the forecourt were being switched off. Several of the attendants began closing the shop. The smiling man in blue overalls reappeared, only this time he wasn't smiling. 'Sorry for this,' he said. 'We are now closed. You must come back tomorrow.'

'What? Do you still have fuel?'

'Oh yes,' came the reply. 'But we are now closing at six.' Because petrol stations were usually dry, 24-hour opening was a thing of the past. Poor John Maponga had failed on his latest attempt to fill up and looked crestfallen. 'They open tomorrow at 7 a.m.,' he said. 'Me, I will sleep in my car.' He seemed quite resigned to this. I hadn't enough petrol to drive anywhere, so I decided to abandon my car, walk home and curse my wasted afternoon on the way. Nearby, the Total pole sign read: 'Petrol, diesel, 24 hours.' I was sorely tempted to add 'None of the above.'

I walked home along the blackness of Crowhill Road. It was dark because the last street light had given out some weeks before. The city council could no longer afford to replace the bulbs and most of Harare's streets were now in darkness after nightfall. But the muggers were probably celebrating.

At 7 the following morning, I retraced my steps, waited another three hours and finally managed to buy 15 litres of petrol – all they would sell. A total of eight hours queuing, spread over two days, for less than half a tank.[7]

This was the most visible consequence of Zimbabwe's economic collapse. No visitor to Harare could have failed to notice the streets clogged with vehicles waiting for fuel. Yet it was only the tip of an ill-concealed iceberg.

Inflation in January 2000 was 58.5 per cent and basic essentials were becoming unaffordable for millions. Over the previous three years, living standards for people fortunate enough to have jobs had fallen by over 30 per cent. But most eked out an existence on the fringes of the economy. Zimbabwe's official unemployment figure was now a staggering 50 per cent. For the 80 per cent of Harare's 2 million people who lived in the townships on the southern ring of the city, life was becoming increasingly unbearable. The gap between Honey Bear Lane and slums like Mbare and Highfield had widened to a yawning abyss. In traditional African fashion, people in the townships were expected to support their relatives in remote villages. But many were now unable to keep this obligation, deepening the poverty in which rural Zimbabwe had always lived. In this way, the discontent of the towns spread into the countryside.

As I wasted my days in fuel queues, Zimbabweans were preparing for a unique chance to make their anger felt. Mugabe had decided to hold the first referendum in Zimbabwean history on 12 and 13 February 2000. Ostensibly, the people were being asked to approve a new constitution. In fact, an opportunity to show what they really thought of their leader suddenly fell into their collective laps. The possibility of losing an election would never have occurred to Mugabe. He was about to receive the rudest, and most unexpected, shock of his life.

★   ★   ★

Why had Mugabe taken this risk? The new constitution he offered to his people was a central part of his strategy for staying in power and securing a Zanu-PF victory in the coming parliamentary election. A handpicked commission of 400 people, over 300 of whom were members of Zanu-PF, had produced a document tailor-made for Mugabe's needs. It kept the sweeping powers of the Presidency and allowed him to run for re-election twice more. Most crucially of all, it removed the central obstacle that had thwarted the seizure of white-owned land. Farmers lost their right to compensation for land seizures; instead, the new constitution laid down that Britain must pay them. Clause 57, inserted at Mugabe's personal insistence, read:

(i)   The former colonial power has an obligation to pay compensation for agricultural land compulsorily acquired for resettlement, through a fund established for the purpose.

(ii)   If the former colonial power fails to pay compensation through such a fund, the Government of Zimbabwe have no obligation to pay compensation for agricultural land compulsorily acquired for resettlement.

At the Lancaster House conference, Mugabe had secured a pledge from Britain to pay for land reform and he passionately believed that London had broken its promise. The new constitution meant that this act of perfidy would not stand in the way of land seizures. It would allow him to grab the land and pay the farmers nothing.

But Mugabe believed with equal passion that he was showing generosity and forbearance to the white community. He was not opposed to the principle of compensation, he just wanted it understood that Britain was responsible for any payments, in accordance with the Lancaster House pledge. If the white farmers joined Mugabe in placing pressure on the British, he was sure they would give way. Remember his ardent conviction that 'very powerful Britons' like 'Lord' Clarke and 'Lord' Rifkind were among the white landowners. If they united behind him, Mugabe was sure that no British government could resist this mighty coalition. In the President's mind, the new constitution was his final offer to the farmers, their last opportunity to join him and carry out land reform together. He would later tell the leadership of the Commercial Farmers' Union (CFU): 'We put in that clause to help you.'[7]

The farmers were, of course, horrified. They believed the sudden insertion of this clause amounted to a denial of their citizenship. They were Zimbabweans, Britain owed them nothing and only their government could provide compensation for land seizures. They feared that Mugabe was moving to strip them of their livelihoods. Moreover, with the election fast approaching, landowners suspected they were being set up as a convenient political punch bag once again. Jerry Grant, deputy director of the CFU, put the point with typical bluntness: 'I don't believe it's the role of the constitution to carry that sort of political rhetoric. This is posturing before the election. Are we developing a constitution for His Excellency or for the people? And who amended the draft, the people of Zimbabwe or one man?'[8] Not for the first time, the farmers and the President were poles apart. Neither had the slightest grasp of the other's viewpoint.

★   ★   ★

In the fortnight before voting began, the Yes and No campaigns moved into gear. To call this referendum a David and Goliath contest does not go nearly far enough. It was a fight between an elephant and a mouse. The Yes camp saturated television and radio with its adverts, helped by a budget of about ZD 60 million (then equivalent to £1 million). Voting Yes was equated with patriotism and loyalty to Zimbabwe. One theme dominated over all others – if the people voted Yes, the white farmers would lose their land and Zimbabweans would reclaim their inheritance. One television advert showed a small boy stopping at a closed gate with a 'No Entry' sign and staring at the lush, green fields beyond. Then the gate suddenly opened and the boy ran into the fertile idyll of the white-owned farm, while a voice intoned: 'Vote Yes.'

Meanwhile, the No campaign consisted of a few thousand badly printed leaflets, handed out on street corners by a handful of activists. Tsvangirai's MDC had little to do with it. Instead, the National Constitutional Assembly (NCA), an alliance of civic groups, ran the campaign on a virtually non-existent budget. Its headquarters was a large, chaotic house in central Harare and volunteers gathered in the living room. The No camp made some tele-vision adverts, but ZBC, the state broadcasting company, refused to show them. Only after a High Court order and vociferous protests were three of the eight programmes broadcast and these were swamped by the blanket coverage given to the Yes campaign. Any visitor to Zimbabwe would have thought that only a Yes campaign was under way.

Mugabe threw his weight behind the drive for a Yes vote on 30 January, when he addressed a rally of 15,000 supporters in the Harare township of Epworth. According to *The Herald,* he drew cheers by assuring his audience the new constitution would 'empower the people'. Mugabe loftily added: 'We are surprised there are efforts to thwart this process.'[9] He followed this up with a television interview on 10 February. 'I think it's a very good draft indeed,' Mugabe told the nation, immediately after yet another barrage of Yes adverts. 'It contains all the elements any constitution should have . . . a Yes vote is important politically.'[10] The President had nailed his colours to the mast. He would share in the glory if the Yes campaign triumphed but could not avoid the blame if it crashed to defeat.

As polling day drew near, the official drive to secure a Yes vote adopted a harsher tone. A few whites had been spotted campaigning for a No. In the suspicious mind of the government, this could only mean one thing. The whites wanted to sabotage the new constitution because of the clause allowing land seizures without compensation. This theme was taken up by the Yes campaign, which shamelessly sought to stir racial hatred. An extra-ordinary example was a full-page advert in *The Herald* which carried a large photograph of a white couple wearing 'Vote No' T-shirts. They were named as John Ayton and Mary Austin of Ridgemont in Gweru and the caption said: 'Don't follow them back to the dark past when they were queens and kings while you suffered. Send a clear message to them by voting "Yes" and take control of your destiny today and for ever.'[11]

Another advert claimed that the No campaign was a front for the whites and the British government. Any blacks urging a No were branded sell-outs:

The same white settlers, with the help of the British government and their International friends are funding Sellout Zimbabweans to buy your rights by urging you to vote No to the draft constitution. WHY SHOULD THOSE WITH LAND URGE THE LANDLESS TO VOTE NO. FOR HOW LONG SHOULD WE CONTINUE TO BE TOLD WHAT TO DO? Vote Yes in the referendum and make a historic change by sending a clear message to the Sellouts and their masters.[12]

Jonathan Moyo, who ran the Yes campaign, drafted these adverts, and much more would be heard from him in the coming months. But on 12 and 13 February, Zimbabweans went to the polls and the Moyo school of political campaigning was put to the test.

★   ★   ★

In the schools and local council offices that served as polling stations across Zimbabwe, there was no sign that a political earthquake was taking place. No queues stretched along the streets, there were no scenes of excitement or drama. More of Harare's residents seemed to be lining up for petrol than waiting to cast their votes. The turnout was low and many polling stations appeared almost deserted.

But anyone who talked to people after they voted realized that something completely unexpected was happening. During an afternoon in Mbare, one of Harare's poorest townships, I met only one man who had voted Yes. He was elderly and leant on a walking stick as he told me: 'I respect Comrade Mugabe and he has asked us to vote Yes. I want us to have our own constitution, so I am voting Yes.' All the other voters were young and there was not a government supporter to be found. 'I voted No. I want to do away with the government,' said Admore Sithole, a 25-year-old who had never had a job since leaving school. Klaas Chandirekera, another unemployed youth, agreed. 'Mugabe is corrupt, I don't want even to see that one,' he said. 'Life is too tough and the government is to blame.' Dhamore Chireu was casting his vote after emerging from a fuel queue. 'Look at the country, there is no diesel, petrol or anything. Everything is just bad, so I am voting No,' he said.

One thing was absolutely clear. No one was casting their vote in response to the question on the ballot paper. The merits of the draft constitution were utterly irrelevant. The referendum had become a test of public confidence in Mugabe and the anecdotal evidence suggested he was losing hands down. Only in the very centre of Harare did queues appear at polling stations. One was sited in a marquee beside the government office blocks on Fourth Street and, because it was closest to the central business district, a large number of whites arrived there to cast their votes. At various points, there was a queue of white voters, clearly visible from the windows of the ministries nearby. That may well explain the conspiracy theory later invented by the government to brush off its defeat.

On the evening of Sunday, 13 February 2000, polls closed and the ballot boxes were gathered together in preparation for the count the following day. Although finding a Yes voter had been virtually impossible in Harare, most observers still expected the government to win. Mugabe had never lost an election and the universal belief was that the No campaign would never be given the chance to prevail. Lupi Mushayakarara, a prominent member of the No camp, told me: 'This government is not ready to lose an election. All this has been for appearance's sake only. The trickster in State House will manufacture the result he wants.'[13]

By the afternoon of Monday, 14 February, the first results were coming in. Journalists were summoned to a gloomy room in a nondescript office block to hear Tobaiwa Mudede, the Registrar General, announce them by parliamentary constituency. Mudede was viewed with deep distrust by the opposition, who accused him of building his entire career on rigging elections for Mugabe. This was unfair, but Mudede made it easy for us to think the worst of him by flaunting his disdain for the press. He treated our questions with brusque contempt and, whenever a journalist came within 100 yards, his facial expression suggested that someone was holding a dead fish under his nose. When Mudede began reading out the results, we expected him to prepare the ground for another Mugabe triumph. Instead, from the very outset it was evident that something was going very wrong.

Mudede seemed hardly able to believe his own voice as he announced the first results from Bulawayo. The No camp had swept 75 per cent of the vote in the townships of Nkulumane, Mpopoma and Luveve. More remarkable were the results in the province of Manicaland, once Mugabe's heartland, where his guerrillas had operated with impunity in the closing years of the war. Seats like Chimanimani and Mutasa, which had returned Zanu-PF MPs with overwhelming majorities at every election since 1980, voted No by 62 per cent and 64 per cent respectively. Even Nyanga, through which Mugabe had escaped to Mozambique in 1975, voted against him by 62 per cent. One crushing rebuff after another was announced, to gasps and whistles of surprise.

When Mudede came to the Harare seats, it seemed that the Yes camp was facing more than defeat – meltdown was a better term. Each impoverished township in succession had voted No by margins of 75 or even 80 per cent. At midnight on Monday, Mugabe was staring defeat in the face. With almost half the votes counted, the No campaign was running at 58 per cent. Zimbabweans could not believe what was happening.

The following morning, Tuesday 15 February, more crushing defeats for Mugabe were announced. The city of Mutare on the border with Mozambique had rejected him with up to 77 per cent voting No. Only in Mashonaland were loyal voters making their presence felt. In Mugabe's home district of Zvimba, 79 per cent voted Yes. The margin of his defeat was falling, but the outcome was no longer in doubt.

Gradually, almost imperceptibly at first, the news spread. Whispers were passed down crowded streets in Harare. 'Mugabe has been beaten,' people told each other in hushed tones. Early on Tuesday morning, I sat in Al Forno's café going through the results. When I told a waiter that the No camp had 58 per cent so far, he appeared to forget the tray laden with cans of coke precariously balanced in his right hand. He beamed and, without saying a word, broke into a spontaneous dance of joy. The elderly, greying man, dressed in immaculate whites, gyrated and jived before a dozen bemused diners. Many in his delighted audience had already heard the news and they broke into a round of applause when the performance was over. The waiter, who had not dropped a single can, bowed politely and rushed to tell his colleagues. More delighted applause came from behind the counter.

Outside, the news was spreading fast. I walked along Samora Machel Street where, as usual, a long line of cars waited to fill up at the Mobil petrol station. Some drivers knew, others didn't. Telling them apart was easy – some were grinning from ear to ear while others sat, slumped and inert, in familiar 'fuel queue' pose. I went up Fifth Street and turned into Herbert Chitepo Avenue, where the NCA had their headquarters. In a cacophony of ululations and whistles, a small whirlpool of humanity was surging along the street. About 200 euphoric people were waving 'Vote No' banners and chanting their joy. Beaming passers-by swelled their ranks, or broke into little jigs on the pavement. Office workers waved from windows as the sounds of triumph passed beneath them. A party of schoolboys, clad in smart khaki uniforms, danced alongside the procession, squealing with excitement.

Charles Chirimambowa, a student, waved his 'Vote No' flag in the direction of State House, Mugabe's official residence which hid behind its barbed wire stockade a few streets away. 'I cannot contain my joy, I am just thrilled,' he said. 'This is the end for Mugabe, at last, at last. We have a new era.' Behind him, the crowd chanted 'Mugabe is finished.' Elizabeth took a break from singing and waving to say: 'I am more than happy. My son, I cannot express my joy to you. We are sick and tired of that liar and cheater. Now he is going, he is going, it is really happening.'

The crowd arrived outside the NCA's headquarters. Never in Zimbabwe's 20-year history had the opposition known anything but defeat, often in the aftermath of ruthless harassment. The garden of the nondescript house was already filled with revellers. Dancing figures covered the lawn and loud music blared over a ghetto-blaster. Inside, every room was thronged with supporters, many in floods of tears. Some danced in the corridors, with an almost manic intensity. There was an unreal quality to the celebrations. People just could not take in what had happened. Few in the No campaign had seriously expected victory and, when it came, the sensation was wholly unfamiliar. Lovemore Madhuku, then deputy chairman of the NCA, told me that he was 'pinching himself' to check whether this was really happening. It wasn't in the script. Mugabe simply did not lose elections. A campaign that amounted to little more than a few tatty leaflets could not defeat the mighty juggernaut of the Yes camp, complete with its wall-to-wall television advertising. And yet the depth of discontent with Mugabe was such that precisely this had occurred.

Priscilla Misihairabwi, one of the leading No campaigners, had just been released from prison. She had spent two nights in jail for delivering 'Vote No' leaflets. A trumped-up charge of campaigning within 100 metres of a polling station was levelled against her and later forgotten. Now, a few hours after her release, she celebrated. 'You can't fight the people, this is a people's struggle and the people always win in the end,' she said with complete, passionate conviction. 'Every dictator loses in the end.' Priscilla burst into tears and I left her, dancing beside the front door.

I drove home, away from the joyous scenes in Herbert Chitepo, past a fuel queue with an unusual number of delighted faces and along Chancellor Avenue, past State House. Here, a dozen of Mugabe's soldiers guarded his official residence, wearing full combat regalia complete with steel helmets, AK-47 assault rifles and fixed bayonets. They appeared more menacing than usual. Like countless people in Zimbabwe on that day, I began nervously pondering how their leader was going to react.

A few hours later, the final result became known. The No campaign had swept 54.7 per cent of the vote, although the turnout had been under 25 per cent. The habits of apathy, imposed by the repressive weight of a *de facto* one-party state, were hard for Zimbabweans to shake off. Yet the defeat could not have come at a worse time for Mugabe. Parliamentary elections would have to be held within the next four months. If this performance was repeated, Zanu-PF would stand little chance against the MDC. Tsvangirai had already exploited his humiliation. 'In the wake of his defeat Mugabe should just step down,' Tsvangirai told me. 'It is a vote of no confidence in him and his government. In any normal democracy, it would mean an honourable exit.'[14] How, I asked myself, is Mugabe going to get out of this one?

★   ★   ★

That night Mugabe broadcast to the nation. Nervous people across Zimbabwe watched as he appeared, perched awkwardly on a sofa, immaculately dressed in one of his blue suits. 'Good evening my fellow Zimbabweans,' he began, reading from a sheet of paper clutched in his hands. Mugabe outlined the history of the constitutional commission and said their work had been 'representative of the diversity of the nation'. He talked of the referendum 'which you and I participated in' and described how 'the Registrar General brought me the final copy of the results this morning'.

Mugabe spoke calmly, if slightly awkwardly. This was not one of his raging, paranoid performances. This was the Father of the Nation speaking. Then he came to the most crucial passage. 'Government accepts the result and respects the will of the people,' he said. Only as Mugabe said 'respects' did the mask slip slightly. He appeared to spit out the word with distaste. But he went on to commend Zimbabweans for voting with a 'sense of order, maturity and tolerance' and said: 'The world now knows Zimbabwe as a country where opposing views and opinions can be found alongside each other peacefully. Let us all, winners and losers, accept the referendum verdict and start planning our way for the future.'[15] The national anthem played and the familiar face faded from the screen. This had been the conciliatory Mugabe speaking, the gracious healer of the country's wounds, the national leader, the Mugabe of 1980. As most people knew, it was the fake Mugabe. When he finished speaking, I remember thinking: 'This is a sham.' He could not possibly take this defeat lying down. The central questions remained unanswered – what would happen next? How would he respond?

Some Zanu-PF heavyweights went into brazen denial. The defeat could simply be shrugged off as a matter of no importance whatever. Didymus Mutasa, the secretary for administration in the politburo, fell into this camp. For him, the concept of Mugabe ever ceasing to rule Zimbabwe was inherently ludicrous. So why did everyone make such a fuss over the referendum result? 'This result was no criticism of us,' claimed Mutasa. 'The referendum had nothing to do with Zanu-PF . . . our government is absolutely popular. It is only our government which has gone to war to fight for the people's rights.' Instead, the people had decided to behave inexplicably by rejecting a constitution that was drafted according to their wishes. 'What is baffling for me is that the people are refusing to implement their own views,' said Mutasa. But he offered words of reassurance. 'Mugabe will rule this country for as long as he likes. There is no question about that . . . it is absolutely mad to think that someone else can govern this country. It is impossible, you cannot even imagine it.'[16]

On 18 February Zanu-PF's central committee gathered at the party's headquarters for a shell-shocked inquest. Mugabe's speeches at these meetings were usually open to journalists and I went along to cover the event. The moment I walked into the hall, filled with 180 members of the central committee, I could sense the tension. The audience was glum, cold and silent. Here were all the Zanu-PF heavyweights summoned, like naughty schoolchildren, to be told off by their headmaster. Eddison Zvobgo, the Minister without Portfolio who had masterminded the whole disastrous, constitution-drafting exercise, shifted uneasily in his chair. Behind him was row upon row of despondent faces. Guilt hung in the air. Zimbabwe's élite cursed the complacency that had brought humiliation.

Everyone rose as Mugabe and his most senior allies made their entrance. The President strode through the hall, looking inscrutable and admirably cool under fire. He took his place on the platform and stood rigidly to atten-tion as the national anthem was played, with the loyal Mutasa at his side. When the martial chords were over, everyone resumed their seats and waited for Mutasa to call on their leader to speak.

I suddenly realized that, apart from the correspondents of the loyal state media, I was the only journalist present. It was hard to blend in with the crowd. Nervously, I watched Mutasa's face scan the audience. His eyes swept from left to right and then caught my own. Mutasa jerked his head with surprise. With the hall in total silence, he stood, left the platform and walked straight up to me. As he approached, a benign smile spread across his face. 'Excuse me,' he said. 'Would you excuse us please?' I have never been thrown out of anywhere in such a polite fashion. 'Of course,' I mumbled. Mugabe eyed me contemptuously as I laboriously gathered my notebook, newspaper and pens. His two Vice-Presidents, most of the cabinet, every member of the politburo and scores of hangers-on stared silently as I stood up and left the hall. My footsteps echoed loudly over the strained faces of Zimbabwe's élite.

It was entirely understandable for Mutasa to throw me out. At this tense meeting of the central committee, Mugabe was challenged in person for the first time and told to leave office. Dzikamai Mavhaire, the MP for Masvingo Central and a Zanu-PF provincial chairman, demanded to know 'what plans the President has made for retirement'. As he spoke those words, a stir went round the room, some people booing softly, others gasping with surprise. Mugabe remained impassive. He replied that it was a 'legitimate question' and he would be making retirement plans in 'due course' but now was 'not the time'.[17] Nothing more was said on the subject. Mavhaire had been a semi-detached member of Zanu-PF ever since he spoke in parliament in 1998 and said: 'The President must go.' That the issue was raised directly with Mugabe showed the new strength of feeling.

Mugabe responded with a speech that blamed his party for the referen-dum defeat. 'We have accepted the people's verdict. We cannot, however, mask our disappointment,' he said. 'It was our duty as a party to have campaigned more vigorously for a Yes vote. Only in a few provinces did this happen and even in those the action programme was embarked on quite belatedly. We accordingly must admit that we fell short on all counts . . . such was our abdication of responsibility.' Mugabe warned his supporters never to be caught 'flat footed in the future' and accused his critics in Zanu-PF of 'despondency and defeatism that may have the effect of crippling the party through abject abdication and complete surrender'.[18] Never before had Mugabe been forced into such an admission of political frailty.

But there was another, more palatable theory explaining the defeat. According to Chen Chimutengwende, the Information Minister, the rebuff had not been the fault of Zanu-PF at all. The historic enemies of the party – unreconstructed whites and black sell-outs – had banded together to inflict the defeat. The way to respond was to hit the enemy hard, not indulge in destructive recriminations. Chimutengwende told the meeting: 'The role of the Rhodesians, neo-colonialists and other retrogressive forces was and is stronger than Zanu-PF thought. This was revealed by the referendum.'[19]

This theory rapidly gained currency as the Official Explanation. It was much easier and more comforting to blame the great conspiracy, a shadowy array of sinister forces, than simply admit that Zanu-PF had gone badly wrong. Jonathan Moyo claimed that the No campaign's victory by a margin of 119,544 ballots was due to a sudden influx of white voters. 'It is clear that some of them came over the weekend, all the way from South Africa, to vote in this referendum,' he said.[20]

But the most crucial consequence of the referendum defeat was the simplest. Mugabe was finally confronted with unmistakable evidence of his own unpopularity and the strength of the nascent MDC. The agony of defeat pushed him into a lethal combination of fury and vulnerability. He realized that unless extraordinary measures were taken, Zanu-PF would lose the parliamentary election. So he resolved to use extraordinary methods against any opponents, real or imagined. The onslaught began.

NOTES AND REFERENCES

1 Speech, Zanu-PF central committee, 18 February 2000.
2 See, for example, his speech at Joshua Nkomo's funeral, 1 July 1999.
3 Press conference, 14 January 2000.
4 Speech, Zanu-PF Congress, 16 December 1999.
5 Zanu-PF campaign speech, Epworth, 30 January 2000.
6 *The Herald,* 28 February 2000.
7 Private information.
8 Interview with the author, 20 January 2000.
9 *The Herald,* 31 January 2000.

10 ZBC interview, 10 February 2000.
11 See *The Herald,* 12 February 2000.
12 See *ibid.*, 9 February 2000.
13 Interview with the author, 12 February 2000.
14 Interview with the author, 15 February 2000.
15 Broadcast to the nation, 15 February 2000.
16 BBC interview, 18 February 2000. I am grateful to Grant Ferrett for allowing me to listen to this tape, not all of which was broadcast.
17 Private information.
18 Speech to Zanu-PF central committee, 18 February 2000.
19 *Ibid.*, see also *The Herald,* 19 February 2000.
20 ZBC interview, 15 February 2000.

Chapter 4

Invasion

February–March 2000

Plece can you help Zimbabwe. We are not safe in this country . . . you are not safe with wore vetrens. Mr Mgabwe just wants the land. Or he will hirt you. (A white farmer's seven-year-old son, writing in his school exercise book, after the onset of the land invasions)

With axes slung across their shoulders, the group of bearded men strode towards us. They wore camouflage jackets, ragged trousers and flip-flops. One sported dark glasses and a curved knife glinting in the sun, thrust into his belt alongside a mobile phone. Looking dour and forbidding, they fanned out behind their leader, a small, stocky, clean-shaven man wearing a flat cap, like a British shop steward from the 1950s. A group of ragged women, children and teenage boys were building shacks with brushwood or lounging on the grass nearby. They were thin, drawn and carrying sticks, clubs and axes. Blue smoke from a cooking fire curled over a sweeping expanse of the high veldt. This field was 'liberated Zimbabwe' and the people around us were the 'war veterans'.

At that moment they were tired, downtrodden and hungry war veterans. Their leader called himself Comrade Jesus and he greeted the white farmer, his deadly foe, politely enough. He shook hands with Anthony Wells in the African fashion, reversing the grip with each shake. Comrade Jesus's five menacing henchmen broke into sinister, gap-toothed smiles and handshakes were exchanged all round. 'Mr Anthony, my friend, we are hungry, please can we have something to eat?' asked Comrade Jesus.

'Yah, all right, I'll find you something,' replied Wells. A few hours earlier, this gang of 40 'war veterans', most of whom were babes in arms when Rhodesia sued for peace, had stormed Wells's homestead. Whipped into a frenzy by a raging Comrade Jesus, they had threatened to hack the farmer to pieces and accused him of hiding arms in preparation for civil war. Earlier, Wells had been punched, sworn at, humiliated and forced to sign away a portion of his farm.

But now Comrade Jesus was in more affable mood. In impeccable English, he told me: 'Mr Anthony has been very generous, he has given us 350 hectares. We are not going to damage anything. We are not going to cause him any harm. Even though this land belongs to me and it has been liberated by the people of Zimbabwe, I will still listen to Mr Anthony.'

'What about the law of Zimbabwe,' I asked him. 'What you are doing is illegal.' Comrade Jesus did not hesitate for a moment. 'The law is just there to benefit the white man,' he replied. 'The courts are the white man's courts. The judges are the white man's judges. A law put in place to benefit one party is not a proper law. We cannot wait until all the whites are dead before we get the land. We want peace and justice for everyone.'

'But you've just grabbed Mr Wells's home and his livelihood,' I said, trying to break through the façade of good humour. I suddenly remembered the stern henchmen toying with axes and thought better of my question, but Comrade Jesus remained affable, with a derisive smile on his lips. 'It is not me who has grabbed the land. White men came here, they grabbed the land from my ancestors. They grabbed the land long ago and they are still sitting on that land. I don't think that is a fair situation. I am just taking back what is mine.' Wells remained diplomatically silent. Then Comrade Jesus announced: 'I must go back to my people.' The interview was over and the leader's praetorian guard escorted him back to his motley collection of followers.

Wells and I returned to his Land Rover. 'I've built a rapport with this guy, it's the only way to handle the situation,' he said. 'I'll shoot an impala for them to eat later. They're quiet at the moment and I want to keep it that way.' Wells seemed remarkably calm for someone who had just confronted a mob at his gates. With all the skill of a master diplomat, he had defused a chilling situation and emerged without injury.

Wells looked and sounded like a typical white farmer. He wore very short shorts, knee-length socks and a shirt open to its third button. His face betrayed years of living under the African sun and most sentences opened with the word 'Yah'. As he showed me the 1,000 hectares of Maunga farm near Karoi, his flat, Rhodesian tones were tinged with pride and emotion. 'We've worked hard on this place, we've built it up from scratch. We've got five dams here, an irrigation network and we've set up a game reserve. There are kudu, impala, eland, sable. We don't cut down a single tree, we protect the place. I've got 130 workers. They all depend on this place and their families too. What would happen to them if these guys took over?' The rains had just ended and the bush was lush and green. As we drove along a ridge, a carpet of rolling grassland opened before us, stretching to the horizon beneath a limitless blue sky. The best farming land in Africa: what had brought the white man in the first place and the cause of all the trouble since.

Wells's father began tilling this corner of the country's agricultural heartland in 1958. When Mugabe came to power, all those words about reconciliation tipped the balance for many farmers and led them to stay in Zimbabwe. Wells bought Maunga soon after independence. To obtain the farm, he had to get a 'Certificate of No Present Interest' from Mugabe's government, specifying that the land was not needed for the resettlement of blacks. This vital piece of paper was issued over the counter and Wells had raised his family at Maunga. He now farmed tobacco and earned hard currency from tourists who enjoyed the peace of his tiny game park. If Comrade Jesus had his way, all this was about to end.

Back at the farmhouse, Dawn Wells was preparing lunch. She was very different from her husband: quiet, immaculate and clearly shaken by what had happened. But despite her ordeal, she was anxious that I would be well fed before I began the long drive back to Harare. 'Do people in the UK know what's going on here? Do they know how bad it's getting?' she asked. When I replied that everyone knew about the farm invasions, Dawn made no attempt to look reassured. Her hands shook as her husband recounted the events of the previous day, Saturday, 4 March.

The roar of a mob surging up their drive was the family's first warning that their farm had been singled out for invasion. Wells moved fast and used the few minutes before the gang reached the farmhouse to smuggle Dawn and their five-year-old son, Ben, out of a side gate, from where the farm manager drove them to safety. Moments later, the crowd massed outside the security fence surrounding the homestead, with Comrade Jesus urging them on. He was incoherently drunk, his breath reeking, his eyes inflamed. As soon as Wells appeared, the mob bayed their anger and pushed against the fence, waving sticks, axes and clubs. 'Open this gate *mabhunu* or we will fuck you up,' shouted Comrade Jesus. His followers were about to smash the flimsy gate to pieces, so Wells opened up and was instantly surrounded. 'You, *mabhunu,* we've come to take our land,' shouted Comrade Jesus.

'I understand what you're saying, but this is my home,' replied Wells. More shouts of anger. Enraged, the mob hurled abuse and one man grabbed the farmer by the nose, while others hit him on the face. Wells was paraded around the garden, to roars of laughter from the gang. They did not often get the chance to humiliate a white man.

'You call this your farm?' slurred Comrade Jesus. 'What do you mean your farm? This land belongs to Zimbabwe.' When they tired of slapping Wells around, the ringleaders sat down on the veranda and ordered him to sign over 350 hectares of land. He had little choice and scribbled out an agreement on a scrap of paper. After 20 years of earnest 'donor conferences', endless seminars and tedious gatherings of worthy experts, this is what land reform in Mugabe's Zimbabwe amounted to. A gang with axes and a terrified farmer signing away his property on a torn piece of A4.

Afterwards the mob left, apparently satisfied with their handiwork. Wells called the local police station but they refused to respond. He could only hope that his visitors would eventually go home. Instead, Comrade Jesus and his followers camped around the farmhouse. They lit a fire, hammered on drums and sang revolutionary songs for most of the night. Chants of *'Pasi ne mabhunu'* echoed around the farm while Wells lay inside his home, listening to the songs of hatred outside.

In the morning, Wells went outside and tried to lock his gate. Howls of protest rose from the mob while he secured the only barrier between the besiegers and the besieged. As he turned and began walking back to the farmhouse, he heard a loud crash. 'They smashed the gate open,' Wells told me, and the mob swamped the garden before surrounding him once again.

Comrade Jesus was still drunk and this time he had a different demand. 'You have got an arms cache here,' he bellowed. 'You are hiding guns for war!' Then his followers flooded on to the veranda and burst inside the house. Wells was convinced his last moment had come. 'I thought this is the end, over and out. Sorry, Wells, you're finished, I said to myself. I thought they were just going to take me out.' Comrade Jesus led the mob through the farmhouse, room by room. Every draw was opened, every cupboard ransacked, every room invaded. Special attention was paid to the bedrooms, and the ringleader insisted on searching the loft.

When they failed to find a stack of machine guns, hand grenades and missiles, or whatever they were expecting, Comrade Jesus looked momentarily crestfallen. But he swiftly decided that Wells was using Maunga's nearby game lodge as his 'arms cache'. So the farmer led the gang through the dense bush to the farm's tiny game park. Comrade Jesus accused Wells of laying land mines all over Maunga and the mob trooped in single file behind him. 'You will be blown up first,' he told the farmer. The squatters were wary and nervous because their leader also suspected that Wells was leading them into an ambush. Once at the lodge, overlooking a small waterhole, they repeated the search and found nothing. Wells seized his chance and managed to get Comrade Jesus to move his gang away from the farmhouse and camp on a field nearby. He hoped that things would somehow get back to normal. When I drove away from Maunga, I passed Comrade Jesus on the farm's dusty track. He raised his hand in a friendly wave.

★   ★   ★

By the time Wells's homestead was stormed, squatters had occupied about 140 white-owned farms across Zimbabwe and this total was growing by the hour. Comrade Jesus became a local warlord, organizing the farm occupations in the Karoi area and earning national notoriety. I was to encounter him, and more frequently his victims, time and again.

This was Mugabe's response to defeat in the referendum. The mob at the gates of Wells's homestead and many others were paid agents of Zanu-PF, the shock troops of the regime. All the paranoid delusions of a thousand Mugabe speeches had been indoctrinated in their credulous skulls. White farmers had organized the referendum defeat and were preparing for civil war, the squatters were told. A new war of liberation, a Third *Chimurenga* (or 'revolution')[1] was starting, hence the obsession with finding the imaginary 'arms cache' and evading the fantasy landmines on Wells's land. His ordeal would become the order of the day for a white farming community that came under siege.

★   ★   ★

Almost three weeks earlier, over 300 miles to the south of Comrade Jesus and his followers, a small column of 'war veterans' filed on to a barren expanse of bush and grassland. They built shacks and sowed crops on the land they claimed as their own. On 16 February, barely 24 hours after the announcement of the referendum result, Yothan farm in Masvingo province was the first to be occupied.

But a white farmer no longer owned its 1,000 hectares. The government had taken possession of Yothan in 1987 and it was handed over to blacks from the overcrowded communal areas. Yet the resettlement was bungled so badly that the new custodians of Yothan, dumped on remote patches of land without water, seed, fertilizer or housing, steadily trickled away until none were left. Like hundreds of other farms taken over by the state, Yothan was left uninhabited and idle.

A party of 20 war veterans occupied Yothan in protest over the referendum result and the official media rewarded them with glowing coverage, conveniently ignoring that the farm was a vivid illustration of the failure of Mugabe's land policies. Their leader, Eston Mupandi, told *The Herald:* 'We sweated, got injured, even died for this land. Those who voted No do not need the land . . . we will invade the farms until we have enough land. This is war and we have started another phase of the liberation struggle.'[2] These words would soon become the lexicon of the land invasions, to be repeated by countless ringleaders across the country.

The invasion of Yothan was reported on 19 February and the government, still shell-shocked by the referendum result, was shown an ideal way of punishing those it blamed for defeat. The following day, Mugabe appeared on state television for his customary interview on the eve of his birthday. In accordance with tradition, the *apparatchiks* of the official media bowled him fawning, adoring questions (Bornwell Chakaodza, editor of *The Herald,* excelled himself with: 'Your Excellency, many happy returns of the day, any special wishes?').

This was Mugabe's first response to the referendum defeat since the conciliatory broadcast on 15 February and his words were sharply different. 'Nobody should rejoice over the defeat the government had on this one,' he warned, momentarily betraying the fury that all those celebrations in the streets of Harare must have caused.

Then Mugabe announced that he would ignore the people's will. They may have rejected his new constitution in its entirety, but he would simply extract the clause allowing land seizures without compensation and insert it into the existing document. That was how he would get around the obstacle posed by the No vote. 'We will take the land, make no mistake about that, because the land question has not yet been resolved,' he said. Then came Mugabe's crucial words: 'The people are angry and if we let the people vent their anger, they will invade the farms and then the farmers will run to us for protection.'[3] It was far from obvious at the time, but Mugabe had announced his response to defeat. From that moment onwards, the farm invasions began in earnest and they had the full support of the state.

On 22 February another two farms were occupied, again in the Masvingo area. The following day the invasions spread north and four farms were invaded near Gutu. The last days of February saw the operation get into its stride. By 28 February provinces and, this time, most were transported in government vehicles, presumably using official stocks of precious fuel. Pickups from the District Development Fund, twin-cabs belonging to Zanu-PF and even police Land Rovers, donated by the British government, were employed. Camera crews from state television were on hand to record the occupations and they were given effusive coverage on official news broadcasts.

Farmers responded stoically. There was no panic, not even much alarm. Invasions of this sort had occurred many times before. Almost every year, a few dozen white-owned farms had been occupied and, after a few days, police usually intervened and restored order. But it was becoming increasingly clear that this was very different. The government was actually organizing the occupations. Moreover, there was no response whatever from the police. At the end of February, it began to dawn on farmers that they were facing something completely new.

As for why it was happening, none had any doubt. I spoke to Jerry Grant, from the CFU, on 28 February. He was open, frank and brutally realistic. 'It's breaking out in all regions and it's clearly being directed by a central authority. We're having difficulty getting the police to react because at the higher level they've been told to stand back.'

'Why do you think this is happening?' I asked.

'This is payback for the referendum result,' said Grant, without hesitation. 'It's a political move to soften up the white community. After all, someone has to take the blame.'

Augustine Chihuri, the Police Commissioner, had spent most of the week avoiding farmers and studiously ignoring their calls for help. On the day I spoke to Grant, he explained his inaction to *The Herald*. The invasions were 'above the police . . . it's a political issue,' he said.[4]

At about this time, two of Mugabe's leading henchmen met their chosen adversaries and rubbed in the message. After the invasions spread to Mashonaland Central province, a group of landowners visited Border Gezi, the Provincial Governor, on 29 February. Gezi had risen from obscurity to become one of Zanu-PF's star performers. Once a lowly clerk with Zesa, the chaotic state electricity company, the plump, bearded figure was now a favourite of Mugabe. Gezi's province covered Zimbabwe's agricultural heartland and he had gone out of his way to stay on friendly terms with white farmers. He was ebullient, approachable and apparently devoid of racial hang-ups. Some white landowners counted him as a friend and all respected his ability to get things done. When Gezi said something would happen, it always did, and that made him unique among Mugabe's ministers. When squatters carried out some half-hearted farm invasions in 1998, Gezi promised farmers: 'We are not going to allow this in my province.' An assurance of this sort from any other minister would have been treated with grave suspicion, but he was true to his word and the invaders were swiftly evicted.

When four farms were invaded near Centenary, in the north of Mashonaland Central, farmers hoped for the same response. Yet when they met their former friend in Bindura, the provincial capital, he delivered a very different message. 'My political ambitions have been damaged by the fact that I have been friends with you,' Gezi told the farmers. 'It has been held against me by my opponents.' He told them bluntly that the invasions would not be stopped. On the contrary, if anyone still harboured doubts, the occupations were 'fully supported by government'. Gezi emphasized his point by using the language of the liberation war. 'This is the Third *Chimurenga*,'[5] he told the farmers. Everyone present at that meeting knew that a crucial watershed had been reached. Immediately afterwards, Gezi became the first government minister to make his support for the occupations public when he told *The Herald*: 'We as a province are behind the invasions . . . these events signal the start of the Third Liberation.'[6]

The following day, 1 March, saw an equally uncomfortable meeting between Peter Longworth, the British High Commissioner, and Vice-

President Joseph Msika. Most Western diplomats thought this solid, reassuring figure a 'realist', a man they could do business with. Once a follower of Joshua Nkomo, Msika was among the Zapu cabinet ministers sacked by Mugabe in 1982. Since the Unity Accord, Msika had buried his differences with Zanu-PF, but he still kept a degree of independence from his leader.

But during a stormy meeting with Longworth, the Vice-President spoke like a raging revolutionary. 'We're fed up with you British and we're going to go our own way,' he said. Msika accused Britain of 'interfering with our political process and organising the MDC'. As for the referendum, all Longworth's denials were angrily dismissed and Msika blamed London for the No vote. 'That was organized by you British and the white farmers,' he growled.[7]

Now all the pieces fell into place. Rather than accept any mistakes or responsibility, Mugabe had summoned his formidable reserves of paranoia and decided that an unholy alliance of Britain and white farmers had inflicted his defeat. It was the perfect explanation – instead of acknowledging that many of his people had turned against him, Mugabe chose to blame the familiar roll-call of enemies. In retaliation, Zanu-PF supporters would be unleashed on white-owned farms across the country. By 2 March, over 70 farms were occupied and the number of new invasions was running at 20 a day.

Across Zimbabwe, one farmer after another found a mob at his gates and tightly knit communities came under siege. A pattern emerged that soon became wearily familiar. The squatters, usually drunk or high on drugs, would order the farmer to sign over his land with threats of violence. To get rid of his tormentors, the landowner would scribble an agreement on a sheet of paper, carefully riddled with mis-spellings, and persuade the squatters to camp on a distant field, well away from the homestead. They would set up a 'base camp', usually marked by a fluttering Zimbabwean flag, and settle down for a long stay. Meanwhile, the farmer would try and get back to work.

Yet it soon became clear that anti-white fervour was only a smokescreen. The squatters began their real business: the brutal work of intimidation. Black farm workers were accused of falling under the influence of their white employers and siding with the MDC. They were brutally 're-educated' by the squatters. Silently, often in the dead of night, hundreds were assaulted. The villages in which the workers lived were raided and known MDC supporters dealt with. Anyone suspected of backing the opposition could expect violent retribution. Rather than seizing the white man's land, this became the consuming task of the mobs on the farms. Everything else was a cover.

★　　　　★　　　　★

Seated in a circle beneath a tree, the group of squatters glared at the farm-house with sullen hostility. The ground was littered with the tools of their trade: sticks, clubs, axes, hoes. They formed the usual profile – a core of men old enough to be genuine veterans of the bush war and a large coterie of hangers-on, male and female, whose only common characteristic was obvious poverty. They sat listlessly, while the target of their hostility stared back with stoical frustration.

Gerald Smith had found a drunken gang of 20 drumming their way up his drive on the previous night. As his wife, Paula, and 84-year-old mother took refuge in the farmhouse, he went outside to confront them. At the gates, he was subjected to a storm of abuse. 'White bastard, white pig,' they yelled. 'Our President, our God Mugabe has ordered us to kill you.' The ringleader styled himself Comrade Doubletrouble and was carrying so much alcohol he was barely able to stand. His followers pounded the fence with their sticks and axes.

Comrade Doubletrouble ordered Smith to open the gates of the security fence surrounding the homestead. When he refused, they simply broke the lock and surged into the garden. Smith retreated through the back door of the farmhouse and grabbed a rifle, an ancient .303 Lee Enfield. At that moment, Comrade Doubletrouble and several of his followers burst through the door and surrounded him. Smith shouted: 'This is my home. Get out or I will shoot.' One squatter grabbed his rifle and started to wrestle with him. Smith kicked his assailant, who pulled him to the floor. As he fell, another squatter brought an axe down on his head. For a few seconds, he was out cold, helpless, sprawled on the floor while the gang gleefully kicked and lashed out at the prostrate farmer. After a few seconds of frenzied violence, the mêlée subsided and the gang inexplicably fled into the night, taking Smith's rifle with them. He was covered with bruises and bleeding from a deep head wound caused by the axe. His distraught wife and mother rushed Smith to hospital. When he returned, with a bandage swathed over his skull, the sullen gang was sitting near his gate.

My arrival caused a stir of interest. A few members of the gang stood up and glared with open hostility, most remained slumped on the ground. Smith told me that Comrade Doubletrouble had disappeared and any attempt to interview his followers would risk stirring the hornets' nest. So we sat in his living room and he talked about the business of running an occupied farm. His workers had been threatened and warned that if any supported the MDC, they would be dealt with. They were too frightened to emerge from their homes.

Smith wore the standard uniform of white farms – short navy blue shorts and an open shirt. His homestead on Nyarenda farm near Karoi was small and modest. He might have been targeted for invasion because of his political views. Until 1987 he was an MP with Ian Smith's Conservative Alliance of Zimbabwe (CAZ), the successor party to the Rhodesian Front. When the old warhorse finally retired, Gerald Smith became the party's leader. In theory, this political force still existed and Smith (no relation to Ian Smith) was one of the foremost politicians in Zimbabwe. In practice, CAZ consisted of him and about three other people. As I walked into his farmhouse, I passed the office – a dusty room with an old-fashioned telephone perched on a shabby desk. The once mighty Rhodesian Front had been reduced to this. The party that had dominated the country now consisted of a handful of people and a few files in a fly-blown office, stuck in a remote corner of the Zimbabwean bush. It crossed my mind that one day the same might be said of Zanu-PF.

But Smith's political background made him more outspoken than many other farmers. 'Mugabe's a monster,' he said emphatically. 'We're dealing with a man who's cornered. If he's removed, people will want answers to questions. There's a lot of blood on his hands. Those people down in Matabeleland won't forgive him and neither will the rest of us.' For Smith, the land campaign was the last gasp of a desperate man.

★   ★   ★

Most of those who sought to farm in the African bush were sufficiently tough and hard-nosed to cope with a mob at the gates. But that was not true of their wives and children. Some were terrified out of their collective minds by the first invasions and never fully recovered. The Henderson family, who farmed amid the rocky outcrops north of Mvurwi, found a band of 200 squatters surrounding their homestead at 6.30 p.m. on a Wednesday evening. Drums beat in the darkness and hundreds of voices roared the songs of the liberation war – songs of hatred against white people. The Hendersons' two daughters, aged four and seven, were woken by the bedlam and their parents pulled them out of bed and put them in front of the television. Ian, their father, turned on top volume in a futile bid to drown the sounds from outside.

The maddening cacophony of drums and songs went on all night without break. It continued through Thursday, while the family cowered, sleepless in their home. Ian Henderson met a delegation of five squatters who ordered him to sign over his land immediately. When he replied that only the government could take his farm, they told him: 'We are the government and we are above the law.' The noise went on for a second night. Camilla, the seven year old, and her mother, Blair, were close to cracking under the strain. 'We didn't get any sleep at all,' Blair Henderson told me. 'I kept thinking they were going to come over the fence and break into the house. It was such a frightening and unpredictable situation.' On Friday morning, the police finally arrived. They persuaded the squatters to free Blair and the two girls, who sought refuge with friends at a nearby farm. When they reached safety, Camilla said to her mother: 'Promise me there are no drums mummy.' Their father remained in the house alone and eventually the squatters tired of their exertions and backed off. They set up camp at the farm's entrance and contented themselves with intimidating the workforce.

In their classrooms, farmers' children began writing plaintive messages. One seven-year-old boy who was unable to return home because of an invasion wrote in his school exercise book: 'What's happening on the farms? Please pray the Lord that can we go home.' Another wrote: 'Plece can you help Zimbabwe. We are not safe in this country . . . you are not safe with wore vetrens. Mr Mgabwe just wants the land. Or he will hirt you.'

★   ★   ★

At the CFU headquarters in Harare, a team of people dropped their usual jobs and tracked the seizures full time. A few miles away, in the city centre, another group saw their lives transformed. Hitler Hunzvi and his War Veterans' Association shot to prominence. As Mugabe's most ardent sup-porters, they had been placed in charge of the invasions and their shabby offices in Equity House, a stone's throw from the British Council building in central Harare, became the nerve centre for the occupations. Later they moved *en masse* into the Zanu-PF headquarters tower block, and their lorries, used for carrying mobs to the farms, were parked alongside the black Mercedes of Zimbabwe's élite.

Hunzvi became the leader of the onslaught and was well rewarded for his efforts. Zanu-PF paid the War Veterans' Association ZD 20 million (then about £330,000) to cover the cost of the occupations. Squatters were supplied with food by government vehicles and paid a daily rate. The amount varied from region to region, but most could expect about ZD 50 (then worth 80p) for every day spent on a farm. Hunzvi appeared on one farm after another, rousing his followers to a frenzy with his anti-white rhetoric.

I climbed the stairs of Equity House to interview him as the occupations began. Hunzvi's office was on the top floor and I found its entrance pro-tected by an iron cage thrown across the stairs and guarded by five bearded men wearing Mugabe T-shirts.

'What do you want?' they demanded.

'I have an appointment to see Mr Hunzvi.' This caused great consterna-tion. Heads shook, eyes rolled, and a muttered conversation took place between the guards. One had a flash of inspiration. 'Who are you?' he asked.

I produced my Zimbabwean press card. This was greeted with a murmur of interest and passed from hand to hand for detailed examination. With their brows furrowed in concentration, each guard subjected the tiny plastic card to close textual analysis. Finally, the cage was opened and I was allowed through.

Keys jangled and bolts rattled as the heavy door beyond was laboriously unlocked. It opened an inch and a bloodshot eye became visible. 'What do you want?' I repeated my request. The door was slammed shut. I waited alongside the morose, silent men in Mugabe T-shirts. Finally, after what seemed like an hour but was probably only fifteen minutes or so, the door was opened and a teenager wearing a 'Vote Zanu-PF' T-shirt led me to a nondescript office, where Hunzvi sat at a large desk.

Sprawled on the floor beside him were two elderly women. They were eating from plates of *sadza,* the maize porridge forming the staple diet in Zimbabwe. Hunzvi was bent over a sheaf of papers, wearing one of his tasteful green suits and an orange shirt with a brown tie. He appeared not to notice my presence. I sat on a rickety chair while the teenager stood beside me. Silence. Then Hunzvi looked up and grinned. 'You, Mr British journalist, ask questions,' he said. Before I could draw breath, he launched into a rant, delivered in a strange, childish voice. 'I will do what the people of Zimbabwe want and they want the land. One thing you British must know is that the land was grabbed from us by you. The land is still in the hands of white people and they are not Africans. These whites who think they are Zimbabwean, we will just deport them back to Britain.' Hunzvi paused for breath.

'What about the law of Zimbabwe?' I asked.

'The law has to fit the people of Zimbabwe and they don't have the land. We war veterans are the policemen of Zimbabwe, we enforce the law, we do not obey the law,' came the reply. Then I asked the burning question that had been on my mind all along. 'Why on earth are you called Hitler?'

'It is my name. My father gave me the name. Hitler has been a victim of Western propaganda. You are only against him because he lost.' Hunzvi burst out laughing.

It was, as usual, almost impossible to get any sense out of him. I was to meet him on about half a dozen occasions, and every time I found it impossible to take him remotely seriously. He was not even a genuine war veteran. He joined Zipra in 1977 but was quickly despatched to Romania and then Poland for training. While in Warsaw, he enrolled at the medical school and claimed to have qualified as a doctor. He returned to Zimbabwe long after independence, having never fired a gun in the struggle, with a Polish wife in tow. She later wrote a book about married life with Hunzvi called *White Slave*. After years of beatings and abuse, she escaped back to her native

Poland, while Hunzvi managed to take over the War Veterans' Association. You could not deny his achievement. But as I left Hunzvi's office, just the thought of his girlish voice intoning the usual gibberish was enough to make me laugh out loud.

★   ★   ★

But no one could deny that 'Hitler' was fast becoming one of the most powerful men in Zimbabwe, far more influential than most of the cabinet. This became painfully clear on 2 March when Dumiso Dabengwa, the Home Affairs Minister, made a valiant attempt to restore order. With 70 farms occupied, he summoned the world's press to his ministry and told us that the 'war veterans' had broken the law. 'I have therefore decided to instruct the war veterans to withdraw from the farms with immediate effect,' said Dabengwa. 'I recognize that farm owners enjoy as much right to protection as any other citizens in this country.'[8]

A short, elegant man with an unblinking gaze, Dabengwa had been a senior guerrilla leader during the war against Rhodesia. As head of intelligence and security for Zipra, Nkomo's rebel army, he was not a man to be casually humiliated. But Dabengwa's humiliation was total and it came at the hands of a man who had served under him as one of Zipra's most junior foot soldiers – and one who never saw action. Even as he tried to restore order, Hunzvi gave a simultaneous press conference for the official media and announced that the invasions would go on. 'They will not result in anarchy,'[9] added Hunzvi piously.

This could have been put down to insubordination, but Mugabe was also briefing the state media and he casually contradicted his Home Affairs Minister. Mugabe appeared on state television and said: 'No, we will not put a stop to the invasions which are a demonstration, a peaceful demonstration and a lawful demonstration by the ex-combatants.'[10] To *The Herald*, Mugabe gave a staunch defence of the invaders. 'They are just demonstrating their greatest disappointment that there was this No vote,'[11] he said. As government vehicles drove yet more invaders on to the farms, it was clear that the squatters had the support of the highest authority in the land.

From that moment onwards, the tempo of the invasions increased. By 6 March, 250 farms were occupied. On 12 March the total stood at 450. The first occupations occurred in Matabeleland and every province was now affected. Farmers despaired of any help from the police. Yet in private, the CFU leadership made contact with senior figures in the government. They received quiet but firm messages of reassurance. All would be well, they were told. But they received one clear warning. If they sought a High Court order declaring the invasions illegal, the situation would be inflamed.

Yet after Dabengwa was tossed aside, Tim Henwood, President of the CFU, decided that going to court was the only option.

On 17 March, Mr Justice Paddington Garwe of the High Court of Zimbabwe issued an order by consent of all parties. The CFU had named Hunzvi, Gezi and Augustine Chihuri, the Police Commissioner, as respondents in the case and they all agreed the following:

1. Every occupation of any property . . . is hereby declared unlawful.
2. All persons who have taken up occupation of any commercial farm . . . shall vacate that land within 24 hours of the making of this Order.

Hunzvi and Gezi agreed not to 'encourage, allow or otherwise participate in' the invasion of any farm. Chihuri undertook to order his police officers to evict the occupiers 'forthwith'. The good Justice Garwe gave the police 72 hours to clear all farms of invaders. What happened next revealed not only a breakdown of the rule of law but the mendacity of those who had consented to the court order. When the ruling was issued, the number of occupied farms stood at 630. By the time the deadline expired, the number was 742. The invasions continued and the law was simply torn to shreds.

★ ★ ★

On the day after the court ruling, I went to Zanu-PF's provincial headquarters in Fourth Street, central Harare, which served as the nerve centre for the invasions. Three filthy blue buses were parked outside the shabby building and a crowd massed around them. Elderly men and women, all wearing the familiar haggard, impoverished look of Zanu-PF supporters, and teenage boys with Mugabe T-shirts – the thugs who did the damage if needs be – milled in every direction. I tried to speak to these sullen, hostile figures and each refused to say a word. One man with a hoe across his shoulder said: 'You must talk to our commander' and then led me through the crowd.

There were some angry murmurs and glares but no real hostility. I was led towards a small, bearded man, wearing a white baseball cap and ragged, brown trousers. 'This is our commander,' said the man with the hoe. The commander glared in my direction and in several others. His squint made it hard to tell whether I was the target of his venomous stare or the people around me. 'You are British?' So he was looking at me.

'Yes,' I replied.

'Tell Tony Blair we will fight for our land.' As his deep, guttural voice emerged from a set of broken, crooked teeth, the commander spat in all directions. I wiped my shirt and asked: 'Are you going to obey the law and stop the invasions?'

'Listen my friend,' came the incredulous reply. 'We are carrying on. We are not bowed by the court order. No matter the courts say anything, we are not going to be limited by courts. If they want war with us, they will get it.'

An angry voice shouted from the crowd: 'The war will start even today.' I was surrounded by a score of morose faces, pushing against me and looking over my shoulder. The commander carried on with a stream of broken English, jerking his head, rolling his eyes and clenching a fist for emphasis: 'We want the law to respect us. No matter the law, we will take the farms. If the farmers provoke us, we will retaliate. They must not clash with us. We are the people who fight for this country. We will not be driven from what is ours. Where was the High Court when this land was taken from us? These whites must watch out if they are causing trouble for us. We can finish them.' The tide of broken English went on and on, with the eyes rotating in a manic, multidirectional stare and spittle spraying in a wide arc from his jaw. My notebook was flecked with tiny white blobs by the time the commander paused for breath. 'Thank you,' there was not much more to be said. 'And what is your name?'

'Commander Joseph Chinotimba' came the reply and the great man turned and lurched away, waving his arms and bellowing at his followers.

A youth grabbed me by the hand and said: 'You must talk to this one.' An old man appeared next to me, his mouth open in a toothless smile, his breath reeking of alcohol. He was painfully thin, with narrow sloping shoulders and wore a large hat made of the spotted pelt of a leopard. 'This is Chief Chiramhora,' his companion announced in a tone of reverence. Then Chief Chiramhora launched into a stream of consciousness. 'In 1896 when the white man came I was standing here. The white man started fighting to take our land. He brought the machine gun to destroy us. The war has not ended. I am crying for the land, we must have our land back, it is the heritage of our children.' He stopped to draw breath and reeled drunkenly. Then the exertion was too much for his elderly frame and he sat down heavily on the pavement. 'He is tired,' said the henchman. 'But you must tell the British what he said.' I promised to do so and walked back to Fourth Street, through the sullen stares of the crowd.

★ ★ ★

In the shade of a thorn tree stood a makeshift shack, surrounded by people cooking, eating and sleeping soundly. A Zimbabwean flag fluttered from the branches overhead and a picture of Mugabe was attached to the tree trunk. His followers showed little willingness to rouse themselves for another day in the vanguard of his revolutionary struggle to seize land from the white oppressor. They spent most of the morning lying on their sides, recovering from the exertions of the previous night. A large pile of empty beer bottles showed that it had been a good party. This group of 20 revolutionaries had recently 'liberated' Parklands farm near Norton and they were charged with the task of invading all of the white-owned farms nearby.

Their leader, Agnes Rusike, took her duties seriously. She wore a 'Vote Yes' T-shirt and a Zanu-PF baseball cap, with Mugabe's face permanently over her forehead. When I arrived at her camp with Paul Grover, a photographer colleague, she greeted us with cries of '*Pamberi ne* Zanu-PF, *Pamberi ne* Comrade President R. G. Mugabe.' Her high-pitched shrieks stirred her followers and some opened their eyes blearily. Rusike went from one huddle to the next, rousing the sleeping figures. Rubbing their eyes, they were persuaded to stand and then Rusike began a vigorous song of support for their leader.

Waking with remarkable alacrity, the group of elderly men, young women and teenage boys danced and clapped their hands while singing a lively ditty that translated as follows: 'As long as Comrade Mugabe stays in power, we are happy. As long as we take the farms, we are happy. As long as we defeat the white imperialists, we are happy.' The two white imperialists who made up their audience applauded appreciatively at the end. Paul and I clapped politely and obeyed Rusike's instructions to wave our fists in the air as the revolutionaries chanted more praise of Comrade Mugabe. Then, with the performance over, most of them dropped like sacks of maize and went back to sleep.

Rusike, however, was anxious that we should understand 'the struggle'. A small figure in her 40s, with short, spiky hair, she spoke with grave intensity. She claimed to be 'National Coordinator of the Liberation War Widows and Widowers Association' and told us that her husband was killed in the guerrilla war. 'We want revenge on the whites. They have been killing us and we are poor because they are rich,' she said. 'Our people live like baboons while these ones are rich, they own 17 farms each, big houses, aeroplanes, silver Mercedes. We want to get what they have.'

Under Rusike's direction, most of the farms around Norton had been occupied and a network of camps established. 'This is the main camp, the information centre,' she told us, pointing at the cardboard shack. 'We liberate all the farms from here.' At that moment a blue Toyota pick-up appeared on a dusty track nearby, driven by an elderly white man wearing a wide-brimmed hat. 'Waaaaaah' shouted Rusike and waved her fist at the passing vehicle. Several of the squatters echoed her howls of derision until the car retreated out of sight. 'That one is the farmer,' she explained. 'He is a very bad man, that one. He does not want us to be here and he is trying to get his workers to kill us. But they are refusing. They are our comrades.'

Rusike then treated us to some new conspiracy theories. Cyclone Eline had just cut a swathe of devastation across neighbouring Mozambique and she had a novel explanation for this disaster. 'The Americans created Cyclone Eline,' she said darkly. 'They have submarines which put a missile under the sea. This created Cyclone Eline so they could send their soldiers to Mozambique. The Americans and you British want to take over the whole world. I read it in *The Herald*.'

As Rusike paused for breath, a small, thin woman with a baby on her back and a toddler clinging to her legs appeared at the fence beside the camp. She was barefoot, wearing a grubby dress and a threadbare blanket. Rusike joined her and the woman waved her fist limply. '*Pamberi ne* Zanu-PF, *pamberi ne* Mugabe' she chanted shyly, in a thin, high-pitched voice. The two women talked quietly in Shona and Rusike produced a grubby, well-thumbed, school exercise book. Writing with the worn stub of a pencil, she took the woman's name and then pointed her down the track.

'I have just given her some land on this farm,' Rusike said. 'She is going to peg some land on the next field.' That was how you got land in Mugabe's Zimbabwe. You approached the local squatters, chanted your loyalty to the master, and then pegged out a few acres. Rusike was being commendably honest. Most of the warlords running the invasions charged anything up to ZD 100 (then worth £1.67) for a plot of land. Then again, perhaps she would have done in the absence of two journalists.

Her fellow ringleader, 'Comrade' Freddy Ruzvidzo lumbered in our direction. He was clearly suffering from the ordeal of the previous night. His eyeballs were shot through with red lines and he lurched unsteadily. He rested his pot belly against the fence while Paul and I introduced ourselves as British journalists. 'I follow British football,' replied Ruzvidzo, brightening suddenly. 'I support Manchester United. Man U, Man U, Man U,' he chanted. 'That one, Roy Keane, he is a very good man.' It made a change from chanting the praises of Comrade Mugabe. Then Ruzvidzo doubled up in a fit of coughing and retching. He heaved, snorted and wheezed against the fence.

When he recovered, I asked him: 'Why do you choose to live in this shack when you're obviously ill?' He bridled at the impertinence of my question. 'Because my commander has told me to,' Ruzvidzo pointed at the picture of Mugabe emblazoned on his T-shirt. 'I always do what he says. I was with him in the bush. I fought for him. I was in Mozambique when Smith's planes came and bombed us and killed us. I am loyal to Mugabe and I fought for land. When independence came, there was meant to be land. But the white man refused. So now we are taking it.'

As Ruzvidzo spoke, the roar of an expensive car engine suddenly drowned his words. A spotless, gleaming Toyota land cruiser drew up beside the shack and six men emerged. They were dressed in a uniform – smart, expensive suits, mobile phones and dark glasses all round. Rusike and Ruzvidzo looked embarrassed and talked quietly in Shona. They walked sheepishly over to the men and exchanged handshakes. But the six looked suspiciously in the direction of Paul and myself and were obviously asking about us. One of the suited figures approached us. 'You are British?' he asked.

'Yes.'

'You British are trying to create war in Zimbabwe. You are here to look at the situation. You are here to assess how to cause trouble.' With that, he turned on his heel and walked back to his companions. Rusike rejoined us a few minutes later. The new arrivals were 'senior Zanu-PF officials' from the party's headquarters in Harare. They did 'not want to see us here'. She advised us to make ourselves scarce and we duly did so.

As we drove away from the cluster of figures around the shack, some in suits, most in rags, it was obvious who was really in command of the land invasions and who would receive the lion's share of the spoils.

★   ★   ★

By the end of March, over 800 farms were occupied and the pace of new invasions showed no sign of easing. After contradicting his Home Affairs Minister and publicly backing the squatters, Mugabe never wavered in his support. In a speech on 10 March he said: 'It was agreed that they can remain on the farms as long as they are peaceful.' He added: 'We want the whites to learn that the land belongs to Zimbabweans.'[12] Even after the High Court declared the invasions illegal on 17 March, with the consent of all parties, including his Police Commissioner, Mugabe's policy did not change and the occupations continued.

At the very beginning, there was little violence, but squatters soon began assaulting farmers and their workers, usually because they were suspected of supporting the MDC. This did not change Mugabe's approach one jot. On the contrary, he blamed the farmers for any violence and placed the onus on them to avoid clashes with the gangs illegally occupying their property. On 27 March, Mugabe said: 'There have been very few cases of violence, but if the farmers start to be angry and start to be violent, then of course they will get that medicine delivered to them. And it can be very, very, very severe, but we don't want to get there.'[13] His rhetoric became steadily more extreme. On 16 March he vented his anger with the 'divisive' forces of the opposition and said: 'Those who try to cause disunity among our people must watch out because death will befall them.'[14]

Mugabe soon devised a propaganda line to explain the invasions. He claimed they were 'spontaneous' popular movements and the government had no hand in them. Moreover, they were 'peaceful demonstrations' and any attempt by the police to bring them to an end would simply cause unnecessary violence. So the solution to the problem was to redistribute land from white farmers to poor blacks as fast as possible.

This line, repeated by Mugabe's ministers to an incredulous media, was a tissue of fabrications and half-truths. The occupation of Yothan farm on 16 February and a handful of the early invasions could well have been spontaneous. But from Mugabe's birthday interview on 20 February onwards, virtually all of the occupations took place with the obvious support of the government. Official vehicles transported and supplied the squatters, while police stood by and watched. Local government officials were seen visiting the squatters and paying them each day. A constant succession of official vehicles brought them food. Zanu-PF offices across the country were used as bases from which squatters mounted invasions. It is a matter of public record that the War Veterans' Association helped run the occupations and did so with ZD 20 million of Zanu-PF funds. By the end of March, the CFU estimated that about 8,000 squatters were occupying farms. Had the invasions been a genuinely popular movement, this total would surely have been many times higher. Over seven million blacks lived on overcrowded communal areas. Why didn't half a million flood on to white farms and swamp every property in the country?

To say that the government supported the operation does not go far enough. The invasions were clearly organized by the authorities and it is impossible to imagine this happening without Mugabe's personal seal of approval. He was convinced that white farmers had organized the No vote and created the MDC. He would punish them for this defiance. Moreover, the two million black people living on their land were votes he had to win for the parliamentary election. Hence the invasions soon escalated into a broader campaign of political intimidation designed to wipe out the MDC. Land was of secondary importance. Smashing the opposition was the crucial objective.

By the end of March, this goal took primacy over all others and a wave of violence was unleashed. The first murder of an MDC supporter occurred on 27 March near Bindura. Edwin Gomo, 16, died after being hit on the head by a stone thrown by a Zanu-PF mob. He had been travelling to an MDC rally. On 28 March, Bindura saw another murder – of Robert Musoni, another MDC supporter killed by Zanu-PF youths. The political terror campaign against the opposition was beginning. It would now engulf Zimbabwe.

Notes and References

1 The First Chimurenga was the uprising of 1896 and the Second was the guerrilla war of 1972–79.
2 *The Herald,* 19 February 2000.
3 ZBC interview, 20 February 2000.
4 *The Herald,* 29 February 2000.
5 Private information.
6 *The Herald,* 1 March 2000.
7 Interview with Peter Longworth, 31 August 2001.
8 Press conference, 2 March 2000.
9 *The Herald,* 3 March 2000.
10 ZBC, 2 March 2000.
11 *The Herald,* 3 March 2000.
12 *Ibid.,* 11 March 2000.
13 Reuters TV, 27 March 2000.
14 Speech, opening of Pungwe water project, 16 March 2000.

Chapter 5

MDC Will Be Crushed for Ever

1–15 April 2000

Those villages who back MDC and bow to the *mabhunu* – we will bomb them! MDC will be crushed for ever. (Border Gezi, Governor of Mashonaland Central, 7 April 2000)[1]

The riot police fanned out across the road, with batons brandished and tear-gas grenades at the ready. Behind the clear visors of their blue helmets, they wore expressions of blind fury. In front of them, a sea of people waved their open palms and chanted: 'Peace'. The crowd advanced with slow, steady determination, towards the screen of helmeted figures and raised clubs. People drew near to the motionless, implacable policemen. One officer betrayed his nerves by swinging his baton and levelling the short-barrelled handgun used for firing tear-gas canisters. No murmur of fear rose from the crowd; instead they pressed on, until their front ranks were pushing against the officers, daring them to do their worst.

I was suddenly reminded of the famous scene in Prague in 1968, when a Czech protester placed flowers down the barrels of machine guns brandished by impassive Soviet soldiers. Behind the impenetrable screen of riot police, I caught sight of a policeman wearing the epaulettes of a senior officer. He held a walkie-talkie in his hand and stood in silence, with his head bowed. Suddenly he looked up and jerked the radio to one side. The officers lowered their batons and moved to the roadside, out of the path of the crowd that immediately surged forward with an audible sigh of relief.

I could scarcely believe my eyes. One minute earlier, I had been bracing myself for the crack of exploding tear-gas canisters and trying to work out which way to run to avoid the noxious white clouds. Having learnt from bitter experience how unpleasant a thorough tear gassing can be, I held my finger in the air, discovered the direction of the breeze and decided to run left, down Samora Machel Avenue. But all this was unnecessary. The march would be allowed to progress through central Harare. Over 50 riot police had decided not to disperse the gathering by the customary method of volleys of tear gas and furious baton charges. Cheered by passers-by, a stream of cheerful, smiling faces embarked on their 'march for peace' on the bright, sunny autumn morning of Saturday, 1 April 2000.

The demonstration had been called by the National Constitutional Assembly to protest against the farm invasions and the accompanying wave of political intimidation. Even the organizers were surprised by the overwhelming response. Over 1,000 people gathered at the outset of the march, black and white, young and old. Some wore MDC T-shirts and waved the open-palmed salute of the opposition. But the banners carried simple messages that, in the hope of the organizers, no one would disagree with. They read 'Peace', 'A Spirit of Peace', 'Tolerance', and 'Truth, Justice and Reconciliation'. They were borne by a remarkable cross-section of Zimbabwean society, probably not seen together since the independence celebrations of 20 years earlier. Impoverished, ragged people from the city's townships walked alongside smartly dressed white businessmen. Nuns and priests joined the students and lawyers of the black middle class. One nun held a banner reading: 'Cry my beloved country'. Many elderly people were visible in the crowd and some marchers carried small children on their shoulders.

I looked from this cheerful, buoyant gathering to the senior policeman with the walkie-talkie. At dawn, a cordon of road blocks had been thrown around central Harare in a failed bid to prevent the throng from assembling. Two marchers had already been arrested. Ten minutes earlier, a High Court order allowing the demonstration to proceed had been presented to this officer – only for him to throw it contemptuously to the pavement. But now he was allowing the joyful mass to stream past. One girl, aged about seven, waved a bunch of flowers in the air. An elderly man was being pushed in a wheelchair. You couldn't tear gas a crowd like this, I thought. That would be too much, even for the Zimbabwean police. That's why you've decided to let them through.

For the next hour, central Harare became a carnival city. The marchers progressed down Second Street, past African Unity Square, crying 'Peace' and laughing excitedly. Some of the younger ones were so overcome with the delight of demonstrating freely in their capital that they took to performing press-ups on every street corner. As the demonstration turned into Jason Moyo Avenue, the long tail of people seemed to grow and grow. Thousands of passers-by joined the march, while others cheered from the pavements. Standing on a traffic island, I saw the entire street thronged with smiling faces and a sea of banners from which one word resounded: 'Peace'. Perhaps 7,000 people had now joined the march and their songs and chants mingled into a single, joyful sound. Meanwhile, the 50 riot police walked beside the demonstration, scowling darkly, with batons swinging limply from their wrists.

The marchers turned and paraded up Julius Nyerere Street, their ranks thinning as passers-by dispersed. By the time the demonstration turned into Union Avenue, one of Harare's main shopping streets, about 1,500 people walked together. In an instant, the mood changed. From near the front rank of the march, I heard cries of 'Peace' mingle with a mounting murmur of fear. People at the head of the demonstration stopped in their tracks. A few hundred yards ahead, above a host of fearful faces, I saw sticks and clubs waving in the air. I pushed forwards, through to the very front of the march.

A gang of 'war veterans' was approaching down Union Avenue. They were instantly recognizable. A Zanu-PF flag fluttered over a mob of about 200, many wearing leather jackets, green caps and Mugabe T-shirts. I noticed the riot police standing in quiet huddles on the pavement, showing no surprise or alarm. Then, with a cry of '*Hondo*' (meaning 'war'), the gang charged. Demonstrators fled in panic as a volley of stones flew towards them. I pushed my way through a boiling mass of running, terrified figures. Seconds later, I reached the relative safety of a shop doorway and turned to see the howling phalanx of attacking thugs collide with the march. Men lashed out at fleeing people, beating them to the ground in every direction. Bodies rolled on the pavement, while spots of blood stained the concrete. Petrified drivers abandoned their cars, shops hastily barricaded entrances, leaving desperate people trapped in the street, while others appeared rooted to the spot with fear. Screams mingled with the incessant screech of car alarms. Bellows of anger blended with cries of pain.

A voice shouted: 'You white people must get away from here, get away, they are after you.' Ducking as more stones flew, I ran to the entrance of Edgars department store and hammered desperately on the glass door. It was barricaded, shuttered and the security guard inside shook his head. Perhaps 20 feet away, a white couple in their fifties were toppled by stones and fell to the ground. Seconds later, three thugs set upon them with clubs. Blow after blow rained down, each aimed at the head. I watched, transfixed, as blood spattered six feet across the pavement. The man tried to get up, but his head jerked forward as the clubs rose and fell. The woman lay on the ground, her head an amorphous mass of red, and with each blow, more blood sprayed around her. Then three policemen drove the attacking thugs away.

Perhaps shaken by the sight of two bodies lying in a vivid, growing pool of red, the guard threw open the door and allowed me to enter. The clothes shop was being transformed into a makeshift first-aid centre. A white man in his forties with severe head injuries lay in a pool of blood. 'I'm dying, I'm dying,' he moaned, as volunteers tended him. Two black women began bandaging his wounds, resting his head on a white cloth, soon to become crimson. From outside came howls of terror and rage as figures ran to and fro, some waving clubs, others intent only on escape. Beside me a tiny, grey-haired, white woman held a bandage to her head. 'What happened to you?' I asked. Trish Swift, 52, replied in a voice filled with suppressed shock. 'They were rushing at us with sticks and stones. They attacked an old man who was lying on the ground, so I went to help. Then they turned on me. They hit me with sticks and then one of them just head-butted me.' She paused and then added: 'This wasn't even a political demonstration. My poster said "Truth, justice and reconciliation." It was a gathering of all Zimbabweans who wanted peace.'

Loud cracks echoed outside and white clouds billowed around the shop doorways. Now that Mugabe's followers had done their worst and dealt with the 'march for peace', the riot police were clearing the streets. I went outside, my eyes stinging, my nose recoiling at the sharp, painful smell of tear gas. Figures ran through the cloud, while the clatter of a military helicopter drowned the screams and cries. The gas cleared and groups of shocked people huddled together, their eyes streaming. Fury and terror were written on their faces. 'Mugabe must go, he must just go. Go, go now,' screamed one woman, her eyes red with tears, her voice cracking with passion. A television cameraman appeared beside me and a crowd gathered around us, roaring their hatred for Mugabe. 'Look what he does here, just look,' said Maxwell Gomera, one of the marchers. 'This is just fascism. Hitler would have done the same thing. This is the worst way anyone can behave.'

Edmore Makore, another marcher, had been caught by the mob and beaten over the head. A student at the University of Zimbabwe, he was tearful, bloodstained and furiously articulate. 'Nothing is respected here, nothing,' he said, while blood ran down his face. 'Look at what Mugabe does. We need sanctions here. We need Zimbabwe to be totally internationally isolated. The world has got to stop this. Look at what this man is doing to us. He is just a dictator, nothing more, and this is how he rules. We have suffered enough in Zimbabwe.'

I stood in the middle of the crowd, scribbling feverishly, recording their anger, while the helicopter circled above and stinging gas floated gently towards the sky. Then an armoured personnel carrier filled with riot police loomed out of the white cloud. An officer shouted in Shona. I paid no attention and carried on writing. Seconds later, the vehicle returned and a policeman casually hurled a tear gas canister into the middle of the crowd. It landed almost at my feet, exhaling a hissing, stinging stream of white. We scattered in all directions. I ran to my car and drove home, through streets filled with swirling white clouds and running figures. A banner lay crumpled in the ditch beside Union Avenue. It read: 'A spirit of Peace'.

★   ★   ★

86

The sequence of events on the morning of 1 April was later pieced together. As the 'march for peace' began its progress through central Harare, a mob of 'war veterans' gathered at Zanu-PF headquarters, under the supervision of Hitler Hunzvi. They armed themselves with pick-axe handles, iron bars, sticks and clubs wrapped with barbed wire. Some tore branches from the trees outside the 14-storey tower block. Then they marched along Union Avenue and attacked the demonstration. Several groups of riot police, totalling perhaps 100 officers, made no attempt to prevent the assault. The mob clearly knew the location of the march and reliable accounts say they were in radio contact with the police, who kept them fully informed.

With the job done, the gang returned to Zanu-PF headquarters and was paid for their morning's work. According to a report compiled by the Zimbabwe Human Rights Forum: 'The mood was self-congratulatory and jubilant. The feeling seemed to be that the MDC had been taught a lesson by the attack on the protestors.'[2] Douglas Mahiya, leader of the Harare War Veterans' Association, told the mob: 'The NCA and MDC must not demonstrate against us. The NCA and other church members should not provoke us. They must respect us.'[3] Persistent enquiries by Joe Winter, the BBC correspondent, forced the police to admit that only peaceful demonstrators were arrested on 1 April. Not a single 'war veteran' was apprehended. Edwina Spicer, a freelance camerawoman, caught the mob on film as they emerged from Zanu-PF headquarters and armed themselves for the attack.[4]

The government took three days to work out a propaganda line to explain away this outrage. On 4 April, Chen Chimutengwende, the Information Minister, gave a staunch defence of the mob to the BBC: 'The war veterans were incensed by what the demonstrators were saying and by their slogans,' he said. It will be recalled that the slogans chosen by the marchers were: 'Peace', 'A Spirit of Peace', 'Tolerance' and 'Truth, Justice and Reconciliation'. Chimutengwende was not asked why these offended 'war veterans' and made them 'incensed'. He flatly denied that the gang had gathered at Zanu-PF headquarters, despite the incontrovertible filmed evidence. Chimutengwende said his government did not 'condone' what had happened, and then added: 'but we understand it'.[5]

Dumiso Dabengwa, the supposedly honourable Home Affairs Minister who had tried to halt the farm invasions, was even more shameless. He claimed that police 'quickly intervened and restored relative order'. In his view, the marchers provoked attack by shouting 'derogatory remarks about the government'. After a morning of chaos caused by Zanu-PF supporters, Dabengwa brazenly accused the MDC of having 'a strategy to create anarchy'.[6] The performance by both ministers showed that Mugabe's government was incapable of telling the truth about any embarrassing incident.

When caught out, they would just lie. Perhaps more alarming was the sub-text of the ministers' remarks: if you were seen to criticize the regime, you would get what was coming to you.

Twelve people were rushed to hospital for their injuries on 1 April. Levias Ruzive, a blind, elderly beggar, usually found strumming a battered guitar beside Union Avenue, was beaten up and robbed of his day's takings. His guitar was smashed to pieces. The man I saw being attacked with clubs was David Payne, a white Zimbabwean. The bloodied figure I found on the floor of Edgars was David Reid, a British visitor to Zimbabwe. He was not part of the march and was set upon while leaving Barclays Bank in First Street.

As calm returned to the streets of Harare, the opposition's response to the riot was weak and confused. On the following day, the NCA struck a note of defiance and announced that it would not be intimidated. Brian Kagoro, its spokesman, vowed that a '100 day programme' of 'peace events' would be held in every corner of Zimbabwe. He told a press conference: 'We are calling on all Zimbabweans to organize peace events, whether they are prayer meetings, marches or demonstrations. We will organize an intensification of mass action, in protest against the political violence which is unacceptable in our society.'[7] Nothing happened. The '100 day programme' became 100 days of complete inactivity. Zimbabwe's opposition bowed to intimidation and never again in 2000 did they even attempt to gather in the centre of their capital. Saturday, 1 April saw a total victory for Mugabe.

★   ★   ★

The riot on 1 April seemed to serve as a starting pistol for Zanu-PF gangs on occupied farms across Zimbabwe. From that day onwards, the crackdown against the MDC escalated. Squatters stepped up their onslaught and reports of new incidents and murders became daily occurrences. Doreen Marufu, who was six months pregnant, was ambushed and beaten to death on 2 April after attending a small MDC rally near Mvurwi. Most of the nearby white-owned farms were occupied and squatter camps served as a network of bases from which gangs intimidated the area.

It soon became clear that black farm-workers were bearing the brunt of this campaign. On hundreds of occupied farms, labourers were rounded up and forced to attend '*pungwes*' – political meetings at which people were browbeaten and threatened into supporting Zanu-PF. These terrifying events have a crucial place in Zanu-PF's folklore. During the liberation struggle, Mugabe gave his guerrillas two objectives – fighting the enemy and 'politicizing the masses' – and the latter often took precedence. Chinese instructors taught Mugabe's forces the methods of indoctrination pioneered by Mao Tse-tung during the Cultural Revolution.

Zanla guerrillas would descend on a remote village after dark and gather all the inhabitants together. Anyone remotely suspected of sympathy with the Rhodesians was dragged forward and tortured to death in front of the crowd. Then the gathering would be made to chant the slogans and sing the songs of the liberation war for the entire night. Those showing enough zeal would be recruited as guerrillas on the spot and taken to the next village, where they would help indoctrinate their neighbours. Anyone lacking enthusiasm would be beaten, tortured or killed. These techniques – employed during a bush war fought among frightened, isolated communities – were now used by Zanu-PF for its election campaign.

★   ★   ★

From the base of the rocky kopje, a sweeping plain curved away to a distant range of blue mountains. Green elephant grass, spotted with trees and bushes, led down to a river and then onwards to the shimmering highlands on the horizon. The landscape was deserted. Not a soul moved and a far-off kraal of conical huts was the only sign of habitation. But Masipula Singano and his companions were still afraid. If the squatters occupying the farm where they worked saw them talking to a strange white man, the penalty did not bear thinking about. To evade the occupying mobs, their employer had driven them to this isolated spot, where I was waiting.

Singano was particularly at risk because he was a known supporter of the MDC. He had voted 'No' during the referendum and urged his colleagues to do the same. When the squatters arrived on the farm near Mvurwi, Mashonaland Central province, they discovered his views and quickly took revenge. 'Five of them came to me with sticks,' said Singano. 'They said "You are MDC, you are a sell-out, you are the white man's dog." Then they beat me. They beat me everywhere.' Singano, 25, was left in a bloody heap on the ground. Other workers were afraid to help him. His mother eventually patched up his wounds. Then the squatters threatened to kill him, so he fled his home and became a hunted fugitive. He wore torn, blue overalls and an ancient pair of wellington boots. He was going to travel to Zimuto communal lands in Masvingo, 300 miles to the south, where his family lived. 'I might be safe there, but even there, Zanu-PF is strong,' he said.

Beside Singano stood Stanley Damusan and two other workers, all of whom had been rounded up and forced to attend a *pungwe*. 'The war vets, the comrades, they came with sticks. They forced us to chant praises of Mugabe,' said Dumusan. The crowd of 200 workers was herded together and led in the customary chants of '*Pamberi ne* Mugabe, *Pamberi ne* Zanu-PF'. Then the squatter ringleader stood in front of them. He wore the obligatory Mugabe T-shirt and a Zanu-PF baseball cap. 'He gave us lessons in how to vote for Zanu-PF,' said Dumusan. 'He took a pencil and he showed how to make a cross beside Zanu-PF. Then he said: 'If you don't vote for Zanu-PF, we will know. We have cameras next to the ballot box so we know how everyone votes. If you vote for MDC, your name will be known. I will come here with my big knife and cut your throats.' The man, known only as Maguti, led several farm invasions in the Mvurwi area and Dumusan had no doubt that his threat was entirely credible. 'That one has killed many people. Killing people was not a problem for him,' he said.

The workers continued chanting Zanu-PF slogans, while squatters patrolled around them, toying with clubs. But one man in the crowd did not display sufficient ardour. 'There was a young guy, he was refusing to sing the songs,' said Dumusan. The man was dragged to the front of the crowd and five men attacked him with clubs studded with rusty nails. 'They were all beating him. He was screaming and crying but none of us could do anything,' said Dumusan. When their victim was on the verge of uncon-sciousness, the squatters placed his bloodied head on an oil drum. Maguti shouted: 'I am going to kill him' and raised an axe above the man's skull. The crowd watched the shining blade hover in the air. Maguti then lowered it and dropped the axe to the ground harmlessly. The man was not killed, but his mock execution had the desired effect on the audience. Dumusan said: 'They are all so afraid, they will vote for Zanu-PF. They know they will be killed if they do not.' The threats, chants and songs went on all night. At one stage, the squatters rubbed in their dominance over the hapless audience by making them perform press-ups and run from one end of the field to the other. Only as the sun rose were they finally released.

Dumusan, 30, was a tractor driver and quietly admitted that he voted 'No' in the referendum. With equal reluctance, he confessed that he would vote Zanu-PF in the parliamentary election. 'I have no choice. These people are killing us,' he said simply. His companions were in a similar state of barely suppressed terror after the *pungwe*. Their fear was such that they remembered more of what Maguti had told the crowd. Smart Sibanda, 22, said: 'Maguti told us, after the election, your white bosses will just be kicked out of Zimbabwe. Those white men who refuse to go will be shot. If you vote MDC, you will go with them or we will shoot you as well. You will be treated the same as your white master. But if you vote Zanu-PF, we will give you the white man's house and his land.' With his hands shaking, Sibanda also said that he would vote Zanu-PF. 'If we want to live, we must,' he said.

An afternoon spent with this group of farm workers convinced me that the MDC could not hope to win the election outright. About 70 per cent of the Zimbabwean electorate lived in remote, rural areas, where Zanu-PF's

mastery of the brutal art of intimidation had no equal. These cruelly effective shock tactics had helped Mugabe win a war. Now they would help him
win an election.

★   ★   ★

The fat man with a bushy beard roared with delight and jumped in the air.
His legs pounded up and down with all the force of pistons, as if he stood on
hot coals. He rhythmically punched the sky with clenched fists, seized the
microphone and began bellowing at the crowd. Border Gezi was giving one
of his customary performances at a Zanu-PF rally. The young, energetic
Governor of Mashonaland Central, once the farmers' friend, now their most
implacable foe, was doing the warm-up act for his master.

A crowd of 5,000 people, some enthusiastic, others sullen and silent,
listened as Gezi expounded Zanu-PF's political philosophy. 'Those villages
who back MDC and bow to the *mabhunu* – we will bomb them! MDC will
be crushed for ever,' he roared. 'This province is a one-party state because
everyone is behind Zanu-PF.' The large, sweating, ranting, dancing ball of
energy continued in this vein for about ten minutes. Any MDC supporters
would be 'dealt with', he bellowed, while stamping the ground for
emphasis. Some of the crowd shouted their approval, most stayed quiet.
With a final rhetorical flourish (he called Morgan Tsvangirai 'a mad, treach-
erous, evil spirit'), Gezi bounded to his seat. I noticed his T-shirt carried a
very large picture of himself. Beneath his glowering countenance was the
slogan: 'BORDER GEZI IS THE PEOPLE'S CHOICE', in vivid, red
letters. Perhaps the words 'OR ELSE' should be added, I thought idly.

Then his master rose to the lectern. For the first time ever, I saw Mugabe
in what passed for casual dress. Instead of his traditional three-piece, Savile
Row number, he wore an olive green safari suit. Friday, 7 April was 'dress
down Friday' for Mugabe, and the people of Bindura in Mashonaland
Central were seeing the relaxed, carefree version of their leader. Personally I
thought his sartorial advisers had made a mistake. The safari suit emphasized
Mugabe's shrunken, hunched shoulders and his surprisingly wide girth. And
the choice of olive green made him look like a military dictator. Admittedly
a leopard-skin hat and dark glasses were needed to complete the effect, but
for the first time it struck me that he looked like a real African tyrant.

Mugabe told his audience that he enjoyed visiting Mashonaland Central
because 'the spirit of the people here has been of great help to me'. The
President assured the crowd that he was in good humour. 'We are happy,
overjoyed and in a mood to celebrate,' he said. In fact, Mugabe looked
weary and care-worn. He leaned heavily on the lectern, blinking incessantly,
as if having difficulty staying awake. Much of his speech was rambling and

incoherent. But the Bindura rally gave the first real insight into why Mugabe was driving Zimbabwe into chaos.

He repeated his unequivocal support for the squatters who, at that moment, had occupied 975 farms. 'Those who have invaded the farms, they are going to stay,' he said. 'I support them, we will not remove them.' Then Mugabe's voice fell and he explained why farmers and whites in general had aroused his fury. For the first time, we got a sense of the anger within him. His words were disjointed, but are worth quoting verbatim:

> In 1980, we said 'Let bygones be bygones', provided the whites are repentant, provided they accept the hand of reconciliation. But, alas, those we thought had accepted the hand of reconciliation have proved they have not done so. Their demonstration of support for Tsvangirai and others and the fact of their rejection in the referendum of the draft constitution – and all to the man the whites voted against it, demonstrating that the white man has not changed. I appeal to the white man to think again. Have they decided to regard us as their enemies for all time? Let them answer that question in their hearts.
>
> We know of their nefarious activities. We know of them ganging together with our opponents. They are pouring money into MDC. They are campaigning for money through internet for MDC. Have they come to the position where they are determined to fight against Mugabe and his government? If that is the position, I will declare the fight to be on and we will win it. MDC can never, never be the government of this country. Once we see the whites as part of the MDC, then we will treat them the same as MDC. They are the monster behind and poor Tsvangirai has become the puppet, they use him to run hither and thither.

The whites had organized Mugabe's humiliation in the referendum. They were the real power behind the MDC. Mugabe's hand of reconciliation from 1980 had been spurned. So now he would wage a relentless struggle to seize their land and crush the MDC. The 'fight was on' and no rules would be allowed. The squatters were his allies and, by implication, every act of humiliation or violence against a white farmer or black MDC supporter was justified. If the whites could not accept this position, Mugabe declared: 'They can just leave Zimbabwe.' To laughter from the crowd, he listed all the border crossings through which they could make their exit and added: 'If they want to have a plane we can accompany them to Harare airport.'

As for the MDC, Tsvangirai was a 'puppet and a traitor'. Mugabe casually blamed him for all the violence and said: 'Tsvangirai is inviting fire for himself and fire burns you. It can actually engulf those who start it. Let him not start the fire that will engulf him.'[8] Mugabe believed he was fighting for the soul of Zimbabwe against a 'nefarious' coalition of black puppets and white racists. He was impervious to reason. All restraint had been abandoned.

★   ★   ★

Black and white Zimbabweans the length and breadth of the country were suffering the consequences of their President's fury. On the morning of 4 April, Constable Finashe Chikwenya, 25, was cycling across the lush fields of Chipesa farm near Hwedza, when he was ambushed by a gang of squatters. They beat him to the ground, stole his pistol and shot him dead. The inevitable consequence of unleashing mobs and placing them above the law had occurred. The land invasions had claimed their first life − not of a white farmer, but a black Zimbabwean trying to do his job.

Chikwenya's capital offence was to have arrested a squatter. On the previous day, he had visited Chipesa alongside several other policemen and made three arrests after Iain Kay, the farmer, was whipped, beaten and nearly killed by a mob. Kay was a prominent supporter of the MDC and, for this reason, Chipesa was among the first farms to be invaded by an especially militant gang. Kay's wife, Kerry, had worked tirelessly to protect farm labourers from Zimbabwe's catastrophic AIDS epidemic, but this brought no sympathy from the invaders.

Kay, 51, was confronted outside the farm's primary school and beaten with clubs, axe handles and a peculiarly ingenious weapon − fan-belts tied on sticks. The pretext for the attack was that a few of the squatters' grass shacks had been knocked down. The farmer tried to escape by locking himself inside the school, but he was quickly dragged out, thrown to the ground, whipped and clubbed. 'Then they tied my hands with wire and demanded to be taken to my house to see how many guns I had,'[9] said Kay.

Stunned and bleeding from deep whiplashes around his head, the farmer was bundled towards some bushes. His assailants probably planned to finish him off in a lonely spot. Suddenly Kay's son, David, came into view riding a motorbike, beyond a nearby dam, and the gang was momentarily distracted. Kay managed to untie himself and dive into the dam. The gang gathered on the verge of the water and hurled sticks and stones at him whenever he came up for air. Kay managed to swim across the dam to his son and escape to safety.

He was rushed to Borradaile hospital in Marondera, his back criss-crossed by red weals and his face scarred with open wounds. The image of a dazed, bleeding, horribly injured Iain Kay went around the world. After Chikwenya and his fellow officers made those three arrests, new orders arrived from police headquarters in Harare. All of the suspects were released without charge. In the aftermath of Mugabe's Bindura speech, police were ordered to back off and let the squatters reign supreme. Chikwenya's murder served as a warning of what would befall any officer doing his duty.

Fired by Mugabe's rhetoric, the squatters sought to humiliate as well as injure. Under the leadership of Comrade Jesus, mobs around Karoi were particularly dangerous and they delighted in rubbing farmers' noses in their absolute power. Adrian Herud and his wife, Marion, found a crowd of 100 massed outside their home on Ardingly farm. So drunk and drugged that many could barely stand, the gang howled '*Hondo*' and waved sticks, chains, whips and axes in the air. The Heruds were dragged on to the lawn along-side the farm manager, Lionel Gundry, and his wife Lialani. A jeering gang surrounded both couples.

'They started beating us with sticks,' Herud told me. 'They were severe blows, they weren't just knocking us about, they were really trying to hurt us. I was completely laid out once. One of them had a club with a nail sticking out of it. He was completely crazy.' Then the two wives were singled out. While the drunken crowd jeered and laughed, the tearful women were forced to dance and chant the familiar roll call of obedience: '*Pamberi ne* Zanu-PF, *pamberi ne* Mugabe.' Both couples were forced to sign a letter of apology to Mugabe and repent for 'having called him bad names'. This scene occurred on 8 April, barely 24 hours after Mugabe's speech. Squatters brought from Karoi in official vehicles had swelled the ranks of his audience in Bindura and all those words about whites had clearly been taken to heart. The gangs were determined to exact revenge from 'the white man' for his 'nefarious' activities.

Neighbouring farmers rushed to the aid of the Heruds and the Gundrys, just as the couples feared they would be murdered. 'They probably saved our lives, it was getting that bad,' said Herud. Delighted by the day's work, the mob dispersed, while their comrades invaded ten more farms around Karoi on a single afternoon, bringing the total occupied to 1,020.

In the Centenary area, gangs simply ordered farmers to pack up and leave – or else. John Hammond was besieged inside his home on Chidikamwedzi farm together with his wife, Marge. On the third day of the siege, I found myself looking at the scene from the homestead on Mtuatua farm, two miles across the valley. Bathed in golden sunshine, the familiar vista of rocky hills, kopjes and fertile plains swept away to the horizon. Across the luxuriant, green valley, spotted with yellow rocks glowing in the afternoon rays, Hammond's homestead was just visible.

Squatters had thrown a cordon of roadblocks around his farm and it was impossible to approach any closer. Most were armed with the usual assort-ment of sticks, axes and machetes, but some had acquired new weapons –

a set of golf clubs. These had been stolen from a nearby farm and the gang besieging Hammond took to attacking any white face with the iron clubs. The only white faces who tried reaching Chidikamwedzi were, inevitably, the foreign journalists who had suddenly flooded Zimbabwe. At least four camera crews were forced to beat hasty retreats in the face of golf-club wielding squatters.

I did not attempt to run the blockade. Instead, I joined Hammond's relatives at their vantage point across the valley. 'The worst thing is knowing that your parents are just there and in danger and there's nothing you can do about it,' said Hilton Thomas, Hammond's stepson. Earlier, the squatters had cut off the homestead's water and electricity supplies. Hammond's phone line was torn down and his only link with the outside world was a radio, whose battery was rapidly running flat. He was 67, his wife 51, and they had been in a permanent state of terror for three days. Taking advantage of their complete control over Chidikamwedzi, the squatters had set about the brutal task of intimidating the black workers. One was attacked with clubs and left with a broken arm. A 69-year-old worker was beaten with a plank driven through with rusty nails. The house belonging to the black farm-manager was raided and wrecked. At night, the squatters hammered on drums and sang incessantly.

But Hammond was determined to withstand the siege, knowing that if he left his home, he would never be allowed back. The cluster of worried relatives across the valley seemed remarkably relaxed. They sat beside a neatly trimmed green lawn, glasses in hand. When I arrived, his son, Neil, was sipping a beer beside Hilton Thomas, as they looked across at their parents' home. After three days of worry, they were drained of obvious anxiety. Dark rings under their eyes were the only visible signs of strain. They just stared, powerless, at the distant roof of the besieged homestead. 'They want dad and the old lady to get out. As soon as that happens, they have control of the house and the whole farm and that's it. So we're not going to let that happen,' said Neil Hammond adamantly. The farm had been in the family since 1939. They were not about to sacrifice 61 years of work. On 9 April, police intervened as mediators and the siege was finally lifted after six days. The squatters backed off from the Hammonds' house. But they kept an iron grip on his land.

★　　　★　　　★

Shards of broken glass crunched underfoot as nervous security guards patrolled the perimeter fence. Inside the farmhouse every room had been invaded, every drawer opened, every cupboard ransacked. Clothes were strewn across the floor and lay amid the glittering fragments of 36 smashed panes. Furniture had been overturned, chairs hurled across rooms and mat-tresses torn from beds. The mob had delighted in raiding the drinks cabinet and carrying off five bottles of whisky.

With an air of restrained, exhausted exasperation, Paul and Liz Retzlaff were trying to restore normality on Lonely Park farm. They talked quietly together, practical instructions like: 'That goes in the corner' mingling with soft words of reassurance. When I arrived, they were buried in the herculean task of clearing the debris left by the mob that had ransacked their home. A quiet, modest, hospitable couple, anxious that I should have a cold drink after my journey from Harare, picking through the remains of their home. They did so while on the alert for another attack. The assault on their home-stead on the night of 11 April had sent a chill through the farming community around Arcturus. As the Retzlaffs pieced the contents of the farmhouse back together, most of their neighbours despatched wives and children to the safety of Harare and patrolled their land with guns.

Liz Retzlaff, 50, settled in a chair and recounted what had happened. Beneath a calm and composed exterior, she was struggling to control her emotions. The sound of a truck crashing through the gate was her first warning that the squatters were about to attack her home. 'When you hear them coming, your stomach goes into a knot and you just feel defenceless,' she said. As a baying mob of 30 surged up her drive, she fled from the farm-house with her husband and son, Anthony, and sought refuge in an adjacent cottage.

Shouting with delight, the squatters immediately set about wrecking the house, shattering furniture and rampaging from room to room, stealing everything they could lay their hands on. 'We could hear them trashing the house, we could hear them breaking everything. But I didn't worry about that. I just worried about our lives. I remember thinking, thank goodness my grandchildren aren't here,' she said. Moments later, the crowd stormed towards the cottage. Liz Retzlaff found it hard to describe what happened next and Anthony took over.

Howling '*Hondo*' and brandishing the usual panoply of weapons – axes, knives, sticks, clubs and iron bars – the mob surrounded the terrified family's hiding-place. Suddenly, they were smashing the windows and trying to break down the door, while screeching threats. 'Can you imagine what it sounded like when they were outside? They were bashing the door and saying: "We're going to kill you. This is war now, it's you against us, this is war".' said Anthony Retzlaff. The family managed to send an emergency message on the radio before a mass of hands reached through the shattered panes and broke the handset. Other hands smashed the telephone, leaving them completely isolated.

By now, the mob's leader was shouting for Paul Retzlaff to go outside and talk. His son said: 'If Dad had gone out, they would have killed us. It would have been over and out.' Pandemonium reigned for about 15 minutes. But unknown to the Retzlaffs, neighbouring farmers had heard the distress call and were rushing to their aid with a rescue party. Hearing the sound of approaching trucks, the besieging mob suddenly panicked and fled, leaving an eerie calm. 'I felt such relief when they went. I thought we were going to die,' said Liz Retzlaff. 'I thought it was all over.' Moments later, trucks appeared carrying three fellow farmers and about 40 of their black workers, who had willingly joined the rescue.

In the gathering darkness, they immediately set off in pursuit of the fleeing mob and followed them to a makeshift squatter camp. Chaos ensued as they charged towards the camp. Rob Brown, a neighbouring farmer who helped lead the rescue party, described a scene of utter confusion. 'It was an absolute shambles, people were running everywhere, my guys were going after the squatters and they were trying to get away. There was smoke and fire everywhere.' Suddenly gunshots echoed over the mêlée. One of the squatters opened fire at the rescuers with an automatic handgun and fired at least five rounds. 'The first was in the air,' said Brown. 'The rest were all aimed towards us. He was clearly trying to do some damage. I could hear the bullets ricocheting over my head.' All the shots missed and the squatters fled, some piling into cars and taking off at high speed.

Squatters had repeatedly been seen with firearms, usually AK-47 assault rifles, but the shots fired in the chaotic aftermath of the attack on Lonely Park were the first. For the farmers, the news was getting worse and worse. The mobs on their land were above the law and now they were firing guns. Every farmer I spoke to was adamant that, unless order was restored, lives would soon be lost.

Earlier, before storming the house, the gang had attacked one of the Retzlaffs' black workers. A frail man in his sixties, he was cutting grass beside the road with a sickle. For no apparent reason, he was set upon and repeatedly slashed with his own sickle. A few hours after I visited Lonely Park farm on 12 April, a handful of squatters appeared in a car and drove at high speed to the homestead. They hurled a brace of petrol bombs at the front door and then sped away. The Retzlaffs immediately left their home and fled for the safety of Harare.

★   ★   ★

As squatters turned the screw on white farms across Zimbabwe, Mugabe completed the tortuous process of stripping his targets of their last legal protection. On 6 April, parliament amended the constitution to allow the government to seize farms without compensation. This clause had been the centrepiece of the draft constitution, and the reason, in Mugabe's mind, for the 'No' campaign allegedly masterminded by the whites. The amendment of the existing constitution neatly side-stepped the referendum defeat. The new clause was identical to the one in the draft – it stated that Britain, as the 'former colonial power', was responsible for any compensation, not the government of Zimbabwe. Parliament passed it by 100 votes to nil, amid chants of 'Zimbabwe was created with blood.'

Yet Mugabe was under heavy international criticism for ignoring the verdict of his own High Court. Although the government had consented to the order granted by Justice Garwe on 17 March, this was simply cast aside. The farm occupations may have been declared illegal and the police ordered to evict all squatters, but the invasions continued with Mugabe's full support. This blatant disregard of the rule of law was becoming increasingly embarrassing. The regime had to wriggle off the hook and maintain some veneer of legitimacy. So Augustine Chihuri, the Police Commissioner, decided to claim that the High Court order (which he had originally consented to) gave him an impossible task. He argued that the eviction of the squatters was, quite simply, beyond the power of the Zimbabwean police. They had neither the manpower nor the resources to do the job. The government had been so good at organizing the farm invasions that now the police couldn't stop them. He asked the High Court to amend the order and absolve the police of any responsibility to enforce the law.

This extraordinary request came before the High Court on 10 April, with Patrick Chinamasa, the Attorney-General, representing the government. Affable and articulate, Chinamasa was a respected lawyer in his own right. His standing in the profession was high – until his performance on this occasion. If Chinamasa felt any embarrassment about appearing before a packed High Court and asking it to tear up the law, he did not show it. Instead, he delivered a speech that would have gone down well at a Zanu-PF rally.

He claimed that the 'police have no resources, no manpower and no equipment to carry out evictions' and that the original order was 'incapable of enforcement'. Chinamasa then blamed a shadowy array of outside forces for the crisis. 'The British, Western countries and white parties in South Africa are coming to the assistance of white commercial farmers here,' he said. 'This nation has been divided along racial lines. The situation has been poisoned racially and internationally.' As for the government's responsibility to enforce the law, Chinamasa was dismissive: 'A law which promotes injustice in society, a law which enforces unjust rights is not in compliance with the rule of law. The rule of law is a political concept. It is a tool which can be used from any political angle.'[10] Shorn of niceties, Chinamasa was saying that the law happened to protect white farmers, so the regime wanted the

High Court's permission to ignore it. Thank you and good night. He sat down to stunned silence in the crowded court-room.

His opponent lumbered to his feet. Adrian de Bourbon, one of Zimbabwe's most senior lawyers, represented the farmers. A large, flamboyant man, de Bourbon did not mince words on any occasion. Having listened to Chinamasa with barely disguised fury, he ruthlessly set about demolishing his opponent. 'We have reached a very sad day,' de Bourbon began, stabbing his finger towards Chinamasa. 'The Attorney-General has stood before this court and asked it to tear up the constitution. The Attorney-General has said that white people are not entitled to the protection of the law. The Attorney-General is telling the man in the street that the rule of law is a political tool. If that is so, lawyers are redundant, courts are redundant and the police are redundant. It is time to remind the Attorney-General of the oath he took.' De Bourbon pointed out that the farm invasions had taken place with the active support of the government. 'Why can't the same official transport that took the invaders to the farms be used to take them out again?' he asked. Flushed with passion, De Bourbon summed up: 'I have to urge the court with all the vigour I can to protect the citizen from the likes of the Attorney-General.'

Throughout the attack, Chinamasa sat with his head bowed. It was almost embarrassing to witness his humiliation. But there was something else about the occasion that struck me. Here was Chinamasa, a black minister, being taken to task by a white lawyer, before an audience consisting largely of white journalists and white diplomats. He would not take this lying down. His dignity was at stake. Even though the judge was black, he would not meekly obey whatever order the court issued. Instead, this hearing would join Zanu-PF's mythology as another occasion when whites behaved with intolerable arrogance in the defence of their privileges.

Moses Chinhengo, the presiding judge, reached his verdict on 13 April. In a detailed and courageous ruling, he dismissed all of Chinamasa's arguments and upheld the original order declaring the farm invasions illegal and compelling the police to evict the squatters. Chinhengo said that Chinamasa's comments about the rule of law made him 'shudder'. The judge ruled:

> The farm invasions are illegal and of a riotous nature. The applicant clearly has a public duty to enforce the consent order . . . if this court were to accede to a variation, amendment or other detraction from the order issued . . . it would not be upholding its sworn duty to uphold the law of Zimbabwe. In independent Zimbabwe, the law should no longer be viewed as being made for us, rather it must be viewed as our law. We have the sovereign right to enact new laws and repeal old laws which we find incompatible with the national interest.[11]

The last point formed the crux of the matter. Zanu-PF had controlled Zimbabwe's parliament for 20 years and could enact, repeal or amend any law it wanted. Chinhengo asked only that the government obey its own laws. But Mugabe had gone beyond the stage where he could be swayed by logical argument. In his mind, if the courts upheld a law that happened to favour white farmers, the courts had joined the Great Conspiracy to protect white interests. Chinhengo's emphatic re-statement of the law made no difference. The invasions went on and the violence escalated.

★   ★   ★

Yet many ministers in Mugabe's cabinet were deeply uneasy about the descent into lawlessness and they now made a concerted bid to haul Zimbabwe back from the brink. On 11 April, the day after Chinamasa's disastrous court appearance, the cabinet gathered in the absence of its leader. Mugabe was attending a summit of developing countries in Cuba, and Joseph Msika, the Vice-President, chaired the meeting in his absence. Msika seized the moment to persuade his colleagues to end the invasions. The cabinet decided to send three ministers – Dumiso Dabengwa (Home Affairs), Sydney Sekeramayi (Security) and John Nkomo (Local Government) on a tour of occupied farms. In the words of George Charamba, Mugabe's official spokesman, their task would be: 'To talk to the war veterans on the need to end the invasions.'[12] On 13 April, Msika appeared at a rare press conference. Although he referred to the farm invasions by their official code as 'peaceful demonstrations', his message was clear. He pointed out that the constitution had been amended to allow the seizure of land without compensation and said: 'It is now no longer necessary to continue with these demonstrations.'[13] Msika's words appeared prominently in the official press.

All of these efforts were completely unavailing. Without instructions from Mugabe himself, the police took no action to restore order and the number of invaded farms crept above 1,100. The three ministers never embarked on their tour. It became painfully obvious that Zimbabwe's entire cabinet and its Vice-President were of no consequence. Only one man mattered. Hob-nobbing with Fidel Castro and an assortment of African cronies in Havana, Mugabe appeared in high spirits. At home, the 'war veterans' had beaten and tortured hundreds of black farm workers and murdered Finashe Chikwenya. When asked about the land invasions on 13 April, Mugabe replied: 'What they have done is merely to stage a demonstration, a peaceful demonstration in most cases, because they have not been guilty of any acts of violence.'[14]

NOTES AND REFERENCES

1 Speech, Zanu–PF rally, Bindura, 7 April 2000.
2 Zimbabwe Human Rights Forum, *A Report on Violence Against Peaceful Protesters*, p. 7.
3 *Sunday Mail,* 2 April 2000.
4 This footage is included in *Never the Same Again,* Edwina Spicer Productions, 2000.
5 BBC World Service, *Focus on Africa,* 4 April 2000.
6 *The Herald,* 5 April 2000.
7 NCA press conference, 2 April 2000.
8 Speech to Zanu-PF rally, Bindura, 7 April 2000.
9 BBC World TV interview, 3 April 2000.
10 Speech to High Court, 10 April 2000.
11 Quoted in International Bar Association report on the rule of law in Zimbabwe, sec 12.15.
12 *The Herald,* 14 April 2000. Charamba later denied he had said this. If so, he was misquoted by the government's own newspaper.
13 Press conference, 13 April 2000. See also *The Herald,* 14 April 2000.
14 *The Herald,* 14 April 2000.

Chapter 6

Full of Anger

15 April–1 May 2000

You are now our enemies because you really have behaved as enemies of Zimbabwe and we are full of anger. (Robert Mugabe on white farmers, 18 April 2000)[1]

On the morning of Saturday, 15 April, a white pick-up drove through the rolling bush country of the Shawa hills in Manicaland. Unfolding beside the road was the familiar tableau of impoverished rural Zimbabwe – clusters of round huts, isolated stone kraals and scattered herds of cattle, tended by boys dressed in rags. The vehicle was heading for Murambinda, a dusty town in the heart of Buhera North – the parliamentary seat then being contested by Morgan Tsvangirai. Inside the pick-up was Talent Mabika, 23, a junior MDC official. In the open back of the vehicle sat Sanderson Makombe, another MDC activist, and at the wheel was Tichaona Chiminya, 38, who served as Tsvangirai's personal driver.

As the car approached Murambinda, the passengers caught sight of a Toyota pick-up driving lazily behind them. Suddenly it accelerated, drew nearer and overtook, showing that 'Zanu-PF Manicaland Province' was stencilled on its side. The pick-up sped ahead and then swerved across the road, stopping abruptly, blocking the passengers' path. Chiminya avoided collision by bringing them screeching to a halt. Everything then moved with bewildering speed.

The passengers were surrounded as men piled out of the Zanu-PF vehicle. They lashed out, punching their victims through the car windows. In desperation, Makombe leapt from the back of the pick-up and managed to escape by dashing into some bushes beside the road. From this hiding place he watched what happened next. He heard Mabika screaming as she was beaten, while still cowering inside the car. Then he heard a male voice call for petrol bombs. Seconds later, he saw two men splashing petrol on their terrified victims and then hurling bottles through the windows. The

102

entire vehicle exploded in a roaring mass of flames. He heard the agonized screams of Chiminya and Mabika, one moment trying to shield themselves from blows, the next set ablaze and converted into human torches. The two flaming bodies kicked and rolled in last, desperate attempts to escape the inferno. Meanwhile, their killers returned to the Zanu-PF pick-up and drove away. Makombe ran to the burning vehicle and tried to pull the bodies to safety. Their skin peeled away in his hands and charred flesh reeked. Chiminya was already dead. Mabika died in agony some hours later.

At about this time, 80 miles north of the swirling pillar of black smoke rising over the Shawa hills, a large force of squatters surged towards the homestead on Arizona farm, near Macheke. They demanded to see David Stevens, the farmer. On the previous day, 14 April, the invaders had assaulted several of Arizona's workers and the labourers retaliated that morning, seriously injuring some of the squatters. Now they wanted revenge. Stevens went to his front gate to negotiate with the mob. Before doing so, he called John Osborne, a neighbouring farmer, on the radio and asked for help. No sooner had Stevens started talking with the gang than he was seized, trussed up and bundled inside his own Land Rover. He was driven away from Arizona in a convoy of three vehicles, including a BMW and a minibus both laden with squatters.

As they roared out of the farm, they passed five of Stevens's neighbours who had answered his call for help. What happened next was pieced together from the traumatized, halting accounts later given by these farmers as they sat, dazed and bleeding, in their hospital beds. They followed the convoy along the winding road, through the lush fields of Zimbabwe's agricultural heartland, until they reached the shabby town of Murewa, 30 miles further north. Here the farmers saw Stevens's Land Rover parked outside the local office of the War Veterans' Association. As they slowed down, a man with a .303 rifle appeared and opened fire on them without warning. He managed to shoot two rounds, before the farmers hurled their cars to the right and drove to the local police station on the edge of the town, intending to seek safety and report Stevens's abduction.

At 4.30 p.m. a gang of 20 squatters strode into the police station where the farmers were talking to several officers. One 'war veteran' carried a rifle, another a handgun. In the words of Steve Krynauw, one of the farmers: 'They took us out of the police building with constant assurances that we were going to be killed. The police just left us.' No officer lifted a finger to prevent the abduction of five people from a police station, in broad daylight, by men toying with guns and making their murderous intentions clear.

Then the farmers were separated. Osborne was driven to the decayed, dilapidated building that served as the War Veterans' Association office, about one mile down a narrow road from the police station. He was thrust into a back room, where Stevens was being held in handcuffs. 'We were knocked about a bit,' said Osborne. 'Then they put David and myself in a sedan car and drove through Murewa.' They were driven about half a mile to the local Zanu-PF headquarters, a shabby, green building, on the outskirts of the town. Here Osborne and Stevens were dragged into some bushes. 'They abused us, they beat us around,' said Osborne. 'A woman nearby said she recognized me and said I should not be hurt because we helped out our communal neighbours quite a bit. A young guy said the same. They put me in the car.' Battered and bruised, Osborne was later taken to safety in Murewa. A chance encounter with someone who remembered an act of kindness had saved his life. But first he witnessed the fate of his friend. Stevens was beaten over and over again and then shot dead.

Meanwhile, the other four farmers had been split into two groups. Steve Krynauw and Gary Luke were hurled into the back of a pick-up, bound with wire, blindfolded and driven out of Murewa. The car lurched to a halt and a heavy object was thrown on top of them. It seemed to have arms and legs, but was limp and silent. They soon realized that it was the body of Stevens. 'He was ice cold,' said Luke. The two captives and their dead friend were driven to a hill north of Murewa, where another mob waited. 'They found I was armed. That's where a lot of my beatings came from,' said Krynauw. 'They said we were stupid for having followed them and for carrying a gun.' The two farmers were driven through the night in a succession of vehicles and whenever they screeched to a halt, they were beaten and tortured. Finally, after being bludgeoned to unconsciousness and rendered unrecognizable by their wounds, the bloodied farmers were tipped into the bush and left for dead.

Some hours later, shortly before dawn on Sunday, 16 April, Krynauw and Luke regained consciousness and managed to untie one another's hands. Barefoot, bleeding and exhausted, they walked ten miles to a farm, only to find that its owner had fled the area. But they broke into a Land Cruiser, drove to safety and were eventually rushed to Borradaile hospital in Marondera.

The other two farmers, Stuart Gemmill and Ian Hardy, were dragged inside the Zanu-PF headquarters building in Murewa and beaten senseless. They were later driven to a remote cave in the surrounding hills, where the torture and assaults continued for the rest of the night. The two men were eventually abandoned. After the Commercial Farmers' Union hired an aircraft to conduct an aerial search for them, they were found by a police detail and taken to safety.[2]

Stevens was murdered at the age of 47. His backing for the MDC was undisguised and it probably cost him his life. He left a wife, Maria, 39, and four children: Marc, 15, Brenda, 13, and two-year-old twins, Warren and

Sebastian. Terrified families were evacuated from all 46 farms around Macheke in the hours after his death, leaving the entire area under the sway of the mobs. As for Arizona farm, the squatters set fire to the vast, cavernous tobacco sheds and the cluster of modest houses where Stevens's black workers lived. All were razed to the ground and the gang took over the charred wreckage of the farm, hurling spears and stones at anyone who approached. The Stevens family lost their father and their home. All 300 of Arizona's black workers became penniless vagrants.

★   ★   ★

With its engines wailing, the Air Zimbabwe Boeing 767 taxied across the tarmac at Harare airport and drew to a halt beside a cheering crowd. The door was thrown open and Mugabe appeared, to a tumultuous welcome. He bounded down the stairs with surprising agility, as if anxious to be back on home soil after his visit to Cuba. This was 9 a.m. on Sunday, 16 April. Stuart Gemmill and Ian Hardy were still lying inside a cave, trussed up, gagged and bleeding from their wounds. The black smoke over Arizona farm and the funeral pyre above the Shawa Hills had barely cleared. Three Zimbabweans lay dead, while another five were recovering from abduction, assault and torture. Hundreds of black Zimbabweans had been rendered homeless, destitute refugees, with a large swathe of the country turned over to marauding gangs. All this had unfolded in the space of eight terrible hours on the previous day.

As Mugabe stepped on to the apron of Harare airport, there were some, myself included, who thought he would now restrain his followers and call a halt to the mayhem. Surely he would heed his Vice-President, most of his cabinet and Zimbabwe's High Court. He would remember his sworn duty as Head of State to uphold the law and protect all of his citizens. With Zimbabwe dominating the world's headlines, he could not remain impervious to international pressure. At last the moment had arrived when the call would be: 'Enough is enough.'

We could not have been more wrong. Even before Mugabe's plane touched down, it was becoming clear that the events of 15 April were merely a bitter foretaste of what was to come. Over 1,000 of Zanu-PF's shock troops had been brought to the airport to greet their leader. Most were squatters, taking a morning off from beating up farm workers. Their breath reeking of alcohol, they glared with open hostility at any white face. Some of the most notorious warlords were present – I caught sight of Agnes Rusike, wearing a red dress covered with pictures of Mugabe, her eyes yellow and inflamed by a potent cocktail of drugs. Shouting with excitement and anger, the crowd waved a variety of banners. 'Zimbabwe will never be a colony AGAIN!' was the most numerous slogan. Others said: 'Down with the naked lies of BBC, Sky TV and CNN.' Some attacked the British Foreign Secretary and his Africa Minister: 'Robin Cook, Peter Hain, stop lying about Zimbabwe.' Others singled out Morgan Tsvangirai: 'Tsvangirai is a Traitor' and 'Tsvangirai is a puppet of the whites'. Another banner summed up all of these messages: 'What is good for the white man is bad for the black man'.

Over a sea of fanatical faces and waving banners, I caught sight of Hitler Hunzvi. He wore a sober, dark suit and a look of immense excitement. He was about to greet his master. Beside him stood Sydney Sekeramayi, the Security Minister. As the man in charge of the Central Intelligence Organisation, this sharply dressed, suave figure knew all about the events of 15 April. This was not going to be an occasion for healing wounds, issuing calls for restraint and restoring normality. This was a victory rally, called to celebrate and revel in the mayhem of the previous day. Zanu-PF was triumphant. The party had just given its enemies a good hiding.

Mugabe walked through the cheering crowd, shaking hands with the hysterical, banner-waving figures. Looking like a pair of deferential schoolboys in their headmaster's study, Hunzvi and Sekeramayi greeted him. Then the two minions delivered the warm-up act. 'All the violence has been sponsored by MDC and white farmers,' screeched Hunzvi. 'We are going to hit back.' His voice seemed even more childish and ludicrous than usual. Standing amid the ecstatic audience, I had to suppress my chuckles. Hunzvi concluded by saying: 'I call on our President to speed up the land reforms. If the whites don't want it, they should leave.' These last words drew a roar of approval.

Sekeramayi spoke next. His voice was deeper and his delivery measured, but the message was identical. The MDC had caused the violence. Tsvangirai was a 'traitor'. His followers would get what was coming to them. Sekeramayi concluded with the words: 'The MDC have slapped a lion in the face and they will be devoured.'

Then it was Mugabe's turn. For a moment he basked in the cheers of his supporters and then spoke in tones of suppressed fury. 'There is an expectation that I will say to the war veterans "Get off the land." I will not do that. I will not do that, until we actually start redistributing the land,' he said. So that was it – the farm invasions would go on, no matter how illegal or violent. But according to Mugabe, they were still entirely tranquil. 'They are peaceful demonstrations, a peaceful campaign by people who are frustrated,' he said, while keeping a straight face. His audience, who knew the absurdity of his words better than any gathering on earth, remained silent.

Then Mugabe turned to the farmers, who at that moment were organizing the evacuation of scores of terrified families in the wake of the 'peaceful demonstrations' around Macheke. 'We warned the white farmers not to be provocative, not to take up weapons. If you do that, you will suffer the consequences. We cannot protect you if you provoke the war veterans. You must accept the consequences,' he said. Any farmer who 'provoked' the war veterans would suffer the fate of Stevens. Then Mugabe added: 'Those who have tried to fight have created problems for themselves.' Was that an oblique reference to Stevens, I wondered. Is Mugabe trying to blame Stevens for his own murder? Then he turned on the MDC. 'They started the violence. You must defend yourselves against the MDC,' he declared. 'Some say, you must turn the other cheek, but I have only two cheeks: after I have turned both, which one do I turn? Don't kill, but hit back mildly.' This drew roars of laughter.

As for the High Court order compelling the police to evict the invaders, Mugabe was dismissive. He referred derisively to the 'little law of trespass' and said: 'This is not a problem that can be solved by the courts. Let the question of the land that the war veterans are now on be settled by us and not the courts. What this must be seen as is a revolution, a struggle that cannot be corrected by the courts.'³ If Mugabe was leading a revolution, his enemies could expect no quarter.

★   ★   ★

On the following afternoon, I encountered something completely and utterly unexpected. Tim Henwood, President of the CFU, walked into a hastily arranged press conference wearing a beaming smile. By nature, Henwood is gregarious and upbeat, but the events of the weekend had left him in the same depths of despair and shock felt by the entire farming community. Yet on 17 April he genuinely believed that a corner had been turned and the land invasions were about to end. Normality would soon return. Henwood opened the press conference by saying: 'Events have moved faster than the hours today. Perhaps the life of David Stevens has been the final catalyst in getting us back to law and order.'

Henwood had just emerged from a meeting with Mugabe. The farmers' leader had been summoned to State House at half an hour's notice, alongside David Hasluck, Director of the CFU, and Richard Tate, Chairman of the Zimbabwe Tobacco Association. Mugabe had welcomed them with great courtesy. He was calm, affable and ostensibly in a mood to listen. He expressed his 'sorrow' at the death of David Stevens. When Henwood described the chaotic situation on the farms, Mugabe listened with apparent concern. He talked in soothing and moderate terms about the need for land reform to happen without violence. His persona could not have been more different from the fist-waving demagogue who had roused his followers at the airport barely 24 hours earlier. The reassuring Mugabe was on display. He gave the farmers one hour and 40 minutes of his time.

There were some moments of tension. In a tone of quiet admonishment, Mugabe made clear his disappointment that most farmers had voted 'No' in the referendum. The clause in the new constitution making Britain responsible for compensating dispossessed farmers 'was put in there to help you', he said. Mugabe wanted the farmers to join him in placing pressure on the British to fund land reform. He bitterly resented their backing for the MDC and wanted it to stop immediately. He warned that if the farmers supported the opposition, he would assume they were opposed to land reform. Yet for all this, Mugabe was very clear that law and order would be restored.

After leaving State House, Henwood said: 'He has given us an undertaking to get things back to normal . . . I really got the feeling that he was fairly determined to get the situation back to normal as soon as possible.'[4] Henwood was left with the impression that Mugabe was on the verge of making a public announcement that would order the squatters to go home and authorize the police to evict any who proved unwilling. The President had given the farmers all they could reasonably hope for.

Before his summons to State House, Henwood had seen Dabengwa and Chihuri. A joint meeting with the Home Affairs Minister and the Police Commissioner was almost unprecedented and both were anxious to appear as helpful and reassuring as possible. Henwood was able to say: 'I have their assurance that no further violent activities will be allowed. The Minister and the Police Commissioner and I are at one.'[5]

After these successful gatherings, Henwood was visibly elated. His private contacts with the government led him to believe that Mugabe's most senior colleagues, notably Msika, were pushing for normality to return. Now Henwood was convinced that the one man who mattered had been won over. In his obvious relief, he chose to regale journalists with an amusing anecdote about how he had dashed to State House for his meeting with the President while wearing a jacket hastily borrowed from a colleague and without any small change to pay for the taxi. ('I just gave the driver the biggest note I had and this guy said: "Can I drive you the next time you go and see the President".') Months later, Henwood told me: 'At that point, we thought it would be sorted out. We thought it would be fixed. We had an assurance from the highest authority in the land. What more could we want?'[6]

★   ★   ★

Less than 18 hours after the amicable gathering in State House, a critically wounded, bloodstained farmer was desperately trying to evade the crackling flames that were consuming his homestead. Bursts of automatic gunfire echoed from outside and a hail of bullets slammed through the thin walls. One round had shattered his right leg, but somehow the farmer improvised a splint and managed to keep moving. With a shotgun and 9 mm pistol, he blazed away at his attackers. For perhaps half an hour, he kept the highly organized, besieging force at bay, limping and crawling from room to room, firing through the shattered windows. Yet the shadowy figures who raked his house with AK-47 assault rifles lurked in the dense bush and were invisible. From carefully prepared positions, they surrounded the homestead and kept up a withering fire. As the shooting continued, they decided to smoke out their quarry.

Petrol bombs fashioned from beer bottles were hurled into the house. As the flames took hold, the heat and smoke became unbearable. Exhausted and bleeding, the farmer was forced to retreat from the spreading, roaring inferno, struggling in agony with his splinted leg. Finally, he took refuge in the bathroom and began running the taps in a frenzied bid to fill the tub and find shelter from the fire. But the acrid smoke and the searing blast that seemed to come from a furnace overcame him. With strength born from desperation, the farmer prised apart the burglar bars covering the window and struggled outside. He lay spread-eagled, bloodied, blackened by smoke and helpless on the ground. The mob surrounded the prostrate figure, shot him over and over again and hacked him to death with knives and axes.

Martin Olds, 43, left a paraplegic wife, Kathy, 44, and two children: Angus, 14, and Martine, 17. By 6.30 a.m. on Tuesday, 18 April, the day when Zimbabweans celebrate their independence, he lay dead beside his home at Compensation farm in Matabeleland. A jubilant gang of 70 'war veterans' looted the house and roared away in a convoy of 13 vehicles. Police waved them through two road-blocks near the tiny, shabby town of Nymandlovu.

News of the attack reached Harare some hours later and early reports suggested that Olds was still alive and fighting back. Together with four other journalists, I flew to Matabeleland in a light aircraft and our pilot circled over Compensation's farmhouse. Surrounded by an endless expanse of parched, brown bush veldt, the tin roof of the homestead glinted in the sunlight, appearing like a large mirror in a desert. From 1,000 feet the scene appeared normal. Matabeleland's cattle-ranching country unfolded below: an arid, harsh tract of Zimbabwe, so different from the cool, verdant fields of Mashonaland. When the aircraft banked steeply and arced downwards for a series of low passes, everything suddenly looked very different. The walls of the homestead were scorched and blackened by fire, its roof had partially collapsed and jagged rows of bullet holes scarred the whitewash. Tiny figures moved to and fro as we circled above, and we wondered whether the siege was still under way. Ten minutes later we landed at Bulawayo airport. It was about 11 a.m. and, as we quickly learned, Olds had been killed before we took to the air.

As the sun reached its zenith, we found the narrow, dusty road that leaves Nyamandlovu and runs past Compensation farm. Matabeleland lies in the same geographical belt as the Kalahari Desert and only the hardiest vegetation survives. Acacia trees and thorn bushes growing from parched soil, tainted by a film of desert sand, stretched away in every direction.

Gathered in a patch of shade were three white farmers. Tense and shaken, they were trying to come to terms with what had happened. Craig Wood had seen Olds's body and was aghast to report that he had not only been shot but also bludgeoned to death. Guy Parkin, the son of a local farmer, heard Olds make a distress call over the radio and approached Compensation at 6.45 a.m., only to beat a hasty retreat when shots were fired over his head. Wally Herbst was one of Olds's closest neighbours and feared that the attack showed that even worse was to come. 'These guys had a mission,' he said. 'They picked on him to provoke a reaction and get a result, perhaps to allow the President to declare a state of emergency. We just can't think what's going to happen next.' But on one point, the sombre, mournful group was adamant. They would not be driven from their land. 'We can't give up, there's no way that I can go,' said Wood. 'I've never been out of Africa. I don't want to sound like a hero but I've no intention of going anywhere.' His companions nodded quietly.

We left the sorrowful huddle and bumped our way along the narrow track to Silverstreams farm, next door to Compensation, where Olds's mother, Gloria, lived. Although aged 67, her first instinct when she heard the gunfire was to defend her son. Fearing that her life would also be lost, neighbouring farmers had been forced to physically restrain the determined grandmother from rushing to his aid. Now she stood at the gates of her homestead: a tall, slender woman with a flowing, white pony-tail, falling almost to her waist. The wives of two neighbouring farmers hugged her silently. Without a word, she turned and walked back inside her modest home. Gloria Olds never spoke to any of her neighbours again.

A degree of mystery still surrounds the murder of Martin Olds. The operation was a professional one, so much so that many farmers are convinced it was the work of the army. But Compensation farm had not been invaded and there seemed no obvious reason why Olds should be singled out. Only after months of quiet investigation was the sequence of events pieced together.

Shortly before 6 a.m. on 18 April, Olds found a convoy of vehicles roaring up his drive, carrying about 70 squatters. In case of trouble, he had already sent his wife and children to Bulawayo and, believing that this was a farm invasion like any other, he went outside the house to confront them.

Olds took a shotgun, but he left the rest of his extensive armoury untouched, inside the homestead. When the squatters massed around the security fence surrounding his home, they may not have appeared any more dangerous than usual. There were probably no guns visible. A separate group of about 20 highly trained individuals armed with AK-47s had taken position earlier, in carefully prepared firing points around the house. When Olds appeared in the open, armed only with a shotgun, they had him cold.

At this point, he was probably shot in the leg. Olds fired back and wounded two men who were among the mob at his gates. They were peppered with shotgun pellets and lightly injured. Then he took cover inside the house and sent out a distress call on the radio. At about 6 a.m. neighbouring farmers heard him say: 'I've been shot and I need an ambulance.' They immediately called an ambulance from Bulawayo and contacted the local police. Meanwhile, Olds managed to grab a 9 mm handgun and fight back, but for some reason he was unable to reach the rest of his armoury. Perhaps the shooting was too intense or the fire began so rapidly that he was forced to struggle away from the flames.

Although Nyamandlovu police station is barely a 20-minute drive from Compensation farm, its officers made no attempt to help. Instead, they threw a cordon of road-blocks across the routes between Nyamandlovu and Bulawayo. The ambulance was stopped at one checkpoint and prevented from passing through. After Olds had been killed, his attackers were allowed to escape through the road-blocks and were sufficiently brazen to stop at a bottle store outside Nyamandlovu and noisily celebrate their success in broad daylight. Later, the police hardly bothered to pretend they were investigating Olds's death. His murder was a clinically planned operation, which clearly had the approval of the state. Whether the army was directly involved cannot be proven. That powerful figures had decided to have another farmer out of the way seems beyond doubt.

Why was Olds singled out? In a bitter irony, he had been called to State House on Independence Day in 1990, exactly ten years before his murder, and decorated with the Bronze Cross of Zimbabwe by Mugabe himself. Olds had rescued a friend from the jaws of a crocodile in Lake Kariba and his feat received nation-wide publicity. Photographs of his investiture show a stern, bearded farmer sitting two places away from an aloof Mugabe. Olds was a tough character with a fiery temper, the pillar of the white farming community in the Nymandlovu area. His murder succeeded in demoralizing all of the farmers nearby and the pace of new invasions in Matabeleland picked up immediately afterwards. To sow terror and confusion was probably the prime purpose.

John Zurnamer, a close friend of Olds, told me: 'They picked out Mart because he was the toughest nut in the area. He was a hard, principled man who didn't take kindly to anyone breaking the law.' Moreover, the attackers probably wanted to provoke a reaction. A man of Olds's temperament could be trusted to fight back and perhaps they wanted some deaths, some martyrs in the cause of land reform. White farmers could then be held responsible and the land invasions presented as legitimate retaliation. In fact, the assault was executed with such professionalism that this opportunity never arose.

No one could possibly doubt that Mugabe's reassuring words to the CFU leadership barely 24 hours before the murder of Olds were worthless. No starker illustration of his insincerity could be imagined. To rub in the message, Mugabe appeared on television at noon on 18 April, less than six hours after the killing, and delivered his annual Independence Day address to the nation. The carefully scripted 26-minute speech was bland and barely referred to the land crisis. But afterwards, Mugabe walked on to the veranda of State House and talked to Reuben Barwe from ZBC. All restraint, all pretence at moderation and reasonableness were abandoned. Waving his arms for emphasis, Mugabe revealed what was running through his mind. He could not forgive the farmers for daring to oppose him in the referendum:

> For them to have banded together to the man in opposition to government and, for that matter, to have gone much further in mobilising, actually it's coercing, their labour forces on the farms to support the one position opposed to government has exposed them as not our friends, but our enemies.

Mugabe then drove the message home. Addressing white farmers directly, he said:

> Our present state of mind is you are now our enemies, because you really have behaved as enemies of Zimbabwe and we are full of anger. Our entire community is angry and that is why we now have the war veterans seizing the land.[7]

Across the parched plains of Matabeleland, hundreds of Mugabe's 'enemies' were leaving their homes. The CFU ordered the evacuation of all farms in the region and scores of small convoys headed along dusty tracks for the safety of Bulawayo. Within hours, most farmhouses were deserted, while the few landowners who insisted on staying slept with guns cocked and loaded beside their beds, taking turns with friends to go on sentry duty. Mugabe's 'enemies' were wondering who would be the next victim of his anger.

★　　　　　　★　　　　　　★

Beneath a portrait of the Queen and posters of rolling English hills, worried people huddled together. Giggling toddlers and silent grandparents, anxious mothers and grim-faced fathers sat side by side. Mugabe's 'enemies' were preparing for the worst. Anyone with a claim to British citizenship was planning an escape route. In the aftermath of the events of 15–18 April, the British High Commission in Harare was besieged as effectively as any white farm. At 6 a.m. each morning, the queuing began outside its offices in a modern, steel and glass tower block. By the time doors opened at 8 a.m., a long line of people snaked around the building.

When I first saw this spectacle, I confess that my reaction was cruel laughter. Here was a collection of affluent, privileged people, who had enjoyed decades of soft living beneath the African sun, complete with swimming pools and servants, and now they were getting up at the crack of dawn and spending cold mornings in a queue. This must be the first mundane, boring task they have ever done for themselves, I thought. The one thing they couldn't get their servants to do. They couldn't ask Samson to wash the car, make breakfast and complete three applications for British citizenship. So distinguished-looking gentlemen who had never changed a light bulb found themselves watching the sunrise and trying to make sense of a bewildering array of forms.

By mid-morning, the reception, corridors, waiting room and consular office were all flooded with people. If they were British expatriates, they clutched their passports and waited to register for 'consular protection'. Zimbabweans carried a sheaf of documents – yellowing, long-forgotten birth, death and marriage certificates – and filled in hasty applications for British passports. The mood in the queues was one of restrained panic. Few of the applicant Britons made any pretence at a stiff upper lip. When I arrived on the morning of 20 April, their nerves were not helped by the television permanently tuned to BBC World News that bellowed from a corner of the reception, alongside a beaming picture of the Queen. Zimbabwe dominated the headlines and the captive audience in the High Commission visibly winced. 'I don't think I've ever felt as insecure as I do now, it's a surreal existence,' Liz Horsfall told me. 'We've been through everything, through the war and sanctions, but I've never felt as stressed as I do now.'

As queues overwhelmed the British High Commission, a mob of 50 squatters surrounded a row of tiny houses and kicked open their flimsy, wooden doors. They hurled burning brands of brushwood through each doorway and roaring, yellow flames soon crackled overhead. The homes of the black labour force on Rudolphia farm were being razed to the ground. Yet another dark pillar of smoke rising over luxuriant, green fields marked a scene of devastation. The gang refrained from burning down the homestead

– instead, they smashed all the windows, ransacked every room and stole everything they could lay their hands on. Glorying in the destruction, they allowed themselves to be filmed by Chris Mazivanhanga, a Zimbabwean working for Associated Press Television, and his pictures were repeated endlessly around the world. His shots of two dogs being beaten to death particularly upset some viewers.

Alan Windram, the owner, had already evacuated Rudolphia and fled for the safety of Harare. He was an open supporter of the MDC and one of his lorries had been used to ferry workers to an opposition rally. The burning of Rudolphia was his punishment. For being accused of attending an MDC gathering, his workers were rendered homeless refugees. A few miles away on the previous day, 19 April, Atlanta farm, owned by Michael Stobart, had suffered the same treatment. Every building was sent up in smoke, including the homestead. The burnt-out shells of both farms were in the Enterprise Valley, a verdant corner of Zimbabwe barely 20 miles east of Harare. The entire area was evacuated and joined the list of regions that were partially or totally cleared of white farmers. By 21 April, this stood at: Matabeleland, Midlands, Virginia, Macheke, Hwedza, Karoi, Chinhoyi and Enterprise. A roll-call of the country's agricultural heartland, encompassing everything from cattle ranches to tobacco farms, had been effectively turned over to the mobs.

I learned from painful experience just how complete and dangerous their control was. On 21 April, I left Harare with Andy Meldrum of *The Guardian* and Horace Kirton, a white Zimbabwean, and we drove east towards the Enterprise Valley. For the first time, the farm invasions had encroached to the outskirts of the capital. Barely five minutes' drive beyond the spacious, whitewashed mansions of the élite suburb of Umwinseydale, makeshift squatter camps appeared beside the main road. Several fields were partially filled by clusters of shacks. The lush meadows that rolled away from the road were devoid of activity. No tractors moved and the only people visible were handfuls of squatters scattered around their ramshackle homes. All the farms had been abandoned.

We turned right and took the dirt road that runs past Atlanta farm. A policeman immediately stepped forward and flagged us down. He looked nervous and told us: 'You must not go further, it is not safe.' We were extremely foolish. We were anxious to see the remains of Atlanta and, after thanking the officer for his concern, we pressed on. Everything appeared normal as the road wound its way through the fields. Ahead was a grove of tall poplar trees and a narrow track that would take us to the farm.

We turned a corner and instantly discovered the reason why the area had been evacuated. A wooden log had been thrown across the road, balanced on two oil drums. Beside the obstacle were 30 men armed with clubs, sticks and axes. They sat or lay on the grass, as if exhausted. We stopped the car and, for perhaps two seconds, the squatters stared at us from a distance of about 100 yards. Then they sprang forward as one and charged, waving their weapons in the air. Other figures leapt from bushes beside the road. For a split second, there was complete silence, broken only by the pounding of running feet on the dusty track. I found myself staring, transfixed, at the mass of waving sticks and clubs that was hurtling in my direction. Then Kirton hurled the car into a three-point turn and we sped off, leaving the squatters in a cloud of dust. The closest got within ten yards before we managed to accelerate away.

Back at the junction with the Harare road, barely a mile from the road-block, we encountered 50 smartly dressed soldiers from the Zimbabwean army. In my naïvety, I assumed they had been deployed to restore order and deal with the gang we had just encountered. But there was something strange about them. They were not armed, some carried maps and a white officer was in charge. He turned out to be Colonel Aubrey-Fletcher from the British military training team that was still helping Zimbabwe's forces. Tall, grey and earnest, he explained that his men were learning 'peace-keeping techniques'. When we told him of the anarchy that prevailed around the next corner, Colonel Aubrey-Fletcher was sympathetic but told us there was nothing he could do. 'If we tried to help, that would probably be frowned upon by the authorities,' he said laconically. While we watched, the highly trained soldiers and their British colonel piled into buses and drove away, leaving the area to the squatters.

The days when the farm invaders were willing to talk to journalists had clearly ended. Later I returned to Parklands farm near Norton, where I had met Agnes Rusike and her band of Manchester United-supporting revolutionaries. My car was immobilized for lack of petrol – an increasingly frequent occurrence – and whenever this happened I hired a taxi driven by Richard Mulindwa. He was a good friend and a genuine war veteran. In his teens, Richard served Mugabe's guerrillas as a *mujibha* – the herdboys who scouted for the rebels, brought them supplies and tracked Rhodesian army patrols. He cordially despised the squatters and thought them faintly ridiculous. 'These ones, they do nothing. They just sit and drink and when they want something, they steal. They are *tsotsis*, thieves, not real war vets. They were not even born in the war,' he would say.

I noticed that Richard's age and bearing gave him a certain authority over the squatters. During our trip to Parklands farm, I became particularly thankful for this. We drove down the dusty track leading on to the property and found no sign of the invaders whatever. The fields were deserted and Rusike's 'base camp' appeared to have been dismantled. We turned and retraced our steps. To my horror, what followed seemed like an action replay of the Enterprise Valley incident. We rounded a corner and there was a road-block, clearly constructed in the last few minutes to block our exit. Six squatters toyed with clubs, beside a makeshift boom balanced on an oil drum. We were so close that escape was impossible.

Richard leaned out of the window and greeted the man who appeared to be the ringleader. He was tall, athletic and wore the standard attire of many squatters – blue overalls with several buttons undone to reveal a Mugabe T-shirt underneath. Richard spoke with him in Shona, using authoritative, even aggressive tones. I understood nothing of their conversation and was astonished when the ringleader laughed heartily, broke into a broad smile and gave Richard a warm handshake. He waved his minions to clear the roadblock and raised his hand as we drove away. I breathed again. 'Phew, Richard, how did you get us out of that one?' His reply was deadpan. 'I said I am a top war vet and this white man is my prisoner. I am taking him to Zanu-PF headquarters for a thorough beating.'

★   ★   ★

'We cannot watch while blood is being shed, day in and day out. Our members and supporters are being brutally murdered with the active support of the state.'[8] Morgan Tsvangirai banged his fist on the table, his eyes blazing with fury. While white-owned farms were being raided and looted, the squatters intensified their most important campaign – the onslaught against the MDC. Anyone suspected of backing the opposition risked being hunted down and murdered, beaten, raped or tortured. The killings of Tichaona Chiminya and Talent Mabika marked a brutal escalation of this crackdown and in the last days of April, MDC supporters were being murdered at the rate of one a day. Between 20 and 25 April, five were killed. Robert Mbudzi was shot dead while addressing a small MDC rally near Mhangura on 20 April. Nicholas Hwindiri, a security guard, was beaten to death in the Harare township of Mufakose on 22 April. Peter Karidza was killed in Shamva on 24 April and reports of abductions and torture came in from all over the country.

Tsvangirai denounced the violence at a furious press conference on 26 April. In the resort town of Kariba, every last MDC activist had been hunted down and murdered or hospitalized (it was later established that two lives were lost). But what enraged Tsvangirai more than anything else was the open sponsorship of violence by the state. Samson Makombe, the survivor who witnessed the attack on Chiminya and Mabika, would later give detailed testimony in the High Court and identify the men who hurled the fatal petrol bombs as Joseph Mwale, an officer in the Central Intelligence Organisation, and Kainos Zimunya, Zanu-PF's election agent for Buhera

116

North. Independent newspapers repeatedly named both men as the killers. They were summoned to appear in the High Court and answer the charge. Neither did so. In April 2001, a judge ordered Andrew Chigovera, the Attorney-General, to proceed with a prosecution. As I write in December 2001, no action has been taken and Mwale and Zimunya are both at liberty. To date, the former remains on the government payroll as an agent with the CIO.

The onslaught in Kariba was organized by Isaac Mackenzie, the Zanu-PF candidate. He gathered 40 squatters from white-owned farms around Karoi, 50 miles down the road, and turned them loose on the MDC in his prospective constituency. The gang based themselves in the Zambezi Valley Hotel, then owned by a relative of Mackenzie, and their leader was none other than Comrade Jesus. The short, plump warlord of Karoi, whom I had met beside his followers on Maunga farm, was enlarging his domain.

I drove to Kariba on 27 April, winding my way through its hinterland of rugged mountains and sweeping plains. After turning a hairpin bend, Lake Kariba came into view: a vast, glittering expanse of blue. It seemed like an inland sea, stretching to an invisible shore beyond the horizon. Later, I was forced to stop while a dozen elephants strode across the road. Graceful impalas and bucking zebras trotted into the bush as I passed the giant trunk of an ancient baobab tree. It was a perfect African scene. But at the end of this idyllic journey lay the human evidence of a brutally successful intimidation campaign.

I went to Nyamhunga township, the scene of the worst violence, and knocked on the ramshackle door of the tiny, concrete house I had been directed to. Inside, the room was dark and baking hot. At first I could barely see anything as I stepped from the harsh, white glare of the sun into the sudden blackness. Waves of heat seemed to radiate down from the tin roof, beating on my head in quick succession. The stale air reeked of the burnt smell of paraffin. My eyes adjusted and the dim shapes around me became two chairs beside a rickety wooden table. Ragged, blue cloth was drawn across the only window and a single beam of sunlight shone through a hole in the makeshift curtain. A girl stood beside the table and her white teeth smiled nervously. 'You are good to come, you must see what is happening here,' she said. 'My name is Epiphania Marufu, you must speak to my sister, Beauty Marufu.' She was about 18 and wore a grubby T-shirt with a blanket around her waist. She spoke quietly, with a nervous tremor in her voice, trying hard to suppress her obvious fear with an artificial smile.

Three steps took us across the room, avoiding cooking pots and chairs. Epiphania opened a wooden door and entered an even smaller room, just large enough for a bed. A strip of cloth covered half of a window. By the sunlight, I saw a shape under a tatty red blanket. A head rested on a dirty pillow, eyes closed, brow glistening with sweat, face drawn with pain. 'This is my sister,' said Epiphania.

Speaking softly in Shona, she knelt beside the bed and poured the inert figure a glass of water. A quiet conversation took place between the sisters, with Epiphania talking in reassuring tones. Then she turned and said: 'Beauty will tell you what happened to her. But we are afraid these people will come back. They might have seen you come. I will watch for them.' She left the bedroom and stood guard beside the front door, drawing back the shabby curtain and peering outside.

There was just enough space for me to kneel at the foot of the bed. A weak voice began speaking quietly, pausing for breath after each sentence. Every word seemed to require a herculean effort. 'I am Beauty Marufu, I am a member of MDC.' A long pause.

'Yes,' I said. 'What happened to you?'

'I was kidnapped by Zanu-PF. They beat me.'

With all the brusque insensitivity of a journalist at a press conference, I interrupted. 'How many Zanu-PF people? Where did they kidnap you from?'

She spoke in staccato sentences, pausing to wince with pain. 'There were 15 and they came here, to this house. They came yesterday. They said, "We are going to kill you because you are MDC." They took me from here. They were already beating me. They took me to Zambezi Valley Hotel. Room 4. They held my arms while three of them stamped on my back. They beat me all over my body. Anyone who wanted to was beating me. They stuffed a towel in my mouth to stop me from screaming. They tied my hands with rope. Now even to move is painful for me.'

I scribbled mechanically as Beauty continued. She had been tortured for seven hours. Her tormentors, armed with whips and clubs, had demanded the names and addresses of all MDC activists in Kariba. In her terror she had told them what they wanted to hear. She had listened to the screams and cries of other victims, as they were tortured in neighbouring rooms of the hotel. Beauty had eventually been thrown into the street, where Epiphania found her.

'How badly are you hurt?' I asked, inanely. Silence. I asked again, nervously. Silence. Then, with one movement, Beauty threw aside the thin blanket. She lay face down and naked. Every inch of her flesh, from heels to shoulders, was criss-crossed with red weals, seeping blood and white pus. Vivid, blue bruises stained the skin in between. No feature of her body could be discerned, beyond one great amalgamation of wounds. She drew deep, exhausted, painful breaths. Her wounds had not even been bandaged. 'You must go to hospital,' I said.

'I am afraid even to leave this house. If I go outside, these Zanu-PF people will see me. They will beat me again.' I realized that Epiphania was hovering beside me, her obvious fear sending a shiver of alarm down my spine. I cursed my stupidity. With blissful ignorance, I had driven into the heart of Nyamhunga and parked my car outside Beauty's house, in full view of the world. Any visitor inevitably draws attention. A cluster of small children had squealed '*Murungu*' as I emerged from my car. By now, most of the township would know of my presence. If the Zanu-PF gang was still nearby, it would descend on Beauty and Epiphania for daring to talk to a white man, let alone a white journalist. With infinite politeness, Epiphania said: 'It is not safe for you to be here. You must go.'

I turned back to Beauty. Epiphania had covered her with the blanket and she lay, silent in the darkness. 'I'm so sorry,' I said, pathetically. Then Epiphania's hand firmly gripped my arm and led me outside. The sun beat down and the harsh light blinded me once more. The toddlers playing in the dust cried '*Murungu*.' I barely registered any of this. All I could think of was the shattered body in the tiny room, her wounds illuminated by shafts of sunlight from the window. All Epiphania could think of was getting me away from her house.

I drove hurriedly away from Nyamhunga, past the Zambezi Valley Hotel[9] and up the hillside to Kariba hospital, barely noticing the scenic views over the lake. I found an entire ward crammed with the victims of Comrade Jesus's gang. They lay in the intense, airless heat with dressings swathed around their broken limbs. More beds had been pushed into the ward to accommodate the casualties and they were packed together, a few inches apart. Flies buzzed around the rusting frames of the beds, and the distinctive, high-pitched cry of a fish eagle soaring over the lake blended with low moans of pain.

I spoke to John Nhema, 25, whose left arm and right leg were both encased in plaster. His brow was covered with sweat and he winced involuntarily, but he spoke with furious energy. He was abducted from Nyamhunga and taken to Banana Charara Estate, a white-owned farm on the outskirts of Kariba. About 30 captives, all suspected MDC supporters, were assembled on a football pitch by a gang of 40 men. They were armed with clubs, sticks, whips and iron bars and Comrade Jesus was their leader. He supervised and participated in what happened next.

The prisoners were ordered to wave their fists and join the customary chants of obedience: '*Pamberi ne* Zanu-PF, *pamberi ne* Mugabe.' Then they were dragged forward, two at a time, and beaten senseless. Nhema was among the first to be assaulted. 'They beat me with clubs and bars all over my body,' he said. 'Then they held me in the air by the arms and legs and beat my buttocks and then the soles of my feet. They hit my leg, all of them were hitting my leg. They were saying "You are MDC, we are killing you because you are MDC, we don't want to see MDC here".' Unconscious and with his right leg broken, John was tossed aside.

His assailants dragged another victim forward and repeated the process, systematically beating all of their captives. Moments later, they threw a bucket of cold water over Nhema to revive him. 'One of them said "You must shout *pamberi ne* Zanu-PF, *pamberi ne* Mugabe". I could not say it and they started again.' For the second time, Nhema was dragged forward and attacked by six men, who broke his left arm with repeated blows from a club. 'When one was tired, another came and took his place,' he said. As a final torment, when the beating was over, Nhema was forced to stand on his broken leg and carry the unconscious body of a friend with his broken arm.

As the gang worked through the victims, they sang constantly. One of their songs was addressed to the MDC: 'You must dig a deep hole under the ground because we are coming to find you. We will find you. We will find you.' Another was a paean of loyalty: 'Father Mugabe, you are the owner of Zimbabwe, you should rule Zimbabwe for ever.' Clubs rose and fell, limbs and heads were broken to the sounds of these words.

After three hours of systematic beatings and torture, the captives were released and some who could still move brought a pick-up and drove the injured to hospital. But two had not survived the ordeal. Nicholas Chatitima and Lux Kanyurira lay dead, both of their skulls crushed. Comrade Jesus's men threw Kanyurira's body into the back of a truck and headed for the centre of Nyamhunga. His corpse was dumped in the dust outside a faded Spar supermarket, as a warning of the price of supporting the MDC.

Nhema described all this in matter-of-fact tones, pausing only to flinch with pain. The patients in the beds beside him recounted similar stories. All had been abducted and taken to Banana Charara Estate or the Zambezi Valley Hotel for torture. In total, 25 people had been hospitalized and two killed on 25–26 April. Perhaps a dozen more had, like Beauty Marufu, been too afraid to seek treatment. That was the end of the MDC in Kariba. All that remained of Zanu-PF's opponents were shattered bodies lying in agony inside the hospital or the darkened rooms of Nyamhunga. Isaac Mackenzie was assured of victory. Luke Sigobele, the MDC candidate, fled the constituency and was never able to campaign again. Violence and terror had delivered the desired result.

At first, the police declined to act against Comrade Jesus and his gang. When John Nhema's family tried to report his assault, the officers at Kariba police station refused to file a report and told them: 'It is political.' But a few hours before my visit to the hospital, police had responded and arrested Comrade Jesus, alongside several of his followers. By that time, the mob had already done its worst. The job was done and Comrade Jesus's followers had served their purpose.

On the following morning, 28 April, I waited outside Kariba's tiny magistrate's court for the appearance of the gang. They arrived in two police Land Rovers, guarded by 20 officers armed with semi-automatic FN rifles. One by one, they climbed out of the vehicles, 5 women and 11 men. All wore the obligatory Mugabe T-shirts and looks of indifference or smug satisfaction. Most were young, in their teens or twenties, and seemed fit and healthy. Then Comrade Jesus emerged, still wearing his white, flat cap. I stood about twenty feet away and for a moment our eyes met and I detected a brief flicker of recognition. He seemed calm, contented and relaxed. A group of 20 Zanu-PF supporters, instantly recognizable in their T-shirts, had gathered to show their support and Comrade Jesus acknowledged them with a raised fist and a smile. Then, surrounded by the guards, he and his followers entered the courtroom for a five-minute hearing. Nervous policemen prevented anyone from witnessing the proceedings and, afterwards, Comrade Jesus sauntered out with his hands clasped behind his back, as if on an afternoon stroll. He joined his gang in the Land Rovers and was whisked away, still wearing a ghost of a smile.

When the policemen had disappeared, I went to see Clara Phiri, the magistrate. She was smiling, friendly and absolutely terrified. 'I don't know what will happen to me,' she said. 'I have just remanded them in custody and I don't know how they will make me pay for that. It is very dangerous to deal with these people.' Comrade Jesus and his followers had been charged with two counts of murder and 'public violence'. Phiri had dismissed their request for bail and ensured they were placed behind bars. But she still feared the consequences. Curiously, I looked down the list of names given by the 16 accused. Comrade Jesus's real name was Chakwana Mueri. Zimbabwe has not seen the last of you, I thought to myself.

★   ★   ★

Beneath the shade of a msasa tree, a small crowd raised their open palms and shouted: '*Chinja*'.[10] They laughed and applauded as the speaker attacked Mugabe and accused him of 'destroying our country'. Morgan Tsvangirai was addressing a rally in Buhera North, the parliamentary seat he was contesting. He spoke on a parched, rocky plateau, 300 miles south of Kariba, to an audience that feared attack at any moment and stole nervous glances in all directions. In the months following the MDC's birth, thousands had turned out to hear Tsvangirai speak at events held across Zimbabwe. After weeks of relentless violence, those numbers had now dwindled to hundreds or even scores.

Only 200 were willing to be seen with him and chant the MDC's slogans on a hot Sunday in Buhera communal lands. Even this modest meeting, held beside a tiny village of conical huts, required extraordinary security precautions. Over 40 youthful MDC supporters arrayed themselves in a protective circle around the audience. Anyone wishing to join in was searched. Five police officers armed with FN rifles were also present and lounged in the shade beside their Land Rover. Tsvangirai's guards viewed them with deep distrust. The screen of watchful, alert youths was the only reliable defence from Zanu-PF mobs.

This was how Tsvangirai was reduced to campaigning. He drove from one small gathering to the next, always surrounded by his guards, who sought to protect the audience as much as their leader. In some villages no one would dare come within 100 yards of him. Tsvangirai would stand on the edge of the circle of huts and speak through a loud-hailer to groups of people sitting on their doorsteps, cooking, drinking or eating. The MDC youths would sing and dance. Their audience would pretend it wasn't an audience and continue exactly as normal. But they would listen with one ear all the same. Earlier on this Sunday, Tsvangirai had driven past the burnt-out, charred remains of the pick-up in which Mabika and Chiminya had died. He paused and stood in silent vigil for a few moments. From the point of view of his campaign, that event marked a crucial turning point. For his prospective constituents, it had been a terrible lesson in the risks of backing the MDC. By killing two, Zanu-PF had terrified 20,000.

When the modest rally was over, I spoke with Tsvangirai under the msasa tree. He was calm, collected and friendly as ever, but his underlying unease was obvious. 'The intimidation is having a terrible effect, absolutely terrible. That's why we didn't see many people here today, they are so afraid. Fear has kept people away, you really cannot exaggerate how terrified these people are,' he said. Then Tsvangirai's voice hardened. 'We know what Mugabe and Zanu-PF are capable of, we know that quite well. We know what they will resort to. We just have to withstand it, we just have to withstand it.'[11]

NOTES AND REFERENCES

1 ZBC TV, 18 April 2000.
2 All quotations from *Daily Telegraph,* 17 April 2000. I am grateful to Anton La Guardia for this account.
3 Speech, Harare airport, 16 April 2000.
4 CFU press conference, 17 April 2000.
5 *Ibid.*
6 Interview with the author, 20 February 2001.
7 ZBC TV, 18 April 2000.
8 MDC press conference, 26 April 2000.
9 The *Lonely Planet* guide to Zimbabwe says of the Zambezi Valley Hotel: 'If

you're looking for all-night African-style action and disco music, this is the place.' Its reputation is 'improving' but the guide warns 'lone women may want to try somewhere else'. (Lonely Planet Publications, Hawthorn, 1997.)

10 Meaning 'change'.
11 Interview with the author, 23 April 2000.

Chapter 7

More Than They Bargained For

May 2000

> They started the violence. Now they are getting more than they bargained for. (Robert Mugabe on the MDC, 3 May 2000)[1]

How to withstand the onslaught? That question dominated the lives of the MDC's candidates, officials, supporters and possible voters. Although no date had been fixed for the parliamentary election, the pressure mounted with every day that passed.

By early May, Zanu-PF's intimidation campaign had reached the capital for the first time. In the Harare township of Budiriro, the party's thugs patrolled the streets, rounding up anyone suspected of backing the MDC. It was the urban version of the rural crackdown, centred on occupied farms, which had been under way since February. Once again, Hitler Hunzvi led the onslaught. During his period in Poland in the 1970s he had, apparently, qualified as a doctor. Every claim Hunzvi made about his life must be treated with grave scepticism, but there is no doubt that he possessed a surgery in Budiriro — a decrepit, red-bricked building, with 'DR C H HUNZVI' written in black above its entrance. There is also no doubt about the purpose this surgery came to serve. A gang of Zanu-PF thugs lived, ate and slept there, using it as a base for their terror campaign in Budiriro. In effect, the surgery doubled as armed camp and prison, where victims were dragged for beatings, floggings and worse.

When I visited Budiriro on Tuesday, 2 May, the streets were silent and empty. There are few more disquieting sights than a deserted, apparently abandoned, African township. Usually, the alleys bustle with ragged children playing in the dust and chattering excitedly, brightly dressed women selling their wares at ramshackle stalls beside the road, and quiet groups of men lying in the shade, with bottles of the ubiquitous traditional brew by their sides. Dogs, goats and even cows are in the streets and all the shabby, identical houses teem with humanity. On this day the contrast could not have been greater. I saw only a handful of people in the open. No one had fled the area – the people of Budiriro were simply too afraid to emerge from their homes. Each of the tiny, square, concrete houses, with their dangerous asbestos roofs, was packed with frightened faces.

I entered the home I had been directed to. There, in the sudden darkness, were five small children, sitting silently in a room crowded with cooking pots, blankets and rickety furniture. Three women, their eyes filled with fear, were among them. One girl of 16 led me behind the house to a shack made of wood and cardboard placed in a tiny garden, where some wilting maize struggled for life in a few square feet of parched soil.

Kudzai Mhlanga hid inside the shanty, a space just large enough to contain a sleeping form. With some reluctance, he left his refuge and talked to me in the garden. He was 35, spoke excellent English and wore the smart, blue overalls of a man with a real job in what remained of Zimbabwe's formal economy. Mhlanga worked for a printing company and earned £25 per month, a good wage by Budiriro standards. Yet his children cowered inside their home and he wore the fearful, hunted expression that I had seen on so many faces.

Three men wearing Zanu-PF T-shirts had ambushed Mhlanga beside Budiriro's shabby shopping centre. They seized him by the arms and asked him where he worked. Mhlanga had no links with the MDC and saw no harm in telling them that he was employed in a factory that made T-shirts. The reply was swift: 'Ah, you are the guy who prints T-shirts for MDC.' Then he was seized and dragged through the streets. It was that simple. Anyone with the faintest connection to the MDC, real or imagined, was being singled out and abducted in broad daylight. Mhlanga was frog-marched to Hunzvi's surgery a few hundred yards away. 'That place, that place is a prison, a torture chamber,' he said. 'They have sticks, electric cables, iron bars, barbed wire.'

Mhlanga found the small building overrun by a Zanu-PF gang of 50, both male and female. He was hurled to the ground and one man planted a foot on his neck, while two others whipped the soles of his feet and beat him across the back and buttocks. 'All the time, they were shouting "Give us names of MDC people. Where do they stay? Where do they meet? Give us names. We want to get these MDC people."' In panic, Mhlanga shouted some false, invented names. As the frenzied beating continued unabated, he named three friends whom he knew were involved with the MDC. When Mhlanga made this confession, a tear rolled from his right eye.

After being beaten almost to unconsciousness, he was dragged along a corridor, unable to walk because of the abrasions on the soles of his feet. Mhlanga was thrust inside a toilet cubicle, crammed in along with three other prisoners. More victims were pushed through the door until eight were packed into the tiny space, forcing some to stand on the toilet itself. The thugs worked through their captives systematically, dragging them out to be tortured and then returning them to the cubicle. Mhlanga was tortured twice more. On each occasion, he was beaten senseless with clubs while a woman whipped the soles of his feet to reopen the wounds inflicted earlier. Two junior MDC officials were among the inmates and they were singled out for special treatment. They were whipped with sticks wrapped in barbed wire and one was kicked repeatedly in the mouth, losing several teeth.

As the cold, winter night fell, the gang tormented their prisoners by pouring icy water on the toilet cubicle's floor and spraying more through the window with a hose pipe. When dawn broke and blood mingled with freezing water, the bleeding, shivering captives were dragged out of the surgery and herded into the back of a white Land Cruiser with 'Zanu-PF Harare Province' lettered on the side. Mhlanga said: 'One of the torturers told us "We can keep you here for a month and the police will never do anything. We can do what we like. If you vote for MDC, we are going to start a war. If you vote for MDC, we will kill you. If you want your life, you must vote for Zanu-PF. Vote Zanu-PF or you will die."' Mhlanga was freed after a 24-hour ordeal, unable to walk because of the lacerations on the soles of his feet. A friend carried him home and his wife treated his wounds. Now he was in hiding, hoping that by staying inside the shack, he would have a few vital minutes to escape if the Zanu-PF gang raided his house.

Yet I sensed there was more to Mhlanga's torment than the unimaginable physical pain. With a degree of insensitivity that I shudder to recall, I asked: 'What happened to the friends whom you named as being involved in the MDC?' He paused. Then came a halting reply.

'Two of them have disappeared. They were taken yesterday. I don't know what has happened to them.' He looked as if he would break down and I cursed my crass impertinence. I noticed that Mhlanga's daughter was hovering by my side. Once again my presence was endangering everyone. As I left, Mhlanga's eyes brimmed with pain and guilt.

I drove through Budiriro's silent streets, carefully avoiding the surgery-turned-torture chamber. I had been warned to steer clear of the shopping centre, where Zanu-PF gangs drank in the bottle stores and occasionally mounted road-blocks. Until now, warnings of this sort had only applied during visits to occupied farms in remote areas of Zimbabwe. Yet here I was, in a corner of Harare, the capital city, the hub of the country, the administrative centre, and it had been turned over to the mobs. One thought drummed through my mind: how could anyone argue that a free and fair election was possible? How could Mugabe and his minions still assert with a straight face that the government did not condone violence? Even Harare was not safe from the gangs.

126

A fortnight later, on 16 May, the inevitable happened. The torturers in the surgery, whose victims ran into scores, if not hundreds, finally killed someone. Takundwa Chapunza was beaten to death and his mangled body dumped at the local bus station as a warning of the price of voting MDC. Police belatedly made some arrests, finally clearing the surgery of its murderous occupants and closing down the torture centre. But Hunzvi himself was never even questioned about what had happened in the surgery that carried his name.

★   ★   ★

If that was the everyday threat hanging over ordinary MDC supporters, the ordeal endured by many of the party's parliamentary candidates was even worse. On 3 May, the day after my visit to Budiriro, a gang of at least 200 descended on a small village outside Bindura. They were looking for Elliot Pfebve, who was contesting the seat for the MDC. The chanting mob, armed and dressed in the usual way, surrounded the modest family home. By chance, Pfebve was not present, so they assaulted his 70-year-old father, dragging him into the street and leaving him seriously injured. Matthew Pfebve, 49, was also in the house and, tragically, he bore a close resemblance to his younger brother. Perhaps believing that they had captured the MDC candidate, the gang bundled him away. Matthew Pfebve's body was found on 4 May. He had been tortured and beaten to death.

In the industrial town of Kwe Kwe, the MDC candidate was perhaps more at risk than anywhere else. Blessing Chebundo was fighting the seat against one of the most feared and powerful men in Zimbabwe. Emmerson Mnangagwa was Justice Minister and a trusted disciple of Mugabe. The two men had known each other since the formation of Zanu in 1963. During the bush war, Mnangagwa served as Mugabe's intelligence chief, and immediately after independence, he became Security Minister. The Matabeleland crackdown of the 1980s was largely the work of Mnangagwa and cemented his reputation for ruthlessness.

Anyone who stood against this quintessential Big Man of African politics would take his life in his hands. Chebundo had already been offered bribes to withdraw his candidacy, and insistent, anonymous voices had delivered numerous warnings. Then, on 9 May, he was following his normal routine and waiting at a bus stop at 7 a.m., *en route* to work. Five men, armed with clubs and iron bars, surrounded Chebundo. One said: 'You are the one who thinks you can beat Zanu-PF. We are going to fix you.' Chebundo was clubbed across the shoulders and his hand was slashed with a knife. As he fell to the ground, someone poured liquid over his head and he realized from the overpowering smell that it was petrol. Chebundo heard the rasp of a match being struck, but it snapped in half and fell to the ground, smoking harmlessly. 'With petrol dripping down my eyes, I went for the guy who was trying to light me,' Chebundo told me. He seized hold of his attacker and held the man in an arm-lock. Then Chebundo shouted to the other men: 'If you burn me, you will also burn your friend.' The gang fled and Chebundo was left on the pavement, wiping petrol from his eyes.

One week later, a gang of 50 surrounded his house at 14 Robert Mugabe Road. They smashed the windows with stones and then hurled petrol bombs through the shattered frames. Crouching in the smoke, as the greedy, roaring flames drew near, Chebundo called the police station barely half a mile away. The officers refused to help. In anticipation of attack, Chebundo had already moved his wife and four children to a safe location and now he tried to flee his home. As he dashed out of the burning building, the gang seized hold of him. Chebundo did not hesitate and stabbed one of his attackers in the chest, forcing four others to carry their wounded comrade to safety. In the confusion that followed, he managed to make his escape. His home was razed to the ground and his family lost everything. Shortly afterwards, mobs attacked the homes of three of Chebundo's supporters and dozens more were assaulted. The MDC soon abandoned any idea of campaigning in Kwe Kwe.

★   ★   ★

On occupied farms, the violence continued unabated. By the beginning of May, more than 1,200 had been invaded and the tide of new incidents showed no sign of slowing. On the afternoon of Sunday, 7 May, Alan Dunn was relaxing in his farmhouse together with his wife and their three daughters. He was a successful cattle and tobacco farmer, employing 180 people on Maasplein farm near Beatrice, 45 miles south of Harare. The Dunn family lived in a modest, single-storey, whitewashed home, surrounded by a luxuriant, carefully tended garden.

Unlike many farmers, Dunn was actively involved with his community. He was elected to the local council as an independent candidate in 1998 and made no secret of his backing for the MDC, becoming one of the party's informal regional organizers. Maasplein farm was near to a communal area and he went out of his way to help his impoverished neighbours, donating seed, fertilizer, transport and advice. Dunn's local reputation could hardly have been better, yet his high profile brought risks. He made enemies, notably the Zanu-PF candidate he had defeated in the local council elections. In the midst of a ruthless campaign aimed at anyone linked with the MDC, Dunn was an obvious target.

At about 4 p.m. on that Sunday afternoon, there was a knock on the back door of the farmhouse. When Dunn went to answer it, he found six men armed with chains, sticks and bricks. The hapless farmer was seized and dragged to a small, open garage beside his home. The gang set upon him, beating and bludgeoning him to the ground with their weapons, striking his head with a large, concrete block they found inside the garage. Dunn's wife, Sherry, and the girls huddled, terrified, inside their homestead and listened to his cries. The attackers did their brutal work in a few minutes and then escaped in a waiting car. Sherry Dunn found her husband lying unconscious in a pool of blood with a fractured skull, his life slipping away.

An ambulance rushed him to the Avenues Clinic in Harare, where he went straight into intensive care, while his distraught wife waited in the hospital's corridors. He died shortly before midnight. Dunn, 45, left three daughters: Kate, 17, Sarah, 15, and Emma, 12. His murder was the seventeenth recorded killing in Zanu-PF's terror campaign.

On the following day, I visited Maasplein farm and found a silent, forlorn group of Dunn's black workers. Wearing smart, blue overalls, they sat in a circle on the ground, six grieving men and two women, heads bowed and faces drawn with sorrow. 'We are all crying for Mr Dunn, he was a good man, he gave us everything,' said Tendai Mahoso, a young tractor driver. He pointed at a six-year-old boy and added: 'Even that small child, he has cried for Mr Dunn. He was a good man, he cared for us. Look at me. When I came here, I was a boy, I had nothing, but Mr Dunn gave me everything.' Mahoso then used a Shona expression translating as: 'This man has given me my beard, my shoes, my food, my home.'

Behind the sorrowful huddle, a tractor drove out to tend Dunn's fields. None of the workers knew whether they would still have jobs or homes, but they were trying to keep Maasplein ticking over. I walked over to the farmhouse. Dunn's family had abandoned their home and it was locked up and empty. A few yards behind the neat, modest homestead, dried blood caked the floor of the garage. A chain and two jagged bricks lay on the ground, near the back door. The dark stains on a large concrete block, so heavy that only a strong man could lift it, showed that it had been the principal murder weapon. Dunn had been bludgeoned within feet of the farmhouse windows, with their white, lace curtains. His distraught family must have heard everything.

Hitler Hunzvi chose the day of Dunn's murder to make another inflammatory attack on white Zimbabweans, whom he referred to as 'British settlers'. Then in a rare moment of comparative coherence, he issued new instructions to his followers. 'This is not Zimbabwe-Britain, this is Zimbabwe on its own,' he said. 'We are now going to search for these people with British passports to leave our country. We are not saying they are welcome to go, they must just leave. They are not Zimbabweans and they are the ones who are causing lots of problems here. They should know they are foreigners and they must leave. By air or ground, they must go.'[2]

Nerves in Zimbabwe's tiny, beleaguered white community were stretched to breaking point. Dunn's murder also coincided with the temporary closure and evacuation of the Rydings School near Karoi, after squatters camped within a few hundred yards of the classrooms and demanded half of its land. Farmers had thought their children safe when they were at the Rydings. Now they were being evacuated for the supposed haven of occupied farms.

Perhaps inevitably, there was an unsavoury case of white retaliation. Chris Mlambo, a black man, was walking along the main Harare road, near the scene of Dunn's death, on 8 May, when three white men, possibly farmers, passed him in a pick-up. They pulled over and beat him up, forcing him to seek hospital treatment. It was the first recorded case of its kind.

In this febrile atmosphere, rumours and false alarms flew thick and fast. I was often telephoned by earnest, well-meaning white Zimbabweans who would regale me with implausible tales in tones of complete conviction. In a single week in May, I was informed that Mugabe had a brain tumour and was on the verge of death. The British would evacuate all their citizens within 24 hours, using a fleet of Hercules transport aircraft secretly deployed in neighbouring Botswana. Mugabe was about to cancel the elections and declare himself President for life. Mugabe was already dead and his anointed successor was Hitler Hunzvi. A farmer was under siege and holding off a force of 500 armed with AK-47s. A mob was beating up everyone in its path in Harare's Westgate shopping centre.

One rumour that was actually picked up by a news agency and sent around the world concerned a supposed incident in Bulawayo. While walking through the centre of town, a white man was allegedly beaten to death in broad daylight. A gang of four men committed the crime while shouting: 'We want our land.' Although this rumour was quickly disproved, it was eventually reported as fact in a book covering the post-independence history of Zimbabwe.[3] This atmosphere of rumour and counter-rumour was a vivid illustration of how jumpy and tense Zimbabweans had become. It reminded me of those stories about wartime Britain, when people famously asserted that the skies over Hastings were filled with German paratroopers dressed as nuns, or trains laden with enemy soldiers were arriving at Victoria Station.

A man whose frustration had reached boiling point was Morgan Tsvangirai. In the three months since the referendum, his party had come under furious attack and now found itself virtually unable to campaign. On 10 May, Tsvangirai vented his anger in public. 'To talk about free elections in the current state of affairs is to fool ourselves,' he said. 'There is violence everywhere, absolutely everywhere, we have no access to the media, we cannot campaign, we are being harassed all the time, how can there be a free and fair election?' Tsvangirai's blind fury exuded from every pore. Yet it was anger born of complete helplessness, for the MDC's options were extremely limited. On this occasion, Tsvangirai chose to muse in public about boy-cotting the election or shutting down the country with a general strike. Neither were remotely feasible – a boycott would simply allow Mugabe off the hook and let him claim that the MDC had no support, while the will to launch a strike simply did not exist. By talking about a boycott, Tsvangirai dismayed his supporters who were still clinging to the hope of unseating Zanu-PF at the election. By talking about a strike and then failing to do anything, he damaged his credibility. The fevered atmosphere was wearing him down, as much as everyone else.

By 15 May, the Zimbabwe Human Rights Forum had recorded the fol-lowing human toll from the wave of political violence since the referendum:[4]

Deaths	19
Assaults (including blunt weapons, gunshot injuries, burns, stranglings)	1,012
Rapes	8

With the exception of the murders, all these figures were conservative esti-mates, based on reports made directly to the Forum. They can be multiplied perhaps ten times over. As for the political loyalties of those responsible, Zanu-PF's followers had committed 86 per cent of the abuses reported to the Forum.

Against a background of this unremitting campaign, a free and fair election already seemed an impossible prospect. Moreover, Mugabe's attitude to the violence was not in doubt. In speech after speech, he was careful to blame the MDC for everything and vigorously fan the flames.

On 3 May, he launched Zanu-PF's election manifesto and formally opened the campaign. Rarely had the Sheraton hotel in Harare witnessed such an extraordinary event. Perhaps inevitably, it began late and we were treated to the sight of Zimbabwe's ageing, corpulent, smartly suited élite looking perplexed and confused. Arranged in neat rows on a large platform, they faced an audience of 300 that waited expectantly for something to happen. Festooned around the hall were shiny, new Zanu-PF banners that defiantly proclaimed: 'Land is the economy and the economy is land' in large, green letters. Mugabe, his two Vice-Presidents, key figures in the politburo and most of the cabinet sat in complete silence. Fingers drummed, quizzical looks were exchanged, Joseph Msika stole a furtive glance at his watch. Proceedings should have begun ten minutes earlier, but the first speaker had failed to turn up and all the Big Men waited in an embarrassed hush. People in the audience coughed and fidgeted.

I watched Mugabe's eyes flick from left to right. Then he raised his forearm, displaying some shiny, golden cuff links, and clenched his fist. '*Pasi ne* British imperialism,' he declared. With obvious relief, his followers punched the air. '*Pasi*,' they shouted. Zimbabwe's entire government then proceeded to fill five minutes with enthusiastic cries of 'Down with the British.' They seemed almost disappointed when Olivia Muchena, the opening speaker, finally bustled into the hall, looking flustered and dishevelled, hastily claiming that an urgent dental appointment had delayed her arrival at the most important event of the official calendar.

That beginning set the tone for what followed. When Mugabe rose to speak, he did nothing but attack his opponents. By voting 'No' in the referendum and backing the MDC, white farmers had shown themselves to be 'raw Rhodesians who have never changed'. In punishment, he would back the squatter invasion of their land. 'I will never order the war veterans to retreat from the farms they are now on,' he declared. 'What are we supposed to do?' Mugabe then asked rhetorically. 'Fold our arms and say, "Ah, you are the ordained ones by the Almighty, by virtue of your white skin and by virtue of your being British, royal blood every one of you, we will not touch your land." No. The end has come, land will now come to the people.' All white farmers were, apparently, British and thus impostors on Zimbabwean soil. As for the MDC, Mugabe's message was unmistakable. 'They started the violence. Now they are getting more than they bargained for,'[5] he said. If anyone still expected the President to urge restraint, they were clearly expecting too much.

★   ★   ★

For the British, Mugabe was becoming an increasingly embarrassing problem. From early April onwards, Zimbabwe dominated the attention of the London press and Tony Blair's government came under unprecedented pressure to curb Mugabe's excesses. Suddenly, his ministers found themselves compelled to think about Zimbabwe, something they had always previously avoided.

A small African country with a collapsing economy had been a natural candidate for the very bottom of the in-tray when Blair took office in 1997. No national interests were at stake, so Zimbabwe was conveniently ignored. But it was evident from the very beginning that trouble was brewing. Mugabe wanted London to pay for land reform, in accordance with the promise made at Lancaster House in 1979. He believed this was an unconditional pledge and expected Britain to furnish him with a cheque. No questions, no ifs, no buts. Under the Conservatives, £44 million had been paid and the last tranche disbursed in 1995. Mugabe wanted this flow of money resumed immediately.

In so far as Blair's ministers thought about the issue at all, they considered land reform to be a development project like any other. If Zimbabwe met the usual conditions, Britain would consider offering funds, but any scheme had to be legal, transparent and focused on helping the poorest. For Mugabe, land reform was an obligation that Britain had a moral responsibility to finance. Any conditions were a violation of Zimbabwe's sovereignty that he would not countenance. This was the heart of the disagreement between Britain and Zimbabwe and, even before the crisis of 2000, the gap between them was probably unbridgeable.

Neither side had the slightest comprehension of the other. For the British, everything about Zimbabwe was mystifying. To understand the place seemed to require a detailed knowledge of colonial history and they were astonished to discover that Mugabe talked of little else. It seemed that the land problem was caused by Rhodes's pioneer column in 1890. Britain's obligation to pay for a solution was, apparently, unfinished business from the dying days of her last imperial entanglement in Africa. For a modernizing, forward looking, New Labour government, this was all rather embarrassing.

Clare Short, the International Development Secretary, put this with singular starkness. In a letter to Kumbirai Kangai, then Zimbabwe's Agriculture Minister in November 1997, she wrote: 'I should make clear that we do not accept that Britain has a special responsibility to meet the cost of land purchase in Zimbabwe. We are a new government from diverse backgrounds without links to former colonial interests. My own origins are Irish and as you know we were colonised not colonisers.'[6] In three brief sentences, Short casually dismissed something Mugabe saw as a solemn pledge and called into question Britain's adherence to one of the cardinal principles of international relations, namely that governments will honour obligations agreed by their predecessors. No more insensitive, derisory rebuff could be imagined. The most charitable explanation for Short's letter is that she dashed out a hasty response on an issue that she, like everyone else in London, was doing her best to ignore.

As for Mugabe himself, the British had no idea what to make of him. One Foreign Office official told me: 'Ministers were baffled. They honestly didn't know how to deal with this guy. There was a very real sense that they didn't know what to do next.' When Zimbabwe began to surface in the red boxes of Robin Cook, the Foreign Secretary, his first idea was to hand the problem over to one of his predecessors. He approached Lord Carrington in 1999 and asked him to go to Harare and talk some sense into Mugabe. As the man who oversaw the birth of Zimbabwe, Carrington still had a degree of moral authority in Harare. He was one of the few Britons whom Mugabe appeared to genuinely respect. Carrington responded favourably, but the Foreign Office eventually talked Cook out of it. According to Carrington: 'They told him it was the stupidest idea they'd ever heard and would only make things worse.'[7]

Mugabe and Blair met only once – at a Commonwealth summit in Edinburgh in October 1997. Their talks were brief and the two men appear to have made a remarkably bad impression on one another. Mugabe would later flaunt his scorn for Blair, while the Prime Minister loftily refused to respond until October 2001, when he mentioned Mugabe in his speech to the Labour party conference and bracketed him alongside Osama bin Laden in the world's pantheon of infamy. It was perhaps inevitable that Blair and Mugabe would not hit it off – two individuals with less in common are difficult to imagine. Apart from a few brief trips to South Africa, Blair had never set foot on the continent and knew little of Zimbabwe. By temperament, a successful British lawyer-turned-politician was never going to bond with a Marxist guerrilla leader-turned-African despot, 19 years his senior.

Yet when Peter Hain was appointed Minister of State in the Foreign Office with responsibility for Africa in 1999, some observers thought that Britain's relations with Zimbabwe could be rebuilt. Hain was Kenyan born and lost no opportunity to proclaim himself a 'son of Africa', while nursing a passionate interest in the continent. He was possibly the only senior figure in the Labour party who genuinely knew and loved Africa.

In his youth, Hain had been one of the prime movers behind the international campaign against apartheid South Africa. He also led demonstrations against Ian Smith's Rhodesia and was, to use his own word, 'elated' when Mugabe won power in 1980. Hain often dubbed himself a 'footsoldier in the African freedom struggle' and his natural affinity with Mugabe was obvious. On 31 October 1999 Mugabe made a private visit to London and met Hain for two hours. According to the accounts of both men, their talks were friendly and relaxed. Mugabe took to patting the British minister on the knee as he made his points, and both seemed to enjoy the other's company.

But on the following day, 1 November, an incident took place that changed everything. Mugabe was emerging from his hotel in Buckingham Gate when Peter Tatchell, a militant gay rights activist and leader of OutRage!, a bellicose protest group, ambushed his limousine. Mugabe's loathing for homosexuals is deep-seated (he once called them 'worse than pigs and dogs'). Tatchell managed to throw open the door of Mugabe's vehicle, grab his appalled victim by the right arm and shout: 'President Mugabe, I am arresting you for torture,' before police seized him and bundled him away.

Mugabe's sense of shock, revulsion and humiliation can scarcely be exaggerated. In Zimbabwe he is whisked from door to door aboard a 22-vehicle motorcade, including lorry loads of soldiers toting AK-47s. A phalanx of bodyguards, security men, troops and assorted henchmen surround him wherever he goes. Anyone foolish enough to try approaching Mugabe is, at the very least, roughly handled. Yet in London, an apparent assailant could go so far as to touch him. Moreover, this assailant was homosexual. In Mugabe's eyes, Tatchell was an unclean, odious figure who should not have been allowed within a mile of the presidential personage. For him to have actually been touched by such a creature was, well, unthinkable and revolting.

In his trauma, Mugabe began to concoct wild conspiracies. A Sky television camera crew had been on hand to film the ambush, probably arranged by Tatchell himself, and the incident took place within a mile or so of MI5 headquarters. Afterwards, Tatchell was not beaten senseless and flung into jail, as he would have been in Zimbabwe, but merely released with a caution. Mugabe put these facts together and concluded that the British government had organized the attack as a way of punishing him for seizing land from white farmers.

Soon after his return to Harare, he summoned a journalist from the official press to vent his fury and outline his new conspiracy theory. Under the headline 'Blair using Gay Gangster Tactics', Mugabe referred to 'this government of little men, Blair and others' and said: 'They are even using gangster gays on us . . . you see, that is the gangster regime of Blair.' The introduction to the story read: 'President Mugabe has described his attack by British homosexuals at the weekend as part of the Blair government's "gay gangster" tactics to scare the Zimbabwean government from proceeding with the land acquisition programme.'[8] That Tatchell is not British (he is Australian) and no one appears to have the slightest control over him, least of all the Blair government, was of no account to Mugabe. This one, bizarre incident did incalculable damage to Anglo–Zimbabwean relations.

Months later, Mugabe was still turning it over in his mind. On 15 June 2000 he gave a BBC interview and chose to re-open the whole affair. He described the incident as an 'assault' and claimed that Hain 'had his Mr Tatchell ambush me'. Then Mugabe added:

I know Peter Hain is reputed to be gay and to be wife of Tatchell, that's what the papers say. And then so if the following morning the husband ambushed me and the previous night I'd had discussions with the wife, so the conclusion I get to is the two had discussed it the night before.[9]

The nature of this accusation is, I suggest, of secondary importance. It is palpably absurd, but no more so than many of Mugabe's public statements. What is striking is how the incident had obviously preyed on Mugabe's mind, troubled him, perhaps kept him awake at night. His hatred for homosexuals and feeling of humiliation by the British government merged into a lethal cocktail.

I wonder whether the farm invasions, the crackdown against the MDC, the language of racial hatred had something to do with this? Did people die because Tatchell tried to arrest Mugabe? Was the law of Zimbabwe torn up because the President felt slighted by Hain? The answer to these questions is almost certainly 'No' – repression in Zimbabwe had a logic of its own, dictated by Mugabe's overriding need to hold power. Yet the extremes of erratic behaviour and the outpouring of bile against white Zimbabweans (who are, in Mugabe's eyes, all British) must have had something to do with his feeling of humiliation at the hands of the Blair government. Hell hath no fury like a Mugabe scorned.

In retaliation, he deliberately set out to goad and infuriate the British. On 9 March he ordered customs officials at Harare airport to break open and search a diplomatic bag imported by the British High Commission. This breach of international law probably stemmed from Mugabe's genuine belief that the British were helping his opponents. His government apparently thought that the seven-ton consignment contained MDC campaign literature or worse. Didymus Mutasa told me: 'the British are trying to bring some very dirty stuff into our country, very dirty indeed . . . they are behaving like a bunch of hooligans'.[10] Chen Chimutengwende told the BBC: 'We know the British government supported subversive elements and opposition elements in this country and them being like that, it could be anything. It could be weapons.'[11] In fact, it was electronic equipment used by British diplomatic missions across the world to prevent unwelcome ears from listening to communications.

The British were furious. If Mugabe's scorn and derision for 'Blair and company' (another of his favourite names for them) knew no bounds, they thought equally little of him. Yet if Mugabe had consciously set a trap for London by provoking the British into a heated response that could later be used against them, Hain stepped right into it. He appeared on the steps of the Foreign Office and delivered a statement that was singularly ill-judged. After outlining how Zimbabwe was guilty of 'unacceptable behaviour', he said:

> This is not the act of a *civilised* country . . . The level of paranoia with which [Zimbabwe] views the international community could not be more ably demonstrated than by its need to open a diplomatic bag

without our consent, against international law and all the norms of sensible *civilised* conduct between countries.[12] (My italics)

Not the act of a *civilised* country? Nothing is more offensive to any African leader than innuendo suggesting that a nation on their continent is uncivilized, doubly so when the impression is created by a former colonial power. Hain, of all people, should have known that. To twice imply that Zimbabwe was uncivilized in the space of a single statement was the height of diplomatic folly. Britain was the wronged party, the victim of an inexplicable act and so had the advantage in the battle for African opinion. With a few sentences, Hain threw that away and handed Mugabe a priceless propaganda line that he would exploit again and again. From then on, whenever any African leader sought to moderate his behaviour, Mugabe would quietly accuse him of bowing to pressure from the 'man who called us uncivilized'.

The diplomatic bag incident sent Hain's frustration boiling over. He summoned the Diplomatic Editor of the *Daily Telegraph* and delivered an attack on Mugabe 'comparable to the rhetoric meted out to Saddam Hussein and Slobodan Milosevic'. Hain said: 'The political leadership is bankrupt . . . the policies pursued by Robert Mugabe are economically illiterate, indeed innumerate . . . after 20 years, Zimbabwe is all but on its knees and there is only one group responsible for that – the ruling party.'[13]

Stan Mudenge, Zimbabwe's Foreign Minister, was quick to seize the opportunity created by Hain's criticism and accused him of mounting an 'unprecedented anti-Zimbabwe crusade' with his 'relentless verbal onslaughts'.[14] This was pompous nonsense coming from a government that had branded Whitehall a 'gangster regime of little men'. But Mudenge was a skilled purveyor of pompous nonsense, and it was often surprisingly effective. The simple fact was that from this moment onwards, no African leader could be seen to side with Hain against Mugabe. Zimbabwe played the anticolonial card, and it worked.

London's central objective was to prevent Mugabe from portraying their dispute as a bilateral tiff, provoked by an old imperial power's pretensions. The Foreign Office wanted to retreat into the background and marshal a coalition of African presidents to restrain Mugabe. Hain's clumsy use of language could not have worked more effectively to undermine this plan.

In fairness, this was probably due to his genuine emotional commitment to Zimbabwe. He felt a deep sense of despair over what was happening, and this probably influenced his response. One official who worked with Hain described him as 'not a very structured person. He's very knee-jerk. He deeply believes himself to be an enlightened white African and he passionately believes in Africa, but this sometimes led him to say things that didn't advance foreign policy.'

When the farm invasions and the terror campaign were at their height, Hain's anger grew still further. He criticized the occupation of white-owned farms as 'incomprehensible. It is resulting in violence and lawlessness and killings. It is an absolutely catastrophic policy.'[15] Hain described the attack on the 'march for peace' on 1 April as 'thuggery orchestrated from on high.'[16] All this was true and Hain deserves credit for censuring Mugabe without equivocation. But verbal condemnation was not enough. What did Britain actually do to contain him?

In practice, almost nothing. Whitehall confined itself to administering a series of pinpricks. On 3 May, Robin Cook announced that Britain would no longer give Zimbabwe free Land Rovers. The 450 still to be delivered would be withheld. Development aid to Zimbabwe was frozen and what remained was channelled through charities, not the government. After British urging, the European Union and Commonwealth issued statements attacking Mugabe. Cook held utterly fruitless talks with Mugabe in Cairo on 4 April and later met three Zimbabwean cabinet ministers in London. None of this made the slightest difference.

There was, of course, more that could have been done. Personal sanctions could have been imposed on Mugabe and his ministers, freezing their overseas assets and preventing them from travelling abroad. Proceedings to suspend Zimbabwe from the Commonwealth could have begun. Steps to isolate the country from any international organization could have been taken. None of this happened because London calculated that this would simply goad Mugabe to unleash yet more violence on the farms and against his opponents. The British were genuinely afraid of what Mugabe was capable of, so they refrained from using all the levers available.

Superficially, London managed to get the worst of both worlds. By strongly criticizing Mugabe, they infuriated him and spurred the excesses. By failing to take all the steps that were available to contain Zimbabwe, they did not succeed in restraining him. By attacking him in singularly inept terms, they made it impossible to build an African coalition against him. But this is too harsh. There was probably nothing that Britain could do. Mugabe was battling for survival. He had a clear strategy which he thought would keep him in power. Nothing would stop him from following it. He was a counsel of despair for diplomats across the world.

★   ★   ★

If the British response to Mugabe failed completely, did anyone else do better? The country with far more at stake and immeasurably greater leverage over Zimbabwe was South Africa. As leader of the continent's economic super-power and dominant political force, President Thabo

Mbeki had an unrivalled ability to turn the heat on Mugabe. South African companies were the biggest investors in Zimbabwe and about 55 per cent of the country's electricity came from Eskom, the South African power giant. Over one-third of Zimbabwe's (woefully inadequate) fuel supplies passed through its most powerful neighbour.

Moreover, Mugabe's excesses appalled influential South Africans, including many who had played prominent roles in the liberation struggle. The two unofficial, moral leaders of the nation were unsparing in their criticism. Desmond Tutu, the former Anglican Archbishop of Cape Town, had this to say of Mugabe: 'He's almost a caricature of all the things people think black leaders do. He seems to be wanting to make a cartoon of himself . . . I know that when he joined the struggle he was an idealistic young man. Now I think that, as he's become increasingly insecure, he's hitting out. One just wants to weep, it's very sad.'[17]

Equally outspoken was Nelson Mandela. The man who kept *Bromley's Family Law* on the bookshelf of his Robben Island prison cell and knew the horror of state-sponsored violence better than anyone, had no time for a leader who tore up the law and sought to crush all opponents. Mandela made no secret of his belief that the best service Mugabe could perform for Africa was to disappear. In a newspaper interview, Mandela said: 'I would have wished that somebody would talk to him to say, "Look, you've been in office for 20 years, it's time to step down."'[18] Mugabe's 'use of violence and the corroding of the rule of law'[19] left him shocked.

On 6 May 2000 Mandela delivered an extraordinary tirade against African leaders who 'once commanded liberation armies and . . . despise the very people who put them in power and think it is a privilege to be there for eternity'. He called on the African people to 'pick up the rifle' and depose such 'tyrants'. Asked whether he was referring to Mugabe, Mandela replied: 'Everybody knows very well who I am talking about. If you don't know who I am talking about, there is no point in telling you.'[20] The headline went around the world: 'Mandela urges overthrow of Mugabe.' The old man made no attempt to correct this impression.

By early 2000 the crisis in Zimbabwe was causing real damage to the South African economy. A vital market for South African exports was in deep, perhaps terminal recession. Tens of thousands of economic refugees were pouring across the border and this human tide threatened to become uncontrollable. The picture of chaos in a southern African country appalled international investors, who saw a president whipping up hatred against an ethnic minority and illegally seizing private property. The inescapable truth was that in the boardrooms of the world, events in Zimbabwe and South Africa were inseparable. A crisis in one country would deter investment in the other. Mbeki's drive to reduce South Africa's crippling unemployment rate of 30 per cent by attracting international companies was being daily undermined by Mugabe's antics.

All of these factors impelled Mbeki to act. Superficially, no one was better qualified for the task. The man who led the ANC's skilful campaign to charm, beguile and ultimately destroy key figures in the white apartheid regime in the 1980s was nothing if not a skilled diplomat. Mbeki's polished negotiating skills had been honed in dealings with the toughest figures of the apartheid era. In her account of South Africa's transition to black majority rule, *Anatomy of a Miracle,* Patti Waldmeir was full of praise for his shrewd prowess at the sly business of backroom dealing. She described Mbeki's 'low, sweet tones of reason' and wrote: 'His greatest weapon was always his charm.'[21]

Thus Mbeki hoped to charm and beguile Mugabe into changing his ways. He would not follow Hain and condemn the Zimbabwean, indeed he would distance himself from the British. Mbeki would be conciliatory in public and subtly effective in private. That was the South African plan for handling the crisis north of the border. So Mbeki held a series of private meetings with Mugabe. They talked in Victoria Falls during a summit of southern African leaders on 21 April. They met in Bulawayo when Mbeki opened the hilariously meagre Zimbabwe International Trade Fair on 5 May. There were various other private contacts between the leaders during the vital period of the farm invasions and parliamentary election campaign.

Yet these encounters revealed a critical flaw in Mbeki's plan. His brand of urbane, pipe-smoking, intellectual charm may have reduced Pieter de Lange, chairman of the *Afrikaner Broederbond*,[22] to helpless jelly, but it failed to impress Mugabe. On the contrary, Mugabe seems to have regarded Mbeki with benign, fatherly contempt. There is an 18-year age gap between the two leaders. Mugabe was running a country when Mbeki was exiled in London and running the ANC's office at the Angel, Islington. Mugabe was a political prisoner and already planning a guerrilla war when Mbeki was a student at Sussex University and penning a dissertation on W. B. Yeats. When the South African took office in 1999, Mugabe was already the second-longest-serving leader in the region.

Whenever I saw the two presidents together, I was fascinated by their body language. Mugabe has no physical presence whatever and he tries to make up for this by assuming lofty, airy, expansive, faintly ludicrous mannerisms. The arms are waved, the nose thrust upwards, the gait measured and brisk. Whenever he met Mbeki, these affectations would be exaggerated. Meanwhile, the South African would wear an expression of smiling, almost meek subservience. I followed them for over an hour as they walked, side by side, around the threadbare stalls of the Trade Fair (patronized by companies from Iran, North Korea and almost nowhere else). The impression was of a headmaster touring his school with a favoured prefect. To anyone who has observed these men together, it is obvious that Mugabe does not take Mbeki remotely seriously.

Mbeki would later reveal that these meetings did yield private assurances from Mugabe that land reform would happen within the law, with illegal occupiers evicted and political violence curbed. Not one of these promises was kept. Mugabe carried on exactly as before. Skilled, charming diplomacy not only failed utterly, but actually became counter-productive. It emboldened Mugabe and allowed him to claim that fellow African leaders were fully behind his policies. This impression was reinforced by a disastrous summit of the Southern African Development Community (SADC) in Victoria Falls on 21 April. This gathering of leaders, including Mbeki, followed the hallowed tradition that no African president ever criticizes a brother African president. The communiqué blandly blamed Britain for every problem afflicting Zimbabwe. President Joaquim Chissano of Mozambique took it upon himself to make the peculiar declaration: 'Mugabe is a master of the rule of law and champions it.'[23] The leaders were happy to leave those words as the message of the summit.

Mbeki was roundly criticized at home and abroad for failing to condemn Mugabe. This is not entirely fair. On several occasions, he made it pretty clear that he regarded the Zimbabwean's approach to land reform as disastrous. When opening the Trade Fair, Mbeki said: 'We are convinced that it would be best that this important matter is dealt with in a cooperative and non-confrontational manner among all the people of this sister country, both black and white, reflecting the achievement of a national consensus on this issue, encompassing all Zimbabweans.'[24] Mugabe was, of course, glorying in his uncooperative, confrontational approach to land reform. He had already invited any whites who disagreed with him to leave the country, and supported the illegal invasion of their farms. Standing a few feet in front of his host, Mbeki's speech amounted to a public rebuke.

Earlier, he had delivered a televised address to the nation and told South Africans that he would work to 'end the violence' surrounding the land invasions and 'create the conditions for the withdrawal from the farms they have occupied of the demonstrating war veterans'.[25] But it was abundantly clear that Mugabe was in no mood to listen.

Like the British, Mbeki had great difficulty in coming to grips with the Zimbabwe problem. There was the personal barrier between him and Mugabe that he found impossible to surmount. But of perhaps equal importance was the presence in South Africa of a sizeable lobby that actively supported the Zimbabwean leader. To many black South Africans on the radical fringe of politics, seizing the whites' land and kicking out any who objected was an eminently sensible policy that should be copied as soon as possible. South Africa had a 'land issue' as well – most of its fertile fields were tilled by a relative handful of white farmers – and Mbeki's efforts to address the problem were moving at a snail's pace. For the radical Pan-Africanist Congress and its allies, Mugabe was not only right, but a model to be emulated.

Reluctant to tackle this lobby head-on, Mbeki was inhibited by another vital factor. As an African president and head of a liberation party, he could not be seen to ally with a bunch of white farmers against a fellow black leader. Thanks to Peter Hain, publicly siding with the British was also made needlessly difficult. Moreover, Mbeki faced subtle yet crucial constraints. In theory, he could pull the plug on Zimbabwe, turn off the lights and cause the final collapse of its shattered economy. South Africa had the power to crush its northern neighbour like an irritating ant. But what would that achieve? Millions of refugees would then head across the Limpopo river and flood South Africa. The big stick that Mbeki supposedly carried in his dealings with Mugabe was illusory. To use it would damage South Africa almost as much as Zimbabwe, and Mugabe knew this quite well. It was a re-run of the Cold War scenario – yes, America could blow Russia to smithereens with nuclear weapons, but only at the cost of suffering the same fate.

So Mbeki failed just as surely and comprehensively as the British had failed. But South Africa paid a far bigger price. In the course of 2000, the Rand lost 18 per cent of its value against the US Dollar and the Johannesburg stock exchange fell by 16 per cent. That was the Zimbabwe effect in action.

★   ★   ★

The world's bid to curb Mugabe reached its modest peak with the arrival of Don McKinnon, Secretary-General of the Commonwealth, in Harare on 15 May. Backed by the collective authority of all 54 nations in the club of former British colonies, he came to say some tough words about political violence and secure Mugabe's agreement for an observer team to cover the elections.

McKinnon was amiable, well-meaning, flustered, inarticulate and utterly ineffectual. During his two days in Zimbabwe, this tall, balding former Foreign Minister of New Zealand wore an expression of permanent bewilderment. McKinnon scampered around Harare, looking ever more dazed. The Human Rights Forum briefed him on the wave of political violence and made it quite clear that, in their view, a free and fair election was impossible. By this stage, 19 murders had been recorded, about 1,400 farms invaded and the tide of daily incidents showed no sign of abating. On the morning that McKinnon arrived, I met a junior MDC official who was on the run, unable to return to his home in the Harare township of Mbare for fear of death. McKinnon met the MDC leadership who repeated the message that continuous violence had already subverted the election.

As for Mugabe, he kept McKinnon stringing along until the last minute. He finally deigned to see his visitor at exactly the time when the Commonwealth delegation was due to leave Harare. Their plane was kept waiting at the airport and even then Mugabe chose to leave McKinnon hanging around at State House for an hour. The Presidential motorcade eventually appeared in a blaze of sirens and McKinnon was favoured with an audience that lasted all of one hour.

Afterwards he spoke to the press, still looking flustered and perplexed, as if grappling with issues of immense complexity. At his shoulder stood the burly, faintly menacing figure of Stan Mudenge, clearly deployed to ensure that he did not step out of line. McKinnon told us the good news. Mugabe had agreed that Commonwealth observers could cover the election. 'I also got from the President that he genuinely wants to see the violence lessened,' said McKinnon brightly, with an air of triumph. Headlines swam into my mind – 'A Little Less Violence Says Mugabe,' or 'Some Violence But Not Too Much Says Mugabe.'

Then in response to a question from me, McKinnon said the words that Zimbabwe's opposition will never forgive him for: 'I believe it is possible to have free elections. That's the reason I came. There are obviously concerns and we need to see the violence go downwards.'[26] So there we had it. As far as the Commonwealth was concerned, after three months of unremitting violence, farm invasions, political murders and the abandonment of the rule of law, a free and fair election was still on the cards. In effect, McKinnon had given Zimbabwe a clean bill of health.

Standing by his side, Mudenge seized the opportunity to regale the world's press with his unique brand of mendacious flannel. 'More than 19 people have been killed in other countries and they have held free elections,' he declared. Like all foreign ministers representing repressive regimes, Mudenge was a consummate actor and his polished performances always juggled 'butter wouldn't melt in my mouth' innocence with self-righteous anger and contrived indignation. In response to Grant Ferrett from the BBC, Mudenge selected his pained innocence expression and asserted: 'We have always had the rule of law in Zimbabwe. The rule of law has always been observed.'[27] The assembled journalists burst out laughing and the hapless McKinnon and his blustering Zimbabwean minder looked momentarily taken aback. Then the New Zealander left for the airport, still looking baffled. 'There is a man who has been eaten for breakfast,' said one of my Zimbabwean colleagues.

A few hours after McKinnon's departure, it was quietly announced that the election would take place on 24 and 25 June. In typical fashion, this crucial piece of news was slipped out in the government gazette, hidden among scores of routine and utterly trivial announcements. State radio managed to announce the wrong dates. The election campaign had been under way for three months, now at least there was a time when the agony might end.

NOTES AND REFERENCES

1 Speech, Zanu-PF manifesto launch, 3 May 2000.
2 Speech, 8 May 2000. Extracts broadcast by *Voice of America* radio.
3 See Peter Stiff, *Cry Zimbabwe*, Galago, Johannesburg, 2000, p. 413.
4 See Zimbabwe Human Rights Forum, *The Unleashing of Violence*, 15 May 2000, p. 44.
5 Speech, Zanu-PF manifesto launch, 3 May 2000.
6 Quoted in *Mail and Guardian*, 22 December 1997. The outraged Zimbabweans released Short's letter to the press.
7 Interview with the author, 11 December 2001.
8 *Sunday Mail*, 7 November 1999.
9 BBC interview with David Dimbleby, 15 June 2000.
10 Interview with the author, 9 March 2000.
11 BBC interview, 9 March 2000.
12 Statement, Foreign Office News Dept, 9 March 2000.
13 *Daily Telegraph*, 8 March 2000.
14 *The Herald*, 15 March 2000.
15 *Daily Telegraph*, 19 April 2000.
16 *Sunday Telegraph*, 2 April 2000.
17 *The Dispatch*, 5 April 2000. Report of remarks made by Tutu after receiving an honorary degree from Uppsala University, Sweden.
18 Interview with *Durban Daily News*, 29 September 2000.
19 *Ibid.*
20 Speech, launch of UNICEF Global Partnership, Johannesburg, 6 May 2000.
21 Patti Waldmeir, *Anatomy of a Miracle*, Penguin, London, 1997, p. 68.
22 The Afrikaner Brotherhood. A secret society of prominent Afrikaners that was a pillar of South Africa's apartheid regime. Mbeki held secret and, from his point of view, highly successful meetings with de Lange in New York in 1986.
23 *Daily Telegraph*, 22 April 2000.
24 Speech, Zimbabwe International Trade Fair, Bulawayo, 5 May 2000.
25 Broadcast, SABC, 4 May 2000.
26 Press conference, State House, Harare, 16 May 2000.
27 *Ibid.*

Chapter 8

No One Was Killed
During Our Election

June 2000

> There is no one who was killed during the Zimbabwean elections.
> (Professor Jonathan Moyo, Information Minister, 10 November 2000)[1]

As we approached the blackened shells of burnt-out huts, I was enormously grateful for the presence of Saddam Hussein. He strode at the front of our party, with an air of purpose and authority. While I poked through the wreckage of the tiny, seemingly abandoned village, Saddam and his six followers fanned out across the field and kept a close watch for intruders. Some kicked and punched the air in an impromptu display of their martial arts prowess. Wearing dark glasses, a trenchcoat and a cowboy hat – apparently his trademark attire – Saddam gave an innocent tree a few vicious high kicks. I'm glad he's on my side, I thought.

When Paul Grover, a *Telegraph* photographer, and I had finished picking our way among the nine destroyed huts, once the homes of suspected MDC supporters, now razed to the ground by a Zanu-PF gang, Saddam and his men gathered around us and we drove away, down a bumpy track, with our bodyguards watchful and alert. 'This is a war zone,' said Luke, a polite, diffident 19 year old. 'We have to be prepared for anything here. These people are killers.'

His impeccable English belied the fact that he hailed from one of Harare's roughest townships and possessed a black belt in karate. During our long journey, Luke recounted numerous tales of memorable clashes and bouts of mayhem, always outlined in the endearingly ponderous English he learned at a mission school. ('This guy was making an attempt to grab me by the throat – so I responded by striking him vigorously on the head. That was the end of the matter. He was finished'.) Tall, muscular and silent, Saddam refused to disclose his real name. He was content to tip the cowboy hat at a jaunty angle and give all the orders.

145

A journey through the craggy bush country of Mberengwa district on 9 June could only be undertaken with an escort provided by Saddam, Luke and company. Taking advantage of its remote, isolated location, hundreds of Zanu-PF thugs had overrun the area and mounted a brutally effective crackdown against the MDC. Texas ranch, an occupied farm, had become the lair of a local warlord known as Comrade Biggie Chitoro. From this headquarters, he commanded a small army of 'war veterans' who soon imposed their dominance on Mberengwa's two parliamentary constituencies. By the time Paul and I arrived, hundreds of people had been assaulted or tortured, nine women raped, 30 teachers driven from the area, seven schools forcibly closed and scores of villagers compelled to flee and become homeless refugees.

In yet another large area, the MDC had been crushed and its campaign shut down. Sekai Holland, the party's candidate for Mberengwa East, could only pay brief visits to her prospective constituency and then only with the protection of 20 of Saddam Hussein's 'Karate Boys'. When Paul and I visited the area, she lent us Saddam and all the 'Karate Boys' we could squeeze into our van – seven in all.

We followed Saddam's advice to the letter. Certain narrow tracks, winding their way through the barren expanse of rocky kopjes, were too dangerous: Zanu-PF gangs had mounted road-blocks and would ambush us. In several tiny villages of mud huts, it was hazardous to pause for longer than 15 minutes. It reminded me of earlier journeys through northern Uganda – an area torn by years of guerrilla war, where the possibility of ambush by rebels from the fanatical Lord's Resistance Army always exists. In effect, the same brand of fanaticism had turned Mberengwa into a war zone.

For some people, the tragedy was as great as anything seen in Uganda. We paused at the village of Faraimose, a circle of huts at the base of a kopje, surrounded by dense bush and thorn trees. A few hundred yards beyond the humble homes of mud stood a house that was very different. It was made of brick, with a flat tin roof and large windows. From a distance, it looked like a remarkably prosperous residence for this impoverished area. As we drew closer, it became clear that this was a cruel illusion. The large windows had been shattered and gaping holes torn out of the tin roof. Shards of broken glass and fragments of stone littered the ground around the house. Beside it were the pitiful, scorched remains of two charred huts. This was what remained of the home of Daniel and Girly Chinyerere, both insignificant members of the local MDC.

Inside the house I met Girly Chinyerere, a small, shy woman of 38. She sat in what remained of her living room, surrounded by splinters of wrecked furniture and clothes strewn across the floor. A nest of ancient wooden shelves had been smashed in half, faded yellow wallpaper torn down in

146

strips, the legs of a table systematically pounded away. Brandishing whips, chains, iron bars and clubs studded with rusty nails, a Zanu-PF mob of 24 had massed outside her home at dawn, when her husband happened to be away, waking the family with cries of '*Pamberi ne* Mugabe.'

While Girly Chinyerere hid in terror, they grabbed her 18-year-old daughter and shouted 'We will beat her until you come out.' She emerged and the gang set upon her. 'They beat me everywhere. On my back, my feet, my legs, everywhere,' she said quietly. All the time, her assailants demanded the names of local MDC supporters and the surrender of her membership card. Then Chinyerere, who was wearing only a nightgown, was thrown to the floor and forcibly spread-eagled. 'Two men held my arms down, one sat on my face and two others pushed my legs apart,' she said and then her thin voice trailed away. I did not ask her to go on.

She looked calm and composed, betraying no resentment of my presence. She had been raped in a country where at least 25 per cent of adults are HIV-positive. Yet she spoke in matter-of-fact tones, with apparently implacable fortitude. Chinyerere quietly resumed her story. When her husband tried to report her rape at the local police station in the nearby town of Mataga, a Zanu-PF mob of 50 men ambushed him. Thugs attacked Daniel Chinyerere with clubs, shouting: 'We will kill you, all MDC people are going to die today.' He was left a bloody heap on the ground, his left arm broken. One week later, the gang paid a second visit to the family home and smashed everything to pieces, stealing whatever they failed to wreck. For good measure, they burned down two adjacent huts that the family used as storehouses.

The Chinyereres had six children, and the youngest boy, who was eight, had witnessed the attack on his mother. Daniel Chinyerere owned a shop in Mataga and had been relatively prosperous. But when I met the family, he was unable to work because of his injuries and lived in daily fear of attack. Lack of money to pay the fees was about to force his children to leave school. After witnessing the fate of the Chinyereres, Faraimose village was terrified, wanted nothing to do with the MDC and would undoubtedly vote for Zanu-PF. A small man, with his left arm encased in plaster, Daniel Chinyerere looked on the verge of tears as he stood beside his stoical wife. The thought drummed through my mind: if Don McKinnon could have spent five minutes in this village talking to these people, he would not have blandly accepted Mugabe's assurances about a free and fair election.

The fear throughout Mberengwa was so pervasive that you could almost smell it. We paused at one secondary school outside Mataga. A Zanu-PF gang had visited the previous day and beaten up two teachers in front of their pupils. No one in the school would show their faces, not a teacher, not a child. It was made clear to us via intermediaries that the best thing we could do for the school was to leave immediately, for our presence was itself a danger. The nine charred and burnt-out huts at the abandoned village some miles away had also had a salutary effect. In the neighbouring village, people hid their faces as we drove past and delivered the same message as the teachers at the school. At the police station, just off the dusty main street of Mataga, a group of eight people, some wearing bandages, queued to report more assaults. The police were simply logging crimes and making no attempt whatever to investigate or rein in the mobs.

Mberengwa provided textbook proof of the effectiveness of political violence. Anyone who visited the place soon realized that Zanu-PF's position was completely secure and based solely on terror. The practical method used to impose this dominance is worth examining. Mberengwa's thugs had a headquarters – Texas ranch – and a leader in the person of Comrade Biggie Chitoro. They were despatched in groups, varying in size from 20 to 100, and ordered to hunt down key MDC figures. Anyone associated with the party was abducted, tortured and compelled to reveal names of fellow MDC officials.

Victims were dragged to Texas ranch for torture and the methods used were hideous. Fainos Zhou, who nominated the MDC candidate for Mberengwa West, was kidnapped and tortured for four days virtually without break, the last three by Chitoro himself. He was bludgeoned with iron bars, and boiling, melting plastic was dripped all over his body. Zhou eventually died of his ordeal on 9 June. His wife, Mavis Tapera, was attacked in her home by a mob led by Chitoro. She was stripped and subjected to a serious sexual assault, involving men ramming an iron rod into her vagina and forcing her to assume sexual positions.

Any surviving MDC officials simply fled the area in terror. In this way, the organizational backbone of the party was destroyed and it was soon unable to campaign or even bring its candidates into Mberengwa. The next stage of the campaign was to terrorize individual voters. That was achieved by picking on people like the Chinyereres and inflicting the most hideous penalties, thereby sowing general fear. As word spread, the price of supporting the MDC became clear to everyone. Teachers were targeted because, as educated professionals, they were assumed to back the MDC and their natural prominence ensured that ripples of terror would be caused by any attack. If you beat up a teacher in front of a class of 100, you terrify the children and their 200 parents. Comrade Biggie's gangs also rounded up hundreds of people for the infamous '*pungwes*' where the indoctrination was perfected. In the space of a few weeks, these thugs wiped out the MDC and created a terrified, cowed electorate, which would duly vote Zanu-PF on polling day.

That was how you won elections in Zimbabwe. Across the country, particularly in remote rural areas, this method was being employed by the likes of Biggie Chitoro and their followers. The effects were devastating. By early June, the MDC had been driven underground across vast areas and Zanu-PF's dominance reasserted by the most brutal methods imaginable. In all three provinces of Mashonaland, plus large areas of Midlands and Masvingo, the MDC effectively ceased to exist.

This brand of political terror owed its origin to the guerrilla war of the 1970s, when Mugabe's army used a combination of intimidation and indoctrination to secure control over a wide area. But in peacetime, the most striking feature of this manual of terror is how it requires the collusion of the state. Closing down the opposition and terrifying the people requires a ringleader and a headquarters. Any competent police force could, of course, eliminate both. All the violence in Mberengwa could have been stopped by the arrest of Biggie Chitoro and his leading henchmen and a quick operation clearing Texas ranch. The police, of course, refrained from doing so, just as they refrained from dealing with Comrade Jesus in Kariba until his work was done, and just as they turned a blind eye to the activities of numerous other warlords up and down Zimbabwe. In most cases, occupied farms were used as bases for the terror campaign and the warlords also served as squatter ringleaders. By failing to end the farm invasions, police allowed the murderous crackdown against the MDC to proceed. That, of course, was the whole point.

★   ★   ★

As terror took hold of much of Zimbabwe, Morgan Tsvangirai found it increasingly difficult to venture outside Harare. By early June, the MDC had classified ten constituencies as 'no-go areas', where all campaigning had been forcibly halted. Any rally held by the MDC was a hazardous event, liable to be attacked. But perhaps most serious were the reprisals exacted against people who turned up for these occasions. Zanu-PF mobs would later hunt them down for severe beatings. Tsvangirai found himself caught in a dilemma – by staging a rally, he not only endangered his entourage and himself, but also his audience and anyone seen to be vaguely associated the MDC. Yet if he retreated into isolation and closed down his campaign, Zanu-PF would achieve its goal. Tsvangirai sought to solve this problem by holding a few, carefully selected rallies and surrounding them with tight security.

Nowhere had been hit harder by the terror campaign than the tiny, shabby, impoverished town of Murewa, 50 miles north-east of Harare. Once again, the gangs worked from well-known bases – the town's Zanu-PF headquarters and an office owned by Zexcom, the company belonging to the War Veterans' Association. David Stevens had been tortured there

149

before his murder and hundreds of other victims imprisoned and beaten in these dilapidated, sinister buildings. Murewa had joined the roll-call of areas where the MDC had been wiped out and its terrified remnants driven underground. Tsvangirai resolved to hold a rally in the centre of the town on 13 June. It was a courageous, risky decision, and one that showed his refusal to be intimidated.

He drove to Murewa in a convoy of eight vehicles, accompanied by 50 youths in MDC T-shirts, acting as his praetorian guard. When I arrived, the town was in chaos. Lurking outside the Zexcom office in Murewa's main street was a Zanu-PF mob of 50, waving clubs, sticks and axes. A few yards away, the MDC youths sang: 'The government is rotten and we will kick them out.' Between them were 50 riot police armed with batons and tear gas. Tsvangirai had begun speaking beside the ramshackle market in the town centre when the Zanu-PF gang had massed nearby. Now everything was jumbled confusion. The MDC youths sang, their bearded opponents howled: '*Hondo*'. Uncertain policemen hovered in between, apparently with no idea of what to do next. Hundreds of terrified townspeople huddled in doorways and tried their best to stay out of the way. I snatched a few words with Tsvangirai as he stood beside his white pick-up, wearing a T-shirt and baseball cap, surrounded by swirling chaos. For the first time, I saw him look nervous and tense. 'What can we do now? This place is just impossible,' he said quietly.

A few moments later, Tsvangirai gave some brisk orders and his supporters piled into their vehicles and drove away from the market to a patch of waste ground on the edge of Murewa's jumble of ramshackle houses. Here Tsvangirai's group reassembled and he began talking through a loudspeaker. His audience consisted solely of the 50 MDC youths. The ordinary people of Murewa were too frightened to approach and some hovered at a safe distance, forming tiny, silent huddles. I suddenly realized that the small, squat, green building a hundred yards behind Tsvangirai carried the letters 'ZANU PF' in black capitals. Here was the headquarters of the terror campaign in Murewa. Then I remembered that David Stevens had been tortured and killed in the bush beside this shabby construction. A dense tangle of grass and thorn bushes ringed the waste ground. Tsvangirai was probably speaking within 50 feet of the spot where the farmer had been shot dead.

The atmosphere was so tense that he was unable to make a coherent speech. Tsvangirai's voice quavered and even his audience of youths was distracted. Fearful glances were shot in all directions and howls of '*Hondo*' from the Zanu-PF mob were still audible. At one point, Tsvangirai pointed towards a group of terrified people nearby and said: 'We know that you are not attending because you will be victimized when we leave. If Zanu-PF are so popular, why do they have to beat people to vote for them?' Then he decided that the risks of continuing were too great. Tsvangirai put down his loudspeaker and gestured to his supporters. Everyone ran for their vehicles and the MDC convoy swept out of Murewa. The rally had lasted for precisely ten minutes.

★ ★ ★

Two days before Tsvangirai was forced to flee Murewa, Mugabe held a 'star rally' and the contrast between the two events could not have been starker. The town of Kwe Kwe was favoured with the presidential presence and all preparations were meticulous. Before the leader's arrival, thousands of smartly dressed schoolchildren were assembled along the route from the airfield to the football stadium. On the terraces of the small grandstand, a quiet crowd of 10,000 had been marshalled. All shops and businesses in Kwe Kwe were closed and the entire town came to a standstill as policemen herded its residents together to greet their leader. A hush fell as the presidential helicopter clattered into view. It settled on the ground amid an expectant silence. Then the Mugabe cavalcade swept past the serried ranks of cheering schoolchildren. Motorcycle outriders with wailing sirens, police cars with blue lights flashing, trucks laden with soldiers toting AK-47s, one gleaming black Mercedes after another. The leader appeared in his limousine, waving benignly from the window. When it comes to aloof, haughty disdain, nothing matches the Mugabe wave. A mere flick of the wrist, accompanied by a ghost of a smile.

Once the 22-vehicle motorcade had entered the stadium, Mugabe was whisked to a podium set before a colourful marquee. As he emerged from his Mercedes, with 'ZIM 1' on the numberplate, the Zanu-PF loyalists erupted in cheers and Mugabe waved his fist in the air. Standing a few feet behind him, I had to bite my hand to stop myself from laughing out loud. Mugabe was dressed in his usual Sunday afternoon attire – a blue, pinstriped, three-piece suit. But someone had advised him to add another feature to this familiar outfit. Thus Mugabe wore a white baseball cap, tipped at a rakish angle. A 76-year-old despot punching the air, while wearing a dark suit and a baseball cap, was a sight I found uncontrollably funny. It was, however, wise to conceal my giggles, for by this stage, foreign journalists were allowed to attend Mugabe's rallies only on sufferance and we were closely watched by his entourage of heavies, cronies and flunkeys.

Before the President treated us to his oration, something unusual happened. Once the carefully organized hysteria had ended and Mugabe was reclining on a vast, red armchair in the marquee, a convoy of a dozen vehicles entered the stadium. They were all Land Rovers and Land Cruisers, of the sort favoured by white farmers. They parked behind the marquee and out stepped a bewildered group of 40 farmers and their wives. I suddenly realized what was going on. No Roman emperor's victory parade was complete without a gaggle of humiliated barbarian prisoners; and henceforth, no Mugabe rally would take place without a silent, fearful gathering of white farmers, compelled to show their faces and pay obeisance to the master who was intent on dispossessing them. This sullen knot of frightened men and women was led to a row of chairs in the marquee, a few feet behind Mugabe. They sat in silence as the speech began.

It was the usual stuff. Reflecting utter boredom, my notes read as follows: 'The whites have spurned the hand of reconciliation BLAH BLAH BLAH the British are waging a vicious campaign against us BLAH BLAH BLAH Tsvangirai is a traitor BLAH BLAH BLAH the British papers are telling lies about Zimbabwe BLAH BLAH BLAH we will take the land BLAH BLAH BLAH.' The audience seemed equally bored and bemused. I amused myself by tallying his references to Britain – only 32 on this occasion, fewer than usual. During his election rallies, Mugabe would eventually average 43 mentions of Britain per speech, roughly one every two minutes. Afterwards, the leader swept away in a flurry of cheers and purring Mercedes, clutching his baseball cap to his head.

I tried to speak with the terrified farmers. They were wary of being seen anywhere near me and only as they left did I manage to snatch a brief conversation. 'The guys occupying our land told us "If you know what's good for you, you will come and listen to the President." So that's why we're here. They dragged us all along,' said one man in his forties with a flowing beard. 'All our workers were dragged along as well,' he added. It suddenly became clear why the crowd had been so lukewarm. Most of Mugabe's audience had been threatened and browbeaten into listening to his diatribe.

As the crowd poured out of the stadium, I found myself pushed alongside a 20-year-old man wearing a Zanu-PF T-shirt. I asked him whether he had enjoyed the speech and he snorted derisively. 'I came here because I was told to,' he said. 'The Zanu-PF youths said "If you don't go, we will beat you." They came to my house.' Mugabe's shock troops had been through the townships of Kwe Kwe on each of the last two days, ordering people to turn up for his rally or face the consequences. My companion, Paul Maswana, had been threatened in person. 'So why are you wearing a Zanu-PF T-shirt?' I asked. Maswana looked at me incredulously.

'For my safety,' came the simple reply. 'If you don't wear it, you are beaten. These guys are beating everyone who does not have a Zanu-PF T-shirt or card.'

'Who will you vote for?'

'I have got nothing to say about Zanu-PF. They are not good people at all. I will vote MDC.'

Beside Maswana, a woman said that she had suffered the same threats. From amid the crush of tightly packed bodies squeezing out of the stadium exit, another voice spoke up. Then another. Then another. It seemed that almost everyone had been threatened and cajoled into attending. After compulsory exposure to a 90-minute Mugabe oration, many would now be voting MDC. The entire rally had been a gigantic, carefully staged sham. I suddenly remembered a phrase that Mugabe had used during his speech: 'The large turnout here in Kwe Kwe is a massive demonstration of the basis of our power.' He was absolutely right. It was a massive demonstration of the power of intimidation, the basis of his rule.

★   ★   ★

'We have defeated British colonialism and we will continue to repulse it in the future,' declared Mugabe, returning to the theme that dominated every one of the speeches I ever heard him deliver. This was to a gathering of Zanu-PF's 120 parliamentary candidates, a fortnight before polling day. I found it a curious sensation to observe this audience. Almost without exception, these men and women were waging vicious campaigns against their opponents. Placing all of Zanu-PF's candidates in one room was like holding a conference of murderers and desperadoes.

Hitler Hunzvi was there, wearing one of his brown suits. He had been selected to fight the seat of Chikomba, and his henchmen were duly imposing a reign of terror the equal of anything in Zimbabwe. Isaac Mackenzie was present, assured of victory in Kariba since the destruction of the local MDC by Comrade Jesus and his gang. Rugare Gumbo listened to his master, undoubtedly confident of overwhelming victory in Mberengwa East, with a little help from Comrade Biggie Chitoro.

Every candidate was slightly more assured of victory because of various other steps taken by Mugabe. All of Zimbabwe's television and radio channels are owned by the state and they were pumping out a relentless diet of propaganda. During the campaign, the main television news devoted 92 per cent of its political coverage to Zanu-PF. The handful of stories about the MDC was unremittingly hostile.

Moreover, the supposedly independent commission appointed to draw up the constituency boundaries had come up with some surprises. Harare and Bulawayo, where overwhelming support for the MDC was obvious to all, each lost one seat. Every African country has seen an inexorable population shift from the rural areas to the cities, and Zimbabwe is no exception. There was only one explanation for this otherwise perverse decision – blatant gerrymandering. This was confirmed when Mashonaland Central province, a Zanu-PF stronghold, gained one constituency.

Zanu-PF's chances were further improved by Mugabe's analysis of Zimbabwe's problems. Without exception, everything was the fault of the British. They were the founts of all evil, the convenient scapegoats for everything that had gone wrong. Mugabe accordingly enlarged his array of conspiracy theories.

He began by deciding that the endless petrol queues were because of an operation by the Royal Navy. The British were intercepting oil tankers bound for Zimbabwe and persuading them to sail elsewhere. 'Right now they are tracking ships bringing fuel here and offering the companies double the money that the government paid,'[2] Mugabe claimed. This theory became a particular favourite and he repeated it during three campaign rallies. It built into his general theme – that Britain had engineered Zimbabwe's economic collapse to prevent the seizure of white-owned farms.

'This country is now under sanctions just because we are simply insisting on equitable distribution of land,'[3] Mugabe told his supporters. Economic sanctions were a convenient figment of his imagination. Yes, Zimbabwe had lost all support from the IMF and the World Bank, but this hardly amounted to an economic blockade of the sort imposed on, for example, Saddam Hussein's Iraq.

But the British were, it seemed, becoming even more desperate. The revelation that London had a contingency plan to evacuate all 20,000 British citizens was greeted by the official press with deep suspicion. They were soon convinced that Britain had already deployed a massive military expeditionary force and hinted that its real purpose was nothing less than the invasion and re-conquest of Zimbabwe. So *The Herald* reported:

> Military contingency plans are being drafted by the British Joint Staff (*sic*) for the possible evacuation of nearly 20,000 people who hold British passports. This 'humanitarian' operation would include Britain's two aircraft carriers and their squadrons of Harrier jump jets and the deployment of several thousand troops, including from the Special Air Services and Special Boot Services (*sic*). A headquarters for the operation has been established in neighbouring Botswana where an undisclosed number of British troops have been deployed.[4]

The Herald added that 'SAS and SBS patrols' made up of soldiers 'born in Zimbabwe' were already on reconnaissance missions inside the country. This story, implying an imminent invasion, with British troops swarming all over Botswana, caused a brief flurry of excitement in the state media. It was relayed on television and, for the first time, I began paying attention to the (crushingly dull) main news programme.

The presenter was a hatchet-faced woman called Dawcus Chibanda, who might have been chosen for her uniquely grating, rasping monotone. Lately, she had been told to lighten up and her broadcasts now began with a cheery greeting. Thus on 17 May, she welcomed me with a beaming smile and said: 'We're half-way through the working week, let's hope it's going well for you and there's a great weekend ahead of you.' I was touched. Then Dawcus's face reverted into hatchet mode and her voice dropped to its customary, lawn mower drone. 'New plot to overthrow the government,' she announced as the main headline. As Dawcus continued, I almost fell off my chair.

'A plot to overthrow the Zanu-PF government of President Mugabe has been hatched in the British capital London,' she intoned. 'Reports made available to ZBC by the authoritative Washington-based Policy Studies Agency News Service says the plot has been masterminded by the Anglo–American policy élite.' So far, so normal. Just another example of official paranoia, I thought. Then Dawcus got the meat of the story. British troops were massing next door. 'The headquarters for the operation, code-named Humanitarian Operation, has been established in neighbouring Botswana,' she solemnly told the nation.

Dawcus's morbid features were instantly replaced by a complex map that purported to show the battle plan for 'Humanitarian Operation'. Thick, white arrows covered the screen, converging on Zimbabwe from all directions. One emerged from the Okavango Delta in Botswana, apparently showing the location of the British aircraft carriers. If this map was correct, HMS *Invincible* was anchored amid the tangled swamps, reeds and elephants of the (landlocked) delta. Her Harrier jump-jets were presumably roaring over the Kalahari Desert. British squaddies were massing for the onslaught amid the safari camps of the Okavango. Gosh. It was a bewildering picture.

While I was still taking it in, Dawcus reappeared, looking remarkably calm for someone who had just announced an imminent attack on her country, and smoothly moved on to the next item. Comrade Grace Mugabe was opening an orphanage, if I recall rightly, but I wasn't paying much attention. I was still trying to get my head around the new bout of official paranoia. Did they actually believe this? Did they expect anyone to take them seriously? What were they trying to achieve?

These questions drummed through my mind as the conspiracies fell thick and fast. Mugabe soon picked up the theme that the British were about to do something drastic. He told the Zanu-PF central committee: 'We are aware that the British are working closely with the opposition MDC and other hostile so-called civil groups to trigger civil unrest in the hope that the Zanu-PF government will capitulate or fall in violent circumstances.' Pretty standard stuff. Then Mugabe added: 'They are even sponsoring hit squads to eliminate some among us.'[5] Hit squads? Elimination? Not content with intercepting fuel supplies, sabotaging the economy and deploying an invasion force, were the British trying to assassinate Mugabe? It seemed that nothing was beneath them. Professor Jonathan Moyo, the regime's chief propagandist, told me: 'Britain has shown quite clearly that it would rather have civil war in Zimbabwe. Civil war would allow them to decide the destiny of Zimbabwe.'[6]

Moyo soon became Conspiracy-Theorist-In-Chief at the court of King Mugabe. In his view, the British were always up to something. Whereas Mugabe gave us paranoia phrased in the ponderous English of the mission school, Moyo, once a respected academic, offered the same theories in the language of the postgraduate seminar. Thus Mugabe would say: 'The British are guilty of vicious and iniquitous acts of economic sabotage';[7] while in Moyo-speak, this became: 'External forces are manipulating our economy in order to induce an artificial crisis.'[8] The words were different, the sentiments identical. They believed it – but did anyone else?

★   ★   ★

As polling day drew near, it was increasingly obvious that a large section of the Zimbabwean electorate felt nothing but scorn for Mugabe. The evidence of his unpopularity in the cities became unmistakable. On 17 June Mugabe held Zanu-PF's final rally of the campaign and chose a location filled with historical resonance – Zimbabwe Grounds in the Harare township of Highfield. On his return from exile in January 1980, this expanse of open field had been overrun by hundreds of thousands of people, who lionized the liberation hero at his 'Welcome home' rally. The turnout was extraordinary, possibly the largest gathering ever seen in the history of the country. People came because Mugabe had not only won Zimbabwe's freedom, he almost counted as a son of Highfield as well.

His personal ties with the dilapidated, heaving streets of the township, filled with tiny, squat, identical concrete houses, were emotional and long-standing. He lived in Highfield for several years in the 1960s and for a few months after his release from prison in 1974. Zanu itself held its earliest meetings in Highfield soon after the formation of the movement in 1963. When Mugabe entered parliament in 1980, he did so as the Honourable Member for Highfield. He still owned a house in one of its shabby streets – a modest, single-storey home, painted in blue. A few weeks after his triumphant return, former Rhodesian soldiers staged a botched assassination bid and raked his house with machine-gun fire. To this day, Mugabe owns this home, and the jagged bullet holes are clearly visible.

I found it almost sad to observe the Highfield rally on 17 June. Where once an immense crowd had roared Mugabe's name, with urchins scaling the poplar trees to catch a glimpse of their future leader, a silent, forlorn group of about 3,000 gathered. In 1980, rousing cheers had swept Mugabe along. In 2000, he was greeted in near silence. Moving among the lacklustre crowd, I realized that this was yet another sham rally. Most of the people I met had been coerced into attendance and would actually be voting MDC. The few genuine Zanu-PF supporters had been bussed in from the party's strongholds outside Harare.

Mugabe looked crestfallen. His every word radiated disappointment and dejection. The speech was longer, more disjointed and more rambling than usual and even his ritual denunciation of the British was limp and contrived. Waving his fist seemed to require special effort. His obvious embarrassment was nothing in comparison to the feelings of his entourage. Tony Gara, chairman of Harare's Zanu-PF branch, was moved to offer a public apology for the pitiful turnout. 'Your Excellency,' cringed Gara, 'many of your people are at work, so they cannot be here today.' As every journalist covering the event pointed out, the rally was on a Saturday and unemployment exceeded 50 per cent. It didn't wash and Mugabe knew it. For the first time, I saw him look a broken man.

I bumped into Didymus Mutasa, about the only politburo member still on speaking terms with British journalists. He made no attempt to conceal his disappointment. 'I was expecting a larger turnout than this. There is definitely something wrong and we feel the people who organized this were too confident and did not tell people about this rally.' Yet Mutasa had no doubts about the outcome of the election. 'Most of us are now very relaxed. We were very jittery after the referendum, but we're relaxed now. The maximum number of seats which Zanu-PF can lose is three,'[9] he declared with absolute conviction. I tried to keep a straight face as I noted Mutasa's bold prediction.

On the following day, Tsvangirai held his final rally of the campaign and the atmosphere could not have been more different. Despite all the threats, intimidation and violence, over 25,000 people thronged the terraces of Rufaro stadium in the Harare township of Mbare. Like his opponent, Tsvangirai had chosen a location filled with historical significance – the scene of Zimbabwe's Independence celebrations in 1980 and the founding of the MDC in September 1999. Unlike his unfortunate rival, this area was now Tsvangirai's heartland. Mbare and the other impoverished townships disgorged their masses to cheer him. Buoyed by the roar of the crowd, Tsvangirai was sufficiently emboldened to declare: 'Victory is certain.' Caught up in the flow of rhetoric, waving his right arm in the air – a trademark gesture – Tsvangirai said: 'Zanu-PF is rotten and should be thrown away. We are gathered here because we want to say enough of corruption, enough of brutality, enough of poverty, enough of racism, enough of Zanu-PF.'[10]

Some in the MDC leadership were literally brimming with confidence. Eddie Cross, the party's economics supremo, solemnly told me that they would win 84 seats. 'This is the end of the Mugabe era. He will probably go next week,'[11] said Cross. With a few exceptions, that was the mood of the MDC leadership. They felt they had come through the inferno of violence and intimidation, survived everything that Mugabe could throw at them, and now they would reap the reward.

I wasn't so sure – and there was another aspect of the rally that I found disquieting. Three times, suspected Zanu-PF supporters were singled out by the crowd and roughed up in front of everybody. One man in his twenties was beaten almost senseless, his face bloody, his panicking eyes filled with terror, like a cornered animal. He tried to escape by scaling the fence of the stadium and was clubbed to the ground, falling heavily, to be kicked and punched where he lay. Only the intervention of three policemen saved him from serious injury or worse. Like Zanu-PF, the MDC had been corrupted by the endemic violence of Zimbabwean politics. Its followers were far from innocent. The human toll of this vicious, appalling election was incalculable, but the psychological cost was perhaps almost as great. A culture of violence nurtured by Zanu-PF had spread to a section of the MDC. On that afternoon in Rufaro, I became convinced that Zimbabwe would never hold a peaceful election.

★   ★   ★

In the final days before votes were cast on 24 and 25 June, the relentless drumbeat of violence continued. Patrick Nabanyama, polling agent for the MDC candidate in Bulawayo South, was abducted from his home on 19 June and has not been seen since. As I write, he is missing, presumed dead. Tichaono Tadyanemhandu, an MDC supporter in Hurungwe, was kidnapped on 20 June and his body found six months later. In an horrific incident in Gokwe on 22 June, Zeke Chigagwa was beaten to death with iron bars for being an MDC supporter. As the polling booths opened, the final tally of the human cost of this election, documented by the Zimbabwe Human Rights Forum, was as follows:

Murders (beating, gunshot, burns, hanging)	37
Assaults (including burns, gunshots, strangling)	2,466
Rapes	27
Abductions	617
Displaced people	Over 10,000
Total number of people affected by violations	**18,696**[12]

With the exception of the number of murders, all these figures are conservative, based on incidents reported to the Forum. The true number of offences was perhaps ten times greater. As for the perpetrators, Zanu-PF's militias committed 90.7 per cent of all offences recorded by the Forum.[13]

★   ★   ★

Yet on the morning of Saturday, 24 June, when the first voters cast their ballots, there was evidence that the intimidation campaign had not terrified every part of Zimbabwe into submission. It was a perfect winter's day, with clear, pastel-blue skies and pleasantly warm rays of sunlight. I travelled to Bulawayo and spent the day in the city itself and in the nearby villages of Matabeleland. From heaving townships to impoverished kraals, it was evident that something remarkable was happening.

At 7 a.m. in the township of Nketa, 200 people waited quietly to cast their votes. It was cold, and some in the queue were shivering. Many had joined the line at first light and there was a tangible buzz of excitement. 'We have nowhere to escape to. We are not ants, we cannot run under the ground,' one man in his fifties told me. 'We cannot hide from Mugabe. All we can do is vote and hope that he will go.' The man had donned his smartest clothes to vote against Mugabe. He stood, shivering slightly, in a dark blazer, with brown patches covering three holes. A desire for change, *chinja*, burned in his eyes. It was the overwhelming sentiment nearby, so strong you could almost touch it. Fear had been conquered – these were people relishing the chance to vote for the opposition.

Standing nearby was the man whom almost everybody in this queue would be supporting – David Coltart, the MDC candidate for Bulawayo South. A softly spoken, tall man in his forties, he was an unusual parliamentary candidate in several respects. Apart from being white, he was also a high-profile figure, who aroused extraordinary hatred in Zanu-PF circles. Mugabe had repeatedly attacked Coltart in public, branding this earnest, courteous figure variously a 'racist', a 'British agent' and a 'saboteur'. Anyone who met Coltart knew how absurd these barbs were. His commitment to Zimbabwe was so heartfelt and genuine as to be almost painful. There was not a racist bone in his body.

Coltart's crime was to have played a key role in exposing Fifth Brigade's atrocities in Matabeleland. He incurred Mugabe's eternal fury by helping to produce the landmark report *Breaking the Silence – Building True Peace*. Coltart's prominence in the MDC and his obvious ability (he is a respected human rights lawyer) led Mugabe and his acolytes to decide that this white man was the prime mover in the opposition.[14] This myth impelled them to take extraordinary steps to sabotage Coltart's parliamentary campaign. As we have seen, Patrick Nabanyama, his polling agent, was abducted and, in all probability, murdered five days before voting began. The boundaries of Bulawayo South were also gerrymandered to replace a middle-class suburb with the teeming, shabby alleys of Nketa. Now this wholly black area was being asked to vote for a white MDC candidate, and the Big Men of Zanu-PF were convinced it would never oblige. But the mood of the queue indicated otherwise, and Coltart was visibly moved by their expressions of support. He remained deeply troubled by the fate of Nabanyama. 'I feel that sense of excitement, but it's tinged by real sadness because I still don't know where Patrick is and it's now five days since he disappeared,' Coltart told me. Mourning disappeared or murdered friends was something that many MDC candidates were doing on that Saturday.

Barely one mile away, in the neighbouring township of Nkulumane, another famous candidate was waiting to vote. Dumiso Dabengwa, the Home Affairs Minister, stepped from his silver Mercedes, a few yards from 150 of his impoverished, ragged constituents, queuing outside the polling station. For a moment it struck me that Dabengwa looked like a classic Big Man of African politics. He wore a fashionable checked shirt and his neatly polished shoes shone in the morning sunlight. He stood beside his gleaming official Mercedes, an authoritative, bearded figure, causing a visible *frisson* among the policemen and officials manning the polling station. Dabengwa has a courtly, softly spoken manner, belying his past as Joshua Nkomo's intelligence chief and a pillar of his guerrilla army.

He readily gave an impromptu interview. Yes he was completely confident of victory and, by the way, the MDC was a party of sell-outs. 'This is a different election from any other because it is an election that challenges the sovereignty and integrity of the country. People are choosing between retaining their sovereignty or losing their grip completely,' he said. As for the violence, Dabengwa blamed 'both sides' and studiously refused to admit that Zanu-PF carried the lion's share of the burden.

Yet when I asked him about Hunzvi, the mask slipped. Dabengwa loathed the war veterans' leader and had, of course, tried and failed to stop his farm invasions. 'Do you feel at all embarrassed by Hunzvi?' I asked.

'I wouldn't be embarrassed by him, he doesn't represent me,' Dabengwa shot back.

'But you're a war veteran and Hunzvi is leader of the War Veterans' Association.'

'He does not represent all war veterans,' Dabengwa replied adamantly. 'War veterans and the War Veterans' Association are two different things. I hope that when Hunzvi succeeds to be an MP he is able to adjust and realize that you shouldn't express yourself in that callous manner.'[15]

For a moment, Dabengwa revealed a sense of the deep unease felt by much of the Zanu-PF élite. Mugabe had turned to someone like Hunzvi, of all people, to keep him in power. That rankled deeply with men like Dabengwa. But if the mood among the line of people barely 100 yards away was anything to go by, the minister was in deep trouble. I could not find a single Zanu-PF supporter. On the contrary, people greeted me with the open-palmed salute of the MDC. Dabengwa's parliamentary career was clearly about to end.

Outside of Bulawayo, in the tiny villages of Matabeleland, the mood was the same. People walked to vote along dusty tracks, where MDC posters hung from telegraph poles. Nowhere else had I seen the open display of MDC literature, and here people were brave enough to say openly that they would be supporting the opposition.

Matabeleland knew the grim consequences of defiance better than any other region, but this time intimidation had failed. After being crushed and humiliated by Fifth Brigade's massacres in the 1980s, nothing could stop the Ndebele from seizing the opportunity to vote for change. I met Pius Ncube, the Catholic Archbishop of Bulawayo and a fearless critic of Mugabe. 'We have reached a crucial moment,' he told me. 'Apathy has been conquered. People here are so fed up and they just want Mugabe out. They want him to go now. They are so disenchanted with the government that terror may not work for Mugabe any more.'[16] The streams of people outside every polling station seemed to prove the archbishop right.

★   ★   ★

On 25 June, the second day of voting, I found myself in a very different area. I returned to Kwe Kwe, the scene of one of Zanu-PF's worst crack-downs. Blessing Chebundo, the MDC candidate, had abandoned his campaign after narrowly escaping a gang's attempt to burn him alive. When the family's home was razed to the ground by a Zanu-PF mob, he fled the constituency altogether, together with his wife and four children. Now he was making his first return, simply to cast his vote – and even this was a hazardous enterprise, requiring careful planning.

I met Chebundo in the shade of a tree beside the main Harare road, on the edge of his prospective constituency. A tall, powerfully built man, he spoke with almost eerie calm about his experience of the election. Barely a single member of his campaign team had escaped assault or abduction. At that moment, one lay in a coma in a Harare hospital, the victim of another mob ambush. Two others had seen their homes stoned, petrol-bombed and burned to the ground. Death threats had poured in thick and fast. On the surface, Chebundo was phlegmatic, but a quaver in his voice betrayed his nerves.

For this lightning return to Kwe Kwe, Chebundo had gathered an escort of two cars, crammed with eight bodyguards. We set off at breakneck speed, forming a convoy of three vehicles, heading for a polling station deliberately chosen for its remote location. The main road runs directly through the centre of Kwe Kwe, so we turned right several miles before reaching the town. A narrow tar road soon gave way to a dusty dirt-track and the convoy bumped through the rolling fields, marked by groves of thorn trees. Finally, we reached an even narrower track that wound its way to Riverlea primary school. This cluster of yellow, sandstone buildings was the polling station.

As the convoy halted, I opened the car door and was about to step out, but Chebundo grabbed me by the arm. Nobody moved until two of his bodyguards, both wearing dark glasses, had completed their reconnaissance. They paced the perimeter of the school, looking under bushes and behind trees. Then they signalled that the coast was clear and Chebundo hurried to cast his vote. We stayed about five minutes, all that was considered safe, before the convoy roared away and the candidate fled his erstwhile constituency yet again. As we parted on the Harare road, Chebundo smiled ruefully and said: 'Even voting for myself is difficult. Imagine how hard it will be for other people to vote for me.' The MDC candidate returned to his hiding place, while I drove back to the capital. During the long journey, Chebundo's words ran through my mind. If a parliamentary candidate viewed the act of voting with trepidation, how would the ordinary Zimbabwean feel?

★   ★   ★

On the afternoon of Monday, 26 June, the first results began trickling through. They were announced in the same dreary room used for the referendum, and the same dreary man was in charge. Tobaiwa Mudede, the Registrar-General, sat behind the desk and wore his most scornful, revolted expression, as if a dead herring festered beneath his nose. Perhaps it was forgivable, for it fell to him to announce the most embarrassing election results in Zimbabwean history. In Bulawayo and Matabeleland, all the signs I had picked up during my brief visit proved entirely accurate – it was a clean sweep for the MDC. Coltart won his seat by a crushing 20,781 votes to just 3,193 for Zanu-PF. So much for the idea that people in Nketa would not vote for a white man. Dumiso Dabengwa crashed to defeat in Nkulumane, managing only 3,644 votes compared to 20,380 for Gibson Sibanda, deputy leader of the MDC. All eight seats in Bulawayo fell to the opposition, with the MDC averaging an extraordinary 80 per cent of the vote.

Across Matabeleland, it was the same story. After suffering the ravages of Fifth Brigade, it was as if the Ndebele had become inured to intimidation.

They seized the chance to oust Zanu-PF with both hands. Of the 23 seats in Bulawayo and Matabeleland, 21 fell to the MDC. The same earthquake rocked Harare. As in the referendum, so in the election: the people of the capital took their revenge on the government. In Budiriro, all the efforts of the torturers in Hunzvi's surgery were fruitless. Terrified people emerged from their homes and crushed Zanu-PF by 21,058 votes to 4,410. All 19 seats in Harare and the neighbouring town of Chitungwiza fell to the MDC, typically by margins of 80 per cent.[17] As Mudede read out one humiliation after another for Zanu-PF, whistles of surprise rose from his audience.

Yet by midnight, when the rural constituencies began declaring, stark evidence emerged of the shattering effects of intimidation in Zanu-PF's heartland. The provinces of Mashonaland East, West and Central had suffered more than anywhere else from the terror campaign, and the desired results were duly delivered. No one could have been less surprised than me to hear the declaration from Kariba. Isaac Mackenzie of Zanu-PF swept to victory with 15,048 votes to a mere 7,332 for his MDC opponent. Comrade Jesus and his gang had done their work well. The people of Mberengwa East and West succumbed to the violent persuasion of Comrade Biggie Chitoro and company. Zanu-PF swept over 80 per cent of the vote in each seat. In Mashonaland Central, where Border Gezi had led the onslaught, Zanu-PF held all ten seats by comfortable majorities. The most powerful testament to the effectiveness of intimidation perhaps came from Buhera North, where Tsvangirai narrowly failed to win the seat by 10,316 votes to 12,850 for Zanu-PF. The murders of Chiminya and Mabika in that horrific pillar of smoke over the Shawa Hills had spread terror far and wide, enough to deny him victory.

Yet there were startling exceptions. Blessing Chebundo, the man in hiding, a candidate unable to campaign or even visit his prospective constituency, pulled off a remarkable victory. He managed 15,388 votes in Kwe Kwe against just 8,352 for Emmerson Mnangagwa, the Justice Minister and one of Zimbabwe's most powerful men. I remembered that rally in Kwe Kwe when Mugabe's audience consisted largely of people threatened and browbeaten into attendance. Now those thousands had refused to be intimidated, and had taken their revenge. In Marondera East, another feared acolyte of Mugabe escaped defeat by the skin of his teeth. Sydney Sekeramayi, the Security Minister (and the man who uttered the immortal words: 'The MDC have slapped a lion in the face and they will be devoured'), came within 63 votes of being devoured by the electorate. He held his seat by 10,692 votes against 10,629 for the MDC. Had his opponent been able to campaign or even visit the area, it is conceivable that he would have picked up the extra 32 votes needed to oust Sekeramayi.

But as Zanu-PF held one rural constituency after another, it became clear that they were going to scrape through the election. Thanks to Mugabe's power to appoint 30 members of the 150-seat parliament, his party needed to win only 46 of the 120 elected seats in order to secure an overall majority. By contrast, the MDC had to take 76 to achieve an outright majority of one. The hurdle for the opposition was, quite simply, insurmountable and the MDC's only real hope was to take most of the elected seats and claim a moral victory. They came within a whisker of achieving this. The final tally of seats was 57 for the MDC, 62 for Zanu-PF and one for the tiny opposition Zanu-Ndonga party. It was an extraordinary achievement for Tsvangirai. No opposition had ever performed so well, Zanu-PF had never sunk lower in public esteem and, most crucially of all, Mugabe's cherished one-party state had been smashed. Comparing the final voting figures with the previous election in 1995 gives the starkest illustration of Zanu-PF's decline:

Party	1995 election		2000 election	
	Elected seats	per cent of vote	Elected seats	per cent of vote
Zanu-PF	118	81.36	62	48.40
MDC	–	–	57	47.02
Other opposition	2	18.64	1	4.58

The MDC, a party just nine months old, had given Zanu-PF an electoral pounding without precedent in Zimbabwean history. Tsvangirai came from nowhere to win 57 seats and almost half of the popular vote. In total, the MDC won 1,171,321 votes, just 34,259 fewer than Zanu-PF. The combined opposition vote actually exceeded that of the ruling party by 79,827. For the first time ever, most Zimbabweans voted against Mugabe and, compared with the previous election, support for Zanu-PF was all but sliced in half. When it came to alienating so many voters so quickly, Mugabe's record was almost without parallel anywhere in the world. John Major's Conservatives suffered their landslide defeat in the British election of 1997 when about one-quarter of their voters abandoned them. Mugabe lost almost twice as many. In Tsvangirai's words, Zimbabwe would 'never be the same again'.[18]

And yet, Mugabe still scraped through. With 30 seats in his gift and already in the bag for Zanu-PF, the ruling party emerged with 92 of the 150 MPs. The ultimate disaster of defeat had been averted. Mugabe retained a workable majority in parliament, although the opposition presence would transform the atmosphere of that supine institution. Strange as it may sound, many in the MDC leadership were still disappointed. They had come

Top: Robert Mugabe addresses a campaign rally in Kwe Kwe. June 2000. © Paul Grover

Bottom: The Harare food riots of October 2000 were suppressed with the utmost severity. Here paramilitary officers from the Police Support Unit attack a man in Mufakose township. © Paul Cadenhead

Left: 'Victory is certain.' Morgan Tsvangirai waves the open palm – the symbol of the MDC – at 25,000 ecstatic supporters thronging the terraces of Rufaro stadium at the last rally before the parliamentary election. Victory was anything but certain. June 2000.
© Paul Grover

Bottom: Agnes Rusike (right), a notorious squatter ringleader, leads her band of revolutionaries in a lively song of support for Mugabe beside their camp on an occupied farm near Norton. I discovered that her fellow warlord was a Manchester United supporter. March 2000. © Paul Grover

Top: Robert Mugabe greets his supporters at a campaign rally in Kwe Kwe. Surprisingly agile for a man of 76, Mugabe lost no opportunity to rouse his followers to fist waving frenzies. Grace Mugabe, the First Lady, responds demurely (right). June 2000. © Paul Grover

Bottom: White farm owners ouside a polling booth. June 2000. © Paul Grover

Top: Morgan Tsvangirai, the MDC leader, addresses fearful supporters in Murewa. A Zanu-PF mob was massing nearby and a few minutes later, he abandoned the election rally and fled the town to avoid attack. June 2000. © Paul Grover

Bottom: Robert Mugabe's face is removed, piece by piece, from the banner overlooking Rufaro stadium in Harare. The urban poor take their revenge on the 'one authentic and consistent leader'. September 1999. © Paul Grover

Top: MDC supporters celebrate their party's sweeping victory in all 19 of Harare's seats in the parliamentary election. The red cards were intended as a signal to Mugabe. It was a signal he was determined to ignore. June 2000. © Paul Grover

Bottom: 'Saddam Hussein' (wearing hat) inside the wreckage of a hut burned down by Zanu-PF gangs in Mberengwa, a fortnight before the parliamentary election. This remote area effectively became a war zone. I could visit only with the protection of 'Saddam' and his friends. June 2000. © Paul Grover

Top: The MDC was far from innocent. Here the party's youths rough up a suspected Zanu-PF supporter at the opposition's last rally before the election. June 2000.
© Paul Grover

Left: Hitler Hunzvi, leader of the War Veterans' Association, in typically pugnacious form. © Rob Bodman

Left: Joseph Chinotimba emerges from the Supreme Court after threatening Chief Justice Gubbay with war. This notorious gap-toothed thug rose from obscurity to become one of the most prominent figures in Mugabe's Zimbabwe. © Howard Burditt

Bottom: The casualties of a brutally effective terror campaign. Children pick through the charred wreckage of their home in Mberengwa, after their village was raided by a Zanu-PF mob. June 2000. © Paul Grover

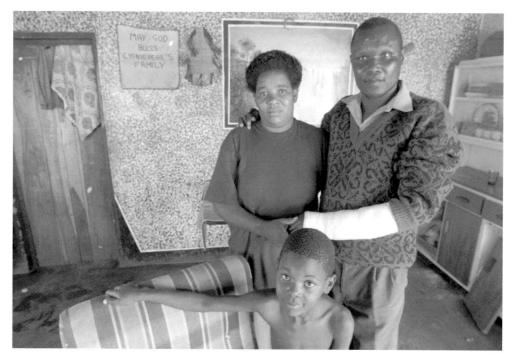

Top: Girly and Daniel Chinyerere, together with their eight-year-old son, shortly after they were attacked by a gang of Mugabe supporters near Mataga. June 2000. © Paul Grover

Bottom: Black farmworkers bore the brunt of Zanu-PF's terror campaign. Oliver Kumfromo, a tractor driver, struggles to a polling station after so-called 'war veterans' attacked him and broke his leg in three places. June 2000. © Paul Grover

through an inferno and harboured a deep sense of grievance. Had the election been remotely free and fair, they would almost certainly have won.

★   ★   ★

There is a patronizing, faintly offensive argument that no election in Africa will ever be truly free and fair. A realist accepts this and realizes that even the most violent campaign does not necessarily invalidate the result. After all, this is Africa and things work differently here. Lord Soames, who as Governor of Rhodesia accepted the 1980 election as the verdict of the people, colourfully expressed this view:

> You must remember, this is Africa. This isn't Little-Puddleton-on-the-Marsh and they behave differently here. They think nothing of sticking tent poles up each other's whatnots and doing filthy, beastly things to each other. It does happen, I'm afraid. It's a very wild thing, an election.[19]

The Soames theory was, curiously enough, implicitly endorsed by many of the African observers who covered the Zimbabwean election. By and large, they argued that widespread violence did not imply that the contest was neither free nor fair. The more fundamentalist among them saw anyone who disagreed as un-African, or even anti-African.

Tony Yengeni, the ANC's Chief Whip in the South African parliament and leader of its observer team, appeared to espouse this view with passion. Mugabe favoured Yengeni with an audience on 27 June and the portly South African emerged visibly star-struck from State House. He breathlessly assured state television that the election had been held in conditions of 'absolute peace'.[20]

When he got round to presenting his brief report to the South African parliament almost three months later, Yengeni revised this peculiar view and accepted that there had been 'incidents of violence and intimidation'. But he claimed: 'The result of the parliamentary elections broadly reflects the will of the Zimbabwean people.'[21] The South African observers gave Zimbabwe a clean bill of health.

Yet the largest observer teams reached fundamentally different conclusions. The European Union sent a group of 190, forming almost half of all the monitors covering the election. Recognizing that the wool would not be pulled over their eyes, Mugabe's government tried every possible gambit to hamper their work. The President declared that no Britons would be allowed to join the teams and this edict was meekly accepted. Pierre Schori, a former Swedish cabinet minister, was chosen to lead the group.

By 10 June, the EU monitors had arrived in Harare and were swiftly enmeshed in a thicket of bureaucratic regulations that kept them kicking their heels in the capital for another five days. By the time accreditation was granted, the election was just around the corner. Not until ten days before polls opened were the EU observers finally given the chance to fan out across Zimbabwe and what they discovered left many deeply shocked. When Schori presented his report, that sense of horror and bewilderment suffused his message. He dismissed the idea that the bureaucratic delays were simply down to incompetence and said they amounted to: 'A deliberate attempt to reduce the effectiveness of independent monitoring of the election.' Schori then delivered his verdict:

High levels of violence, intimidation and coercion marred the election campaign. An assessment of violence and intimidation since February 2000 made by the EU Election Observation Mission, together with reports from EU observers operating throughout the country since early June, indicate that Zanu-PF was responsible for the bulk of political violence. Zanu-PF leaders seemed to sanction the use of violence and intimidation against political opponents and contributed significantly to the climate of fear so evident during the election campaign . . . Overall, the conduct of the government has failed to uphold the rule of law and compromised law enforcement agencies.[22]

Under questioning, Schori went further. 'The term "free and fair" is not applicable in these elections,'[23] he said. Schori chose to release his report at midnight on 25 June, and this curious timing was deliberate. When Schori spoke, nobody knew the outcome of the election. On purpose, he released the EU's conclusions after the close of polls but before the onset of the count. He wanted to pre-empt accusations that the EU had condemned the election simply because it disapproved of the result.

Mugabe's propagandists cheerfully accused him of this anyway. Moyo decided that Schori's verdict showed: 'The EU has joined the forces trying to overthrow President Mugabe's government.'[24] For Mugabe's apologists, the most embarrassing facts about the election were the surrounding violence and that Zanu-PF had emerged with a minority of the popular vote. Moyo simply chose to deny both of these. In a BBC interview he said: 'There is no one who was killed during the Zimbabwean elections.'[25] When Brian Donnelly, the new British High Commissioner, pointed out that the opposition won most of the votes cast, Moyo told him: 'I am surprised that after six months in the country you are peddling an ordinary lie . . . we have the pleasure of sending you a correct version of the full election result if you want.'[26] I am not sure if this ever happened. It would be fascinating to see Moyo's 'correct version' of the result.

As for Don McKinnon's Commonwealth observers, they reported in similar terms to Schori, but stopped short of declaring that the entire contest was neither free nor fair. General Abdusalami Abubakar, the former military ruler of Nigeria, and someone who knew a thing or two about flawed elections, led the 40-strong team. Their report condemned the violence and pinned the blame squarely on Zanu-PF:

> There was violence, intimidation and coercion in many parts of the country, especially in rural areas . . . there were incidents where opposition parties carried out acts of violence. But it would appear that most of the violence was directed against the opposition parties, especially the Movement for Democratic Change . . . the violence which disfigured this campaign was employed systematically as part of a strategy to diminish support for the opposition parties.[27]

In other words, a terror campaign had occurred and all the evidence suggested that it had worked. With a vicious use of violence, Mugabe had bought his own survival. The purpose of this campaign was clear. He would complete the unfinished business of seizing land from the whites.

NOTES AND REFERENCES

1 BBC Radio 4, *Today,* 10 November 2000.
2 *The Herald,* 2 June 2000.
3 *Ibid.,* 1 April 2000.
4 *Ibid.,* 19 May 2000.
5 Speech, Zanu-PF central committee, 29 September 2000.
6 Interview with the author, 4 May 2000.
7 He was always saying this. See for example his speech at the Independence Day ceremony, 18 April 2001.
8 Interview with the author, 4 May 2000.
9 Interview with the author, 17 June 2000.
10 Speech, MDC rally Rufaro stadium, 18 June 2000.
11 Interview with the author, 18 June 2000.
12 Zimbabwe Human Rights Forum, statistical summary of offences, circulated on 27 June 2000. The starting point for this record was the referendum result on 15 February 2000.
13 *Ibid.*
14 Moven Mahachi, Mugabe's late Defence Minister, took me aside during the Zanu-PF Congress of December 2000 and told me with complete conviction: 'Coltart is the true leader of MDC. Don't you know that? You don't know that?

Eeeeh. Coltart is the one behind everything, absolutely everything. He is the one causing all our problems.'

15 Interview with the author, 24 June 2000.
16 *Ibid.*
17 Stan Mudenge, the Foreign Minister, told me on 7 June: 'It is almost impossible for us to lose seats in Harare.'
18 Interview in *Never the Same Again,* Edwina Spicer Productions, 2000.
19 BBC interview 1984, also quoted in Ken Flower, *Serving Secretly*, John Murray, London, 1987, p. 256.
20 ZBC news, 27 June 2000.
21 Report to South African parliament, 14 September 2000.
22 Interim report, EU Observer mission, 25 June 2000.
23 Press conference, 25 June 2000.
24 *Financial Gazette,* 27 June 2000.
25 BBC Radio 4, *Today,* 10 November 2000.
26 *The Herald,* 1 December 2001.
27 Quoted in International Bar Association report on the rule of law in Zimbabwe, sec. 8.5.

Chapter 9

Land for the People

July 2000 and before

In Zimbabwe, none of the white exploiters will be allowed to keep an acre of their land. (Robert Mugabe, 1976)[1]

The joyful gathering in the midst of an endless plain burst into song. Female soprano and male bass blended into a tuneful hymn that floated across the vast, open grassland. 'We thank our ancestors for answering our prayers,' went the words. 'You have delivered us from our suffering and we give thanks.' The 11 men and 4 women making up the impromptu choir danced as they sang: slow, dignified, rhythmic arm movements, a shuffling of feet and hips. All were carefully turned out in their Sunday best. Bright, colourful dresses and headscarves adorned the women, while their male companions wore jackets, ties and an assortment of hats, ranging from flat, workmanlike caps to objects that resembled tea cosies. Yellow rays of spring sunshine bathed a scene of perfect happiness.

The prayers triumphantly answered by the ancestors were prayers for land. Swallowed by the immensity of the veldt, these euphoric people were the winners in Mugabe's Zimbabwe. They were about to be given land from a white man's farm. A tall, silver-haired figure stepped forward, his face wreathed in smiles. 'This is a day for all of us to remember, a day for history to remember,' he said. 'At last, after 20 years, the land is coming to the people today.' Cheers from the men and ululation from the women greeted his words and another round of singing began. A paean of praise was offered to the land itself: 'The land is our mother and our father, we cannot live without it.' Then the elderly, authoritative man held a battered, brown hat in the air. Each of the new owners of Vlakfontein farm near Gweru came forward and picked a scrap of paper, like a raffle ticket, out of the hat. This showed which plot of land they had been given, and the men and women sang once again.

As Cephas Msipa, Governor of Midlands province, put aside the hat, he

169

appeared as delighted as the new owners of this expanse of Zimbabwe's soil. A genial, kindly figure in his late sixties, looking just like the headmaster he once was, Msipa had quiet, affable words for everybody. He was even conciliatory about the neighbouring white farmers, whom he felt sure would help the new owners of Vlakfontein. When Msipa spoke to me, he managed to go a whole conversation without mentioning the evils of the British. I found the absence of hectoring aggression, so wearily familiar from the Big Men of Zanu-PF, quite disconcerting. 'We want to live as Zimbabweans together. There is enough land for everyone, all we want is a fair distribution. We have begun bringing about that fairness today,' he said. Msipa then gravely told the gathering that he would do 'everything possible' to help them farm successfully and give them, as he put it: 'clinics, roads, schools, proper houses and a good life'.

Vlakfontein ranch was the first white-owned farm to be seized in Midlands province and handed over to blacks under the 'Fast Track' resettlement scheme. On 15 July, barely three weeks after Zanu-PF's narrow election victory, this programme had been launched. As Mugabe never ceased to proclaim, the whole purpose of his government (and presumably of the violence and terror that sustained it) was to allow ceremonies of this sort to take place. What I had just witnessed was, so the propaganda went, the *raison d'être* of the Mugabe regime, the defining testament of what Zanu-PF stood for. Land, the white man's land, was at the heart of everything. Mugabe's passionate crusade was designed to correct a monstrous injustice bequeathed by colonial history. What I had seen, so Msipa told me, was one small step towards putting that right.

★   ★   ★

What were the origins of the bitter sense of grievance that infused Mugabe and his followers? When Cecil Rhodes's pioneer column laagered their wagons in 1890 and raised the Union Flag for the first time in what is now African Unity Square in central Harare, this bunch of adventurers and desperadoes had been promised a reward of land. Rhodes had pledged 3,000 acres for each of the 200 pioneers (and 15 gold-mining concessions into the bargain).

He had, of course, cheerfully offered land already inhabited by the Shona and Ndebele peoples, not that this appears to have worried him. The new white settlers gathered their loot using the simplest of methods. A hardy pioneer from the British South Africa Company would carry the white man's civilization into the New Rand of Rhodesia by riding his horse north for a day and sticking a peg into the ground at sunset. Then he would ride east for a day and leave another peg, then south and west until he had marked out the corners of a square. That would be his farm. If any unlucky people already lived on 'his' land they would be moved, often by the simple expedient of burning down their village. In the 12 months after Rhodes's invasion of Matabeleland and the formation of the Southern Rhodesian colony in 1893, over 10,000 square miles of rich, high veldt soil were staked out. At least 230,000 head of cattle were also stolen, on the pretext that they all belonged to Lobengula, the vanquished King of the Ndebele, and so became spoils of war.

But the white settlers arrived in a country that was almost empty, with a widely scattered population of under half a million, and some of their apologists have seized on this as a plea in mitigation. There was plenty of room for the odd 3,000-acre farm, goes the argument, so what was the problem? The pioneers simply marked out virgin tracts and began earning a living. According to this defence, most blacks were unaffected by the sudden inflow of settlers.

In fact, it took Rhodes and his followers only three years to provoke the first nation-wide war of independence ever seen during the European conquest of Africa. Both the Shona and Ndebele rose in revolt in 1896, after the wholesale looting of their best land and cattle, together with the imposition of punitive taxes, rendered them impoverished and desperate. It actually took a perverse genius for the pioneers to spark so much hatred so quickly. As Thomas Pakenham wrote in his masterly epic, *The Scramble for Africa*: 'If the whites were planning to produce an explosion, they could not have worked more effectively.'[2] With the help of the Maxim gun, the inevitable explosion was dealt with in a matter of months and the First *Chimurenga*, as it later came to be known, crushed with the utmost ruthlessness. But any idea that the white man's arrival was a non-event, scarcely noticed by the far-flung people of the new colony, was clearly nonsensical.

As more white settlers headed north, so their demand for land grew. In a searing account of his experiences during the Rhodesian bush war, *Kandaya*, Angus Shaw wrote of his family's arrival in the country:

> My grandfather pegged out his good land at the turn of the century and it became his for the price of a sixpenny revenue stamp from the British South Africa Company, then the administrators of the colony. The stamp covered the cost of the title deeds and the red sealing wax. There was no need to consult anyone who might have been living on the land at the time.[3]

To cope with the arrival of Shaw's forebears and thousands of others, the government formally divided Rhodesia along racial lines in 1930 with a Land Apportionment Act. A white population of barely 40,000 was given

20 million of the very best hectares, while the 900,000 blacks were left with just 16.3 million hectares, mainly in barren Native Reserves. In theory, hundreds of thousands of blacks inhabiting land set aside for white farmers would be forcibly moved. Yet the Native Affairs Department in the Rhodesian government was far from oblivious to the possible consequences. With great prescience, its officials warned that any attempt to enforce the letter of the Act would, quite simply, provoke another uprising. So the authorities trod softly for another 15 years and made no attempt at the full implementation of their law, which would later earn a special notoriety in the legends of African nationalism.

All this changed after 1945 for the simplest of reasons – thousands of new white settlers were flocking to Rhodesia and many had been promised farms by the British government. Demobilized soldiers were offered the chance to farm in Africa as a reward for service in the Second World War, and Rhodesia opened up new tracts to provide for them. Even today, a group of prize farms near Mvurwi, which I had the good fortune to visit frequently, is known as the Victory Block – in memory of the fact that this beautiful, fertile area, set in a bowl of green hills, was marked out after 1945 and given to victorious British soldiers.

Quietly, with no fanfare, vast numbers of blacks were moved to make way for the new settlers. As one historian wrote, the Native Affairs Department 'could no longer resist the clamour for mass movements of natives'.[4] No fewer than 85,000 black families were evicted between 1945 and 1955, totalling perhaps 425,000 people.[5] Considering that the black population in 1945 barely exceeded 1.5 million, something approaching 30 per cent of all 'natives' were moved from their homes. Perhaps most astonishing is that this forcible mass migration did not provoke a full-scale revolt. When about 100,000 people were evicted in similar circumstances in Kenya, the direct result was the Mau Mau uprising of 1952–54. In Rhodesia, it took Ian Smith and UDI to channel these grievances into a struggle for liberation.

But a burning sense of grievance certainly existed. Land had been stolen, with blacks herded into 'Native Reserves' while their white rulers took possession of the most fertile fields. The best land was denied to the most people. Land of immense traditional importance – where ancestors lay buried and chiefs once held sway – was under the dominance of outsiders. In her story, *The Old Chief Mshlanga*, Doris Lessing goes to the heart of the matter. A white landowner, the father of the narrator, summons Chief Mshlanga after a herd of goats from an African village strays on to his farm:

> It was now in the late sunset, the sky a welter of colours, the birds singing their last songs, and the cattle, lowing peacefully, moving past us towards their sheds for the night. It was the hour when Africa was

most beautiful; and here was this pathetic, ugly scene doing no one any good.

At last my father stated finally: 'I'm not going to argue about it, I am keeping the goats.' The old chief flashed back in his own language: 'That means my people will go hungry when the dry season comes.'

'Go to the police then,' said my father, and looked triumphant.

There was, of course, no more to be said.

The old man sat silent, his head bent, his hands dangling helplessly over his withered knees. Then he rose, the young man helping him, and he stood, facing my father. He spoke once again, very stiffly; and turned away and went home to his village.

'What did he say?' asked my father of the young man, who laughed uncomfortably and would not meet his eyes.

'What did he say?' insisted my father.

Our cook stood straight and silent, his brows knotted together. Then he spoke. 'My father says: all this land, this land you call yours, is his land and belongs to our people.'[6]

Lessing's story ends with the deportation of Chief Mshlanga's people:

Next time the policeman came on his rounds, he was told this story. He remarked: 'That kraal has no right to be there, it should have been moved long ago. I don't know why no one has done anything about it. I'll have a chat with the Native Commissioner next week. I'm going over for tennis on Sunday anyway.'

Some time later we heard that Chief Mshlanga and his people had been moved 200 miles east, to a proper native reserve; the government land was going to be opened up for white settlement soon.

I went to see the village again, about a year afterwards. There was nothing there. Mounds of red mud, where the huts had been, had long swathes of rotting thatch over them, veined with the red galleries of the white ants.[7]

This folk memory, lodged in the consciousness of millions of black Zimbabweans, pervades and complicates the 'land issue' to this day. When Mugabe and Nkomo led the guerrilla war, or Second *Chimurenga,* of the 1970s, one slogan united these bitter rivals: 'Land For the People.' Reclaiming the white man's land, taking his fertile farms and returning them to black people, lay at the heart of the struggle.

★   ★   ★

But when I arrived in Zimbabwe in 1999, little had been done. Mugabe gave passionate speeches about taking land from the whites – a consistent feature of his rule – while taking no action whatever. After 19 years of independence and Zanu–PF dominance, fewer than 4,000 members of the Commercial Farmers' Union (CFU), the vast majority of them white, owned 8.6 million hectares of land, or 21 per cent of the entire surface area of Zimbabwe. Meanwhile, about 7 million blacks, over half of the population, lived in 'communal areas' covering 16.3 million hectares, or 41 per cent of Zimbabwe. Under the *status quo*, these millions were condemned to lives of poverty.

With these facts in mind, it is important to squash a persistent myth. Mugabe and his minions lost no opportunity to recite a mantra that white farmers owned '70 per cent of the land'. Even more extravagant claims were often made. A petition given to the British High Commission by Zanu–PF demonstrators on 1 June 2000 claimed that '80 per cent of our land is owned by white farmers who are all British citizens'. It is worth bearing in mind that the actual figure is 21 per cent and the overwhelming majority of these landowners are Zimbabweans. Mugabe has, for years, shamelessly exaggerated the scale of the problem. His 70 per cent figure has acquired totemic significance and is repeated endlessly, although it has no basis whatever.

Yet his point stands. The case for land reform is unanswerable because it is patently unjust for large tracts of an impoverished country to be the preserve of a privileged few. The crucial question is: why was Mugabe content to ignore this problem right up until 2000? The Official Explanation is recounted so frequently with such fervour that it has become almost symbolic of the Mugabe era. It can be summed up in a few words. Land reform didn't happen because of the perfidy of the white farmers and their British masters. Mugabe did all he could, but his valiant efforts were sabotaged by this wicked coalition.

There are several stages to the Official Explanation. The first concerns the Lancaster House conference of 1979 that framed the constitution for independent Zimbabwe. Here, Mugabe agreed a deal on land that fell far short of what he had sought. He had wanted a Zimbabwean government to be able to seize land compulsorily from white farmers and pay no compensation. He got the exact reverse – a constitution that protected farmers by ruling out compulsory land acquisitions and guaranteeing full compensation. Moreover, these clauses would be set in stone and shielded from amendment for ten years. Mugabe signed up to this reluctantly, in order to bring peace to his country.

Then we come to the Official Explanation's second stage. In return for endorsing this legal protection for white farmers, Mugabe got the British to agree to pay for land reform. If the landowners were guaranteed compensation, the British would buy them out and pay all the costs of resettling blacks in their place. That was his understanding of the deal. But the miserly British paid too little and even this money stopped altogether in 1995. Tony Blair's government broke Britain's promise and refused to renew payments. So the whole land reform process was hamstrung from the start and the white farmers, scarcely believing their luck, concentrated on making money hand over fist.

Stage Three of the Official Explanation brings us up to date. After 20 years of no progress and with thousands of 'war veterans' invading farms, Mugabe decided to go ahead with land reform his way and tell the British and the whites to take a running jump. So he stripped farmers of their right to compensation with the constitutional amendment of 6 April 2000 and he went ahead with compulsory land seizures and resettlement, under the 'Fast Track' scheme launched in July. On Vlakfontein farm, I had seen the first steps.

So much for the Official Explanation. As an apologia for 20 years of failure, it seems detailed and convincing, but there is one problem. All of the above is a shameless distortion of the truth. The idea that Lancaster House was an insuperable barrier to land reform is another myth, although a strangely persistent one, put about by some historians. In *The Road to Zimbabwe*, Anthony Verrier wrote that the constitution produced by the conference 'denies any fundamental change in the pattern of land owner-ship, except in terms which are clearly beyond Zimbabwe's financial resources'.[8] But despite all the constraints of Lancaster House, Mugabe's government managed to acquire 3.5 million hectares of land from white farmers, almost 30 per cent of their total holding, in the 18 years after inde-pendence. Virtually none of this land was seized compulsorily – over 98 per cent was conceded willingly in return for full compensation, paid largely by donor countries. The miserly British coughed up £44 million towards the cost of resettlement. With a modicum of competence, this could have gone a long way towards solving the problem. Yet it failed completely.

For all his sound and fury about land reform, Mugabe appeared to lack the first idea of how to go about it successfully. Broadly speaking, two models were adopted. The first approach was in tune with Mugabe's brand of Chinese-style, agrarian socialism. 'Village collectives' were formed, of the sort that had failed disastrously in Tanzania, China, Cambodia, Ethiopia, the Soviet Union and everywhere else foolish enough to try them. They duly failed in Zimbabwe. Placing people on land over which they have no right of individual ownership and expecting them to grow food for the 'collec-tive', with inadequate water, seed and fertilizer, has always been the worst form of farming imaginable. The hapless beneficiaries of these schemes in Zimbabwe usually ended up poorer than they had been at the start and most trickled away or desperately sought jobs from neighbouring white farmers.

All over Zimbabwe you can find the shattered ghosts of farms that were acquired by the government back in the 1980s, turned into collectives and finished up wrecked and abandoned. At Grazely farm near Arcturus, one of the very first to be taken after independence, I found a scene of devastation 20 years later. What was once a pleasant garden was littered with the wrecks of burnt-out cars, and weeds had long since submerged the ruins of the farmhouse. Grazely had been among Zimbabwe's most productive dairy farms, and Ben Harding, the former owner, employed almost 100 people. When I visited, about 20 people scratched a living amid the dereliction and decay. Clumps of maize here and there were the only signs of cultivation, while most of the farm's 2,400 acres, some of the best land in Africa, were wild and unkempt. The farmhouse had, apparently, been dismantled because selling the bricks was the only way the new inhabitants of Grazely could earn a living.

With some exceptions, this is generally what happened to the 3.5 million hectares made available to the government. Why was this disastrous model adopted? The reason was simple. Apart from being ideologically pure, it brought the maximum political gain by allowing large numbers of people to be dumped on the land in short order. Mugabe could quote impressive figures for the quantity of people resettled and then set grandiose, ambitious targets. An 'Accelerated Resettlement Programme' launched in 1982 aimed to provide land for 162,000 families in three years.

Done properly, land reform is a slow, complicated process. So it was done badly in order to maximize the political impact. In the restrained words of an assessment by Britain's Department for International Development: 'The record on improving incomes . . . was patchy and some settlers, especially women, ended up in poverty.'[9] The unfortunate people who 'benefited' from a Mugabe resettlement scheme generally disappeared and returned to their former homes after a few months. Only 71,000 black families had been resettled by 1997, a fraction of the target and fewer than the number deported by the colonial government in the ten years after the war.

The second model of land reform adopted by Mugabe had nothing to do with helping poor people. Quite the reverse. The Commercial Farm Resettlement Scheme was designed to help his rich friends. In the words of George Charamba, Mugabe's spokesman, its purpose was 'changing the racial complexion of commercial farmers. There is no God-given right for whites to be the best farmers.'[10] In other words, a farm would be taken from a rich white man and given to a rich black man. With endearing honesty, no one pretended that reducing poverty had anything to do with it.

There are no prizes for guessing what kind of people won from this scheme. In fact, Charamba was among them. An official list released by the government in March 2000 showed that he had been leased a farm near Kadoma. Among the other winners were two cabinet ministers, the Speaker of parliament, two High Court judges, two deputy ministers, a provincial Governor and a retired General. An Ordinary Tenant Farmer Scheme was also used to favour the élite with farms. Among the 'ordinary tenants' was Air Marshal Perence Shiri, commander of the Air Force, who earlier in his distinguished career had led the notorious Fifth Brigade and masterminded its murderous crackdown in Matabeleland during the 1980s.

In short, land reform failed because farms were either handed out to the élite or resettled in a singularly disastrous way that managed only to increase poverty. But, crucially, it did not fail because of lack of land. On the contrary, not all of the 3.5 million hectares were actually used. When Mugabe launched his drive to seize white-owned land in 2000, his government still possessed 70 farms, covering over 300,000 hectares, which lay empty and idle because no one had bothered resettling them. From 1980 onwards, anyone selling a commercial farm had a legal obligation to offer the land to the government first. Over 80 per cent of Zimbabwe's white-owned farms have changed hands since independence, and the authorities could have acquired any of them. They declined to do so. Lack of land was never the problem. Lack of willingness and ability to resettle the land properly was the real failing.

Despite the passionate rhetoric and the burning sense of grievance, all the evidence suggests that Mugabe did not take land reform seriously. Astonishingly, £3 million provided by the British to help pay for it was returned, unspent, by Zimbabwe.[11] Quite simply, he was content for land reform to languish at the bottom of the in-tray. Until 1987, Mugabe's consuming obsession was securing his grip on power by crushing Zapu and imposing a one-party state. Directing the murderous repression of Matabeleland left little time for ensuring that land resettlement went ahead successfully. Once his dominance had been assured after 1987, Mugabe still attached little priority to the problem. He was, of course, aware that white commercial farmers were the backbone of Zimbabwe's economy and he had no wish to put this at risk. But the most convincing explanation for his inactivity is that during this period, white farmers posed no threat.

In fact, Mugabe maintained a cosy relationship with the CFU leaders, while the vast majority of rank and file farmers took no interest in politics. Some even backed Zanu-PF and a few were elected to parliament on the ruling party's ticket.[12] Powerful interests bound Mugabe and the farmers together. Mugabe could not forget that the landowners employed 300,000 black workers and, taking families into account, almost two million people lived on their land. This was a huge constituency that had to be kept behind Zanu-PF, and the only way of guaranteeing this was by enlisting the farmers as allies, or at least benevolent neutrals. As for the farmers, after independence the CFU leadership had decided that securing their future demanded reconciliation with Mugabe and support for land reform.

This explains Mugabe's post-independence drive to reassure the farming community, which so impressed many observers. It will be recalled that Denis Norman, the CFU chief, became Zimbabwe's first Agriculture Minister, and in the early years leading farmers were able to visit the most powerful office in the country at the drop of a hat. Jim Sinclair, who was President of the CFU from 1981 until 1983, had numerous meetings with Mugabe and described him as 'friendly, easy to talk to and easily accessible. We had an easy relationship with him.' Ordinary farmers were not forgotten and Mugabe would tour the country, addressing gatherings of landowners in colonial-era country clubs. In Sinclair's time, Mugabe spoke to four big meetings each year and also attended the CFU's annual Congress.

Sinclair recalls accompanying him to Lower Save in 1982, where he addressed 40 landowners in a country club and told them that their future was secure. 'My role was to un-demonize Mugabe in the eyes of farmers, because he had been demonized during the liberation war,' explained Sinclair. 'But it was equally important to un-demonize the farmers in his eyes. That's why we had these meetings and they worked. He would say, "Look, we need you, you're part of the future for us. But you've got to look after your workers and support land reform." He made a good impression and farmers were reassured and they stayed and prospered.'[13]

All very commendable – and it is easy to see how Sinclair, one of the few white farmers to welcome the birth of Zimbabwe and give his all to the new country, was ideally suited to this task. But while Mugabe and the CFU leadership were getting along so well, land resettlement was falling apart. Sinclair stresses how farmers 'showed willingness to support land reform' and made available large areas for the purpose. But virtually all of this was misused and a disastrous pattern emerged. The CFU would hand over farms, the government would wreck them and the donors would foot the bill. While Mugabe and the white farmers were on backslapping terms, each confident that the other posed no threat, impoverished rural Zimbabweans became poorer still. The few 'beneficiaries' of land reform found themselves trapped on Maoist collectives that served only to make them even worse off.

No one emerges well from this catalogue of blunder and failure. Blaming Mugabe is not enough. What were the farmers and the donors, especially Britain, doing as resettlement schemes collapsed the length and breadth of Zimbabwe? The unfortunate answer is: very little. All of the powerful players thought they had a good deal. Mugabe was able to quote bogus figures for the number of people resettled, while ensuring that white farmers caused no trouble. The CFU leadership believed it was earning credit by supporting land reform and demonstrating its dedication to Zimbabwe. Britain was handing out enough money to keep the Lancaster House pledge, and while it was mainly wasted on failed, madcap schemes, the sums involved were too small to cause serious embarrassment. Everyone was happy, except those impoverished millions in the communal areas for whose benefit the whole exercise was supposedly intended.

This equilibrium survived, after a fashion, right up until the late 1990s. What happened to upset the balance? The British tired of handing out money that achieved nothing, save making poor people poorer. When the flow of funds for land reform dried up in 1995 and the newly elected Labour government refused to resume it, showing crass insensitivity into the bargain, Mugabe was enraged. One pillar of the equilibrium had collapsed by 1998.

Then in 2000 came the referendum defeat and the rise of the MDC. As we have seen, Mugabe was convinced that both were the work of white farmers, and by April 2000 they had ceased to be apolitical bystanders and became, in his words, 'enemies of Zimbabwe'. What rankled most was Mugabe's conviction that they were turning those 300,000 black workers against him. So the old bargain fell apart, to be replaced by a new, more sinister dispensation. Land reform now became inseparable from Mugabe's ruthless quest to hold power at whatever cost. He would crush the white farmers, and therefore, in his own mind, crush the MDC. And he would offer their land as a reward to his supporters. Mugabe's new battle-cry can be simply paraphrased: 'The white man is the enemy. Keep me in power and you will get his farms.'

★   ★   ★

And so the onslaught against white farmers began. In justification, Mugabe lost no opportunity to invoke those bitter folk memories of the wholesale theft of land by the pioneers back in the 1890s. He went out of his way to link the white farmers of today with the rapacious followers of Rhodes. 'They are the ones who succeeded the robbers of yesterday,' said Mugabe in a television interview. 'If you succeed the robbers of yesterday, you are no better than the robber.'[14]

Once again, the facts were not allowed to restrain the oratory. I never met a white farmer who owed his land to the largesse of Cecil Rhodes, as bequeathed by a great grandfather who rode with the pioneer column. Rarely did I meet a farmer who had possessed his property for longer than ten years. Over 80 per cent of white landowners had bought their farms since independence, under the laws of Zimbabwe. All they had in common with the original settlers was their skin colour, nothing more. Many were

179

not even of British origin. I have met white farmers whose ancestors were Greek, Italian and Afrikaner. Even the crudest form of retributive justice cannot demand that these people suffer because of the sins committed by a few thousand whites over a century ago. Yet in Mugabe's mind, the fate of black people in the 1890s justified the campaign against white farmers from 2000 onwards. There was a dreadful symmetry between what happened then and what would happen now.

As we have seen, the land invasions marked the first stage of the campaign. But with the election on the horizon, Mugabe moved towards the official seizure of white-owned farms. On 2 June, he filled seven pages of *The Herald* with a list of 804 farms identified for 'compulsory acquisition'. A target was set for the seizure of 5 million hectares of land.[15] Within three weeks of Zanu-PF surviving the election, 'Fast Track' resettlement began. The name of this scheme gave the game away. Back in 1992, Mugabe had passed a Land Acquisition Act that provided for the compulsory seizure of farms. But the procedure enshrined in this law was lengthy and cumbersome – a farm would have to be listed under Section 5, the owner served with an occupation order under Section 8 and then the whole matter would go to court before, finally, perhaps a year or two later, the farmer would get three months to pack up and leave.

This was too much for Mugabe. He wanted to evict his enemies and hand out their land on a 'Fast Track'. So he just grabbed the farms illegally and ignored the rules. Mugabe had, of course, supported the illegal invasion of white-owned land. Now he took the breakdown of the rule of law one step further and began the illegal confiscation of farms wholesale. What was the justification? Well, that was how those white people did it back in the 1890s. 'Where was the rule of law when our land was seized by the Rhodesians?'[16] Mugabe would ask rhetorically, with a gleam of triumph in his eyes. That was his trump card. The ghosts of the pioneers justified any act of plunder. I doubt if Mugabe or his minions ever realized the irony of this position. He was choosing to take his moral standards from, of all people, Cecil Rhodes. What was good enough for the greatest robber baron of the nineteenth century was, apparently, good enough for Mugabe.

To no one's surprise, the 'Fast Track' scheme did not proceed as planned. In theory, the local authorities would select a group of poor black people and take them to a white man's farm. For appearance's sake, this property should have been listed for seizure, so at least the first stage of the law was abided by. Then the new settlers would take over the land, till the fields with seed and fertilizer provided by their government, and support themselves happily ever after.

In fact, they would do better than feed themselves. If the Agriculture Ministry was to be believed, they would reap a bonanza and propel the whole country into an economic boom without parallel anywhere in Africa. In total, the festival of prosperity would add at least ZD 13.5 billion (then worth £225 million) to Zimbabwe's economy. National crop volumes would soar by 50 per cent. Agricultural exports would shoot up by 50 per cent. Maize and grain production would surge by 3.75 million tonnes. Even the national livestock herd would mysteriously expand by 2.1 million animals.[17]

What actually happened? A white farmer would find a convoy of perhaps a dozen government vehicles roaring on to his land. Often his property had never even been listed for seizure. About 40 or 50 people would gather on one of his fields, supervised by a local bigwig, sometimes the provincial Governor himself. Anyone who saw this happening would immediately notice that none of these people were particularly poor – they were usually well dressed and many possessed cars. A witness would hear the familiar melody of Zanu-PF songs and see the traditional, fist-waving denunciations of the MDC. Clearly these people were fans of Mugabe.

Then the local bigwig would make a show of handing out pieces of paper, on which plots of land were supposedly marked. Once the ceremony was over, the 40 or 50 settlers would fan out across the farm, sticking pegs in the ground, marking out their new home. The bigwig would inform the bemused farmer that his land had been 'Fast Tracked' and was now the property of the government. If the landowner was foolish enough to point out that this was illegal, he would be reminded of the activities of Cecil Rhodes and company. Then the new settlers would get on with creating the promised economic bonanza for Zimbabwe. Or perhaps not.

Usually, the farmer would wake up a day or two later and find that they had all disappeared. He would quietly revert to working as normal. Sometimes a hard core remained and would periodically shut down the farm with threats and assaults. They would besiege the odd homestead, assault the occasional landowner, wreck fences, burn crops, steal maize, vandalize storehouses and beat up the workers. All this was, of course, wearily familiar. The official 'Fast Tracking' of a farm was indistinguishable from an invasion by squatters. In fact, it was often led by the same bigwig who had organized the local farm invasions, using the same official vehicles.

In its early months, 'Fast Track' resettlement was done purely for show. Night after night, Dawcus Chibanda's gravelly tones would announce on the television news that another dozen farms had been resettled, accompanied by pictures of happy, prosperous people waving their fists. Visit one of these farms a few days later and everything would look entirely normal, without a settler in sight. Certain curiosities came into play. Some farmers found their land being 'Fast Tracked' several times over. When all the settlers disappeared, it became rather embarrassing, so the local bigwig would order a repeat performance, sometimes three or four times.

I had the great privilege of watching the 'Fast Tracking' of Insingisi farm near Bindura. It was a hazardous enterprise because the happy settlers were such fervent supporters of Zanu-PF that they appeared to believe all of Mugabe's rhetoric about the evils of the white man. Colin Taylor, the farmer, had rightly warned me not to approach them, but I foolishly decided to risk it. The crowd of 40 smartly dressed people (some of the men wore shiny leather jackets and Armani sunglasses) was not pleased to see me. I was surrounded by an angry group, perhaps a dozen strong, who shook me by the shoulder while muttering about the '*mabhunu*'. A ringleader stepped forward; he wore a baseball cap, dark glasses, smart blue jeans and a Mugabe T-shirt. 'Where are you from?' he roared.

Inspiration struck me. Without a moment's pause, I deadpanned: 'Norway.' This caused great consternation, the hands fell from my shoulders as the group discussed this remarkable piece of news. I heard 'Norway, Norway, Norway' being repeated by a dozen voices. People split into twos and threes, brows furrowed in concentration, discussing this strange word 'Norway'. I took the opportunity to turn and walk quietly to my car. The ringleader in dark glasses was not satisfied. He knew something was amiss. 'You say Norway?' he asked incredulously, as I retreated towards the car. 'Yes, Norway,' I replied. 'I'm a visitor and Zimbabwe is such a beautiful and safe country, isn't it?'

'Oh, of course, of course, it is only the British liars who say we are not.'

By this stage I was turning the key in the ignition and vowing never to watch the 'Fast Tracking' of a farm ever again.

From the safety of a parking place by the main road, I saw what happened next. The 40 people who had just been given land on Insingisi boarded their convoy of eight vehicles, most of them bearing Zanu-PF insignia, and roared next door to Pimento Park farm. Oliver Newton, the owner, told me that all had been given plots on his land as well. This became another curiosity of the 'Fast Track' scheme. Land on two or three different farms would be handed out to the same individuals. Presumably the local bigwigs couldn't find enough people to resettle all the farms they wanted to 'Fast Track'. Either that, or the settlers were bribing their way into collecting multiple plots of land.

From the government's point of view, everything was working out well. Sham, pretend resettlement was much faster and cheaper than the real thing. After four months, Joseph Made, the increasingly shameless Agriculture Minister, kept a straight face while claiming that 26,000 families, or 130,000 individuals, had been resettled on over 1.7 million hectares of land.[18] Presumably the lucky people I saw getting plots on both Insingisi and Pimento Park were counted twice (even though most disappeared from both properties within days). Presumably the combined acreage of both farms was counted as resettled, although everything continued much as normal.

The 'Fast Track' scheme was flawed on every conceivable level. Once again, the beneficiaries were not the impoverished masses of the communal areas; far from it. Farmers soon discovered that the people allocated their land were policemen, army officers, civil servants, local officials or nearby shopkeepers. Many of those fortunate enough to pick up plots on several different farms promptly sold them and made a fast buck. A farmer once drove me around the tiny town of Glendale, pointing out the businesses and smart cars owned by the dozen people on his farm.

Yet all the winners had one thing in common – they were supporters of Zanu-PF. The Mugabe model of land reform 'Fast Tracked' members of the black middle class with the correct political connections. The 7 million in the communal areas were, once again, ignored. In a way, this was quite fortunate, for the hapless individuals given land were offered no help whatever. No seed, fertilizer, training or finance came their way. It was, therefore, impossible for them to earn a living from the land and they were wholly reliant on their various other sources of income. Any genuinely poor people would have been left high and dry.

★   ★   ★

The ceremony on Vlakfontein farm ended as the sun began to sink and dark shadows lengthened across the veldt. When the settlers sang their joy, my scepticism had momentarily vanished, to be replaced by a faint feeling of guilt. These people were happy, they were getting their land, what was the problem? Perhaps Mugabe was right to brand British journalists as cynical onlookers, willing Zimbabwe to fail. But as I looked around, it was impossible to dismiss the verdict of common sense.

The ranch's 2,000 acres were a grandiose expanse of veldt: scenic, picturesque and utterly inhospitable. There was absolutely nothing there. The main road was reached after a ten-mile drive along a narrow, bumpy track. Travel another 40 miles and you arrived in Gweru, the nearest town. The 14 settlers were being offered no help or support whatever. They were being dumped on a desolate patch of dry grassland with no housing, water, seed or fertilizer, let alone schools, clinics or proper roads. Moreover, Vlakfontein had historically been a cattle ranch, for the very good reason that nothing but grass would grow in its parched soil. Only two of the settlers possessed any cattle; the rest would be demonstrably incapable of earning a living.

What kind of people were Vlakfontein's new inhabitants? Immediately after the ceremony, an autoelectrician from Gweru shook my hand and announced he had no intention of living on his newly acquired land. A clerk from the High Court admitted, in worried tones, that he had no farming experience whatsoever. None of the settlers were from the impoverished communal areas, and only two had ever lived off the land. They were former employees of a white farmer. Strangely enough, all were supporters of Zanu-PF. Dumping them on this land with no help or support could only end in disaster.

I made a point of returning to Vlakfontein two months after witnessing the handover. The veldt was still grandiose, scenic and almost completely empty. Only two of the settlers still lived on their newly acquired land. The rest had disappeared. Perhaps three or four appeared at weekends, when they rested from their jobs in Gweru by going hunting. Herds of impala that were scattered across the plain when I last visited had disappeared.

I met Otilia Hungwe, one of the remaining settlers. She sat beside a cooking fire outside her mud hut, a ragged blanket wrapped around her waist, while her three-year-old son, naked save for a torn T-shirt, played with bottle tops in the dust. She had 19 cows and managed to scratch a living with her husband and two children. I remembered Cephas Msipa's promise of 'clinics, roads, schools, proper houses and a good life' and asked whether anyone had given her family any help. Hungwe shook her head silently. No officials had even visited Vlakfontein since the handover. The place had simply been forgotten.

For almost three hours, I toured the empty wreck of a once-thriving cattle ranch. Paulos Viljoen, the former owner, once employed 15 workers and exported beef, earning hard currency for Zimbabwe. Now, nothing was happening and, in the final absurdity, all of those labourers had lost their jobs and homes. More people had been displaced than resettled. The losers out-numbered the 'winners' and the 'winners' either disappeared or lived in absolute poverty. With perverse genius, land reform Mugabe-style managed to create no real 'winners' at all. Everybody ended up losing. My feeling of foreboding at the end of the joyful ceremony two months earlier had been sadly vindicated.

Multiply the fate of Vlakfontein several thousand times over and you get an idea of the catastrophic consequences of this brand of land reform for Zimbabwe. By June 2001 about 90 per cent of white-owned farms had been listed to suffer the same. The engine of the whole economy was in the process of being disabled. Commercial farms provided, either directly or indirectly, about half of Zimbabwe's entire economy, 40 per cent of its export earnings, and homes and jobs for 300,000 families. All that was in the process of being swept aside, with nothing put in its place. Disaster was totally, completely predictable. In 1980 land reform was crucial in order to change for the better the indefensible situation that Mugabe had inherited. He proceeded to make everything far, far worse.

Notes and References

1 Quoted in Smith and Simpson, *Mugabe*, Sphere, London, 1981, p. 95. He was speaking at the abortive Geneva conference of October 1976.

2 Thomas Pakenham, *The Scramble for Africa*, Abacus, London, 1994, p. 498.

3 Angus Shaw, *Kandaya – Another Time, Another Place*, Baobab, Harare, 1993, p. 49.

4 Terence Ranger, *Peasant Consciousness and Guerrilla War in Zimbabwe*, Currey, London, 1985, p. 103.

5 *Ibid.*, p. 104. The figure of 425,000 assumes five people per family.

6 Doris Lessing, *The Old Chief Mshlanga* in *This Was the Old Chief's Country*, HarperCollins, London, 1994, p. 24.

7 *Ibid.*, pp. 24–5.

8 Anthony Verrier, *The Road to Zimbabwe*, Cape, London, 1986, p. 307.

9 DFID Background Briefing, *Land Resettlement in Zimbabwe*, March 2000.

10 Interview with the author, 28 March 2000.

11 See speech by Baroness Amos, House of Lords, *Hansard*, 12 December 2001. Britain actually provided £47 million and only £44 million was used.

12 For example, Jacobus de Wet, Zanu-PF MP for Kadoma West until 2000. Timothy Stamps, an appointed Zanu-PF MP and still in Mugabe's cabinet as Health Minister, owns a dairy farm near Mazowe.

13 Interview with the author, 19 November 2001.

14 ZBC interview, 10 February 2000.

15 Mugabe usually said he was 'only' taking 5 million of the '11 million hectares' owned by white farmers. Sometimes he claimed they owned '12 million'. I once heard him say '12 or 13 million'. Zanu-PF's election manifesto went for 13 million. As we have seen, the actual figure was 8.6 million hectares. The number 11 million was repeated endlessly but, like the famous 70 per cent figure (or 80 per cent on a good day), had no basis whatever.

16 He said this so often, it is scarcely worth providing a reference. Pedants can see his speech at the Zanu-PF Congress on 14 December 2000.

17 See Zanu-PF's parliamentary election manifesto, June 2000, pp. 18–19.

18 *The Herald*, 24 November 2000.

Chapter 10

Reconciliation Revoked

August–December 2000

> The national reconciliation policy we adopted in 1980 is threatened, gravely threatened, by the acts of the white settlers in this country and we shall revoke that national reconciliation, we shall revoke it. (Robert Mugabe, 25 October 2000)[1]

A heat haze shimmered over the crumbling pot-holes scarring a narrow road and danced on the tin roofs of the shacks. Twisted metal and boulders littered the ground, some piled together to form makeshift barricades. Black smoke curled from burning tyres, shards of broken glass glittered in the harsh glare of the sun and three street urchins huddled beside the gutter, eyes wide with fear. In every direction stood young men: thin, drawn, ragged and carrying stones. A few elderly women retreated hurriedly inside the ramshackle houses, casting terrified glances over their shoulders. Fearful faces peered through the windows of tightly packed, shabby homes. They ducked and disappeared when the staccato crack of exploding tear-gas canisters echoed from a few streets away.

Then, through the heat haze, a white police Land Rover roared into view, with its occupants leaning out of the windows. Lazily, as if following a boring routine, the officers hurled tear-gas canisters left, right and centre, lobbing the shining, hissing, metal circles at anyone they happened to pass. The Land Rover was a high-speed dispenser of noxious, stinging gas, and within seconds the street ahead was filled with billowing white clouds. As the vehicle hurtled towards us, the men armed with stones scattered in every direction. Figures dived over bushes and climbed through windows. I stood, rooted to the spot, transfixed by the sight of the speeding Land Rover leaving clouds in its wake.

An urgent voice beside me said: 'You must come this way, quick, quick.' One of the rioters was smiling and motioning with his arm. He held jagged bricks in both hands. I followed him without hesitation, as did my companions. We dashed down a narrow, muddy alley running between two shacks, escaping around a corner as the gas billowed behind and the Land Rover swept past. More car engines roared nearby and voices shouted orders, while booted feet pounded on the road. The riot police were unloading and pursuing their quarries on foot. 'No problem,' said the man with two bricks. 'They can't find us here.' We ran along another winding path, jumping over open sewers, racing past tumbledown walls and brushing against the yellow, wilting shoots of maize that grew between every shack. In one direction, a cloud of white floated upwards, obscuring clear blue sky.

We paused to catch our breath and the man with the bricks smiled broadly. His chest heaved and his brow glistened with beads of sweat. 'These ones, these police, they don't know this place. They can't find us. They can't stop us from doing this,' he said. By 'this', he meant rioting. In my dispatch later that day, I described people like him as 'stone-throwing youths'. Yet this rioter, like many others, could not have been more friendly. Curiously enough, we journalists often had little to fear from 'stone-throwing youths' – but the forces of law and order had to be avoided at all costs. Mugabe's police would take any chance to administer a good hiding to an 'enemy of Zimbabwe'.

The voices receded and the Land Rover engines revved once again. The police were moving off. With one street transformed into a gas chamber and a few baton charges complete, they were satisfied with their handiwork and heading to the next trouble-spot. There were plenty to choose from, for on 17 October Harare's ramshackle townships were rocked by a second day of rioting sparked by a 34 per cent rise in the price of bread. Almost every slum, from Mabvuku in the east to Dzivarasekwa in the west and Highfield in the south, was engulfed. Touring the townships with three colleagues, I found streets strewn with debris and filled by angry mobs.

After being shown an escape route by the man with two bricks in Ardbennie township, we had barely gone half a mile before hitting the next trouble-spot. Police had already lost control of Mbare by the time we arrived and even the lightning dashes of the tear-gas dispensing Land Rovers had become too dangerous. Mobs blocked the streets around Rufaro stadium and Mbare Musika, the bus station and market forming the hub of southern Harare, was a no-go area.

On Remembrance Drive I watched from a distance of a few hundred yards as a gang of 20 stoned any car foolish enough to drive past. Boulders had been rolled across the road to form a primitive barricade in the shadow of Rufaro's terraces, although a skilled driver could still weave his way to safety. A yellow car swerved violently as a brick shattered its windscreen and a volley of stones rained on to the bonnet and roof. Lurching to a halt, the dazed and disoriented driver partially opened his door. Five men surrounded him and wrenched open the door, seizing the car's radio and grabbing the man's bag. He abandoned his vehicle and fled. His running figure was soon lost amid the tangled maze of shacks and tiny, tin-roofed houses.

The next victim was not so fortunate. The driver of a white pick-up was brought screeching to a halt by the same method, with stones smashing his windscreen. He was dragged out of his seat, flung to the ground and beaten by the roadside, while the mob set about looting the vehicle. All this I watched from a distance of about 300 yards, together with a small crowd of frightened people. I wondered why we seemed to be relatively safe and then realized that we stood at the gates of a run-down police station. No officers were in sight, but nonetheless, the building appeared to afford some protection.

The crowd around me cried out with alarm as people were beaten and robbed a stone's throw away. When a few cars managed to dodge the barricade and run the gauntlet of hails of bricks, they whistled and clapped with admiration. But none had any doubt about where they stood on this chaotic day. They stood with the rioters. One man in his twenties shook his head with disgust as the man in the pick-up was robbed. He was smartly dressed in neat, blue overalls and introduced himself as Isaac Mupandawana. 'This food rioting is a protest against these price rises. Food, bus fares, cost of living, all are going up and we cannot cope any more. What people are calling for is complete change,' he told me.

'So you think the riots are justified?' I asked.

'Yes, these will continue until Mugabe goes. He must go. We have nothing to eat, we are suffering and he wants to stay in power for ever. What kind of man wants to stay in power for ever? He is evil. That one must just go. I don't want even to see him.'

As he spoke, Mupandawana's voice rose with passion and his clenched fist beat against his open palm. He worked as a mechanic in a garage in central Harare, but would not be going to work today. 'None of us are working today. Everybody is staying at home. It is not safe to go to work while these troubles are happening,' he said. Almost every shop in every township was closed and barricaded with metal shutters. The few who were lucky enough to have jobs were being prevented from going to work, yet their support for the rioters was unhesitating, and everybody, absolutely everybody I talked with, linked the unrest with one simple demand – Mugabe must go.

But the forces of law and order had other ideas. As we left Mbare, a military helicopter clattered overhead, flying at a height of no more than 100 feet. Later, it dropped tear-gas canisters on the crowds below, an aerial bombardment that filled whole townships with noxious, billowing clouds. Large doses of tear gas can be fatal for young children and at least one baby was killed by suffocation as the helicopter hovered over the streets, carpet-bombing the rebellious poor of Harare with vicious canisters.

On the following day, 18 October, police formally announced that they had lost control and the army was deployed in the townships. They set about dealing with the rioters in typically ruthless fashion. Several hundred soldiers wearing the red berets of the Parachute Regiment and armed with clubs, whips and batons swept through the streets of Dzivarasekwa, Mufakose and Kuwadzana. Everyone who crossed their path was assaulted.

At about 10 a.m. I spoke to Richard Mulindwa, my regular taxi driver, who was cowering inside his home in Dzivarasekwa. 'These soldiers are beating everyone who moves around, we are just staying at home and hiding,' he said. 'These army guys are like the war vets, they are just *tsotsis* now. Look at these people, it's terrible. This one, Mugabe, he must go, he must just go.' For the first time, I heard Richard sound worried. In broad daylight, he was forced to huddle inside his house with his three children – hiding not from rioters but from soldiers supposedly charged with keeping the peace.

Later, troops began dragging Richard's neighbours out of their homes for beatings. A three-year-old boy was severely injured when a rifle butt was plunged into his face. As they did their brutal work, soldiers shouted: 'We are beating you for voting MDC, we are going to beat everyone who is MDC.' As I heard reports of this sort from all over southern Harare, everything suddenly fell into place. The military operation was designed to punish an MDC stronghold and wreak vengeance on those who had dared vote against Mugabe during the election, as much as to crush the riots. The 'stone-throwing youths' had afforded an excuse for the government to take revenge on the urban poor. Whole families were being assaulted in the streets.

An hour after 100 soldiers had rampaged through Kuwadzana township, I found myself among its teeming shacks. Barricades had been cleared from the roads and no mobs of youths were visible. Instead, bewildered people huddled together, with fear written over their faces. The atmosphere of shock reminded me of the aftermath of the 1 April riot, only this time an attack by fully trained troops had been endured.

Margaret Mujuru stood outside her tiny home with tears running down her face. She was in her forties, dressed in a thin, red dress and a five-year-old boy wearing only a pair of ragged shorts clung to her legs. She sobbed softly, while holding her head in her hands. As another woman placed a consoling palm on Mujuru's shoulder, she told me in halting tones what had happened. Her 18-year-old son, Simbarashe, had been in the street when the soldiers came. 'They beat him with sticks. He was just here, doing nothing. They beat him. Then they put him in a lorry and took him away,' she said. Other young men had disappeared from Kuwadzana. After being selected, seemingly at random, soldiers threw them into trucks. A few hundred yards away, another mother cried noisily and a cluster of small children sobbed by the side of the road. Fearful faces hovered at the windows of the houses. Kuwadzana had not seen the worst of the rioting – far from it – but over 78 per cent of its people voted MDC in the election. Nothing else mattered.

Among the other victims of the army were four of my colleagues. Vincent Murwira, a presenter from the South African Broadcasting Corporation and Peter Maringisanwa, his cameraman, visited Dzivarasekwa with Rob Cooper and Chris Mazivanhanga, photographers from Associated Press. Over 30 soldiers forced them to the ground and beat them with whips and clubs, leaving them covered in bruises and vivid, red weals. The army was clearly anxious that no one should witness or report its violence.

The riots should not have come as a surprise. Zimbabwe's economic crisis had turned Harare's townships into combustible powder kegs. Most people were jobless and destitute, and inflation, then running at 55 per cent, ensured that basic essentials grew more expensive by the day. Life was becoming impossible and, in retrospect, it is remarkable that the grinding hardships did not spill over into rioting more frequently. Yet the sub-text of all this was plain: since the people of Harare's crushing rejection of Zanu-PF in the election, the regime saw them as the enemy. The first sign of unrest would be used as a pretext for general punishment. Margaret Mujuru's son was one of countless victims.

★   ★   ★

The vicious response to the October riots delivered a message that was unmistakable and devastating – Mugabe may have scraped through the election and held control over parliament, but nothing would return to normal. To my surprise, credulous Harare diplomats, a few naïve farmers and even some journalists had spent the pre-election period claiming that everything would miraculously come right after polling day. They predicted that, with victory in the bag, Mugabe would send conciliatory signals to the rest of the world, clear the farms of squatters, conclude a deal with the IMF and generally restore common sense. Eric Bloch, a Bulawayo economist who attacked Mugabe week after week in his column for the *Zimbabwe Independent,* became the unlikely high priest of this school of thought. Three days before the election, he assured me that an 'economic recovery' would start by the end of 2000. Bloch forecast that Zimbabwe would be back on terms with the IMF by September. 'Everything that is being said and done now is for the sole purpose of winning the election. Once that is accomplished, the situation will change completely,' he said.[2]

I sensed that many Zimbabweans clung desperately to this optimism because the alternative – more repression and accelerating economic collapse – did not bear thinking about. The alternative was what they got. In Mugabe's mind, the election was not a signal for him to relax, ease the pressure and restore normality. On the contrary, it was a further startling display of the strength of the MDC and a call to arms for a renewed offensive against his opponents. Moreover, there was another election on the horizon, one with immeasurably higher stakes. A presidential poll would have to take place by 1 April 2002, deciding Mugabe's future once and for all. With the June contest over, he turned his mind to the next hurdle and firmly kept the heat on his perceived enemies.

White farmers faced yet more pressure. In the ten days after the election, another 30 farms were invaded, raising the number under chaotic occupation to 1,150. The daily litany of squatter violence continued. Police made no attempt to curb the usual round of crimes – theft, vandalism, arson, assaults on black workers. One of the most odious incidents of the entire crisis occurred on the night of 5 August when a gang of 20 squatters raided a school on Blackfordby farm, ten miles south of Harare. Seventeen children, all aged between 12 and 14, were kidnapped and dragged, frightened and screaming, to a squatter camp. The mob toted axes, knives and handguns and they fired two shots over the heads of their terrified captives. Once at the camp, the children were forced to dance and chant all the familiar slogans: '*Pamberi ne* Mugabe, *pamberi ne* Zanu-PF.' Yet the real purpose of the abduction soon became clear – the ten girls were singled out and sexually harassed by drunken squatters.

Police arrived on the scene within two hours of the kidnapping, but were in no hurry to free the children. Only after they had suffered a three-and-a-half-hour ordeal, much of it in the presence of police officers, were the captives finally released. But in the final humiliation, the squatters demanded that their parents, all of them farm workers, surrender in return. With no intervention from the police, who appear to have agreed to this request, these terrified people were held at the squatter camp overnight, forced to chant the slogans of Zanu-PF and severely beaten.

A teacher at Blackfordby's school recounted this to me in a halting, fearful voice. He was too afraid to give his name, or even meet me in person. A snatched conversation on a crackling phone line was all he could risk. When he had finished his description, the man said: 'I am in hiding, I cannot go home. I cannot believe what is happening here, even our children are not safe. The police are not helping us. There is nothing we can do.' Then his voice faded away and the phone line was cut off. I never spoke to this man again, or discovered his name.

★   ★   ★

Like a hapless politician charged with mediating peace talks in the Middle East, Tim Henwood, President of the CFU, had a good claim to having the worst job in the world. A tall, heavily built, fair-haired figure, he looked and sounded like a typical white farmer. Yet he was more ebullient, personable and optimistic than most and managed, despite everything, to remain resolutely upbeat. Henwood vested all hope in the belief that the land invasions would stop after the election. He told farmers that polling day would mark the end of their long ordeal. When it came and went and Mugabe showed no sign of calling off the mobs, Henwood was reduced to issuing plaintive statements saying: 'Invasions, threats and violence have escalated, and the situation on farms is untenable . . . it may soon become impossible for farming operations to continue nation-wide.'[3]

If more proof was required, Mugabe showed once again that he was utterly impossible to deal with. Henwood could not forget the assurances given by the President on 17 April, immediately after the murder of David Stevens, and casually broken less than 24 hours later. It was now Thabo Mbeki's turn to receive the same treatment. On 2 August, the South African leader arrived in Harare for a full day of talks with Mugabe.

Mbeki's agenda was clear. Turmoil in Zimbabwe was still pushing down the Rand and frightening international investors away from South Africa. Enough was enough, the election was out of the way, it was time for order and normality to be restored. During a meeting held in the Sheraton hotel, Mugabe duly gave him the assurances he sought. Land reform would happen within the law, with the 'war veterans' removed from all farms that had not been listed for resettlement. Mugabe would look favourably upon an initiative announced by the United Nations Development Programme (UNDP) that aimed to resolve the land problem in a consensual, orderly fashion, with the co-operation of donor countries.

Afterwards, the two presidents sat side by side and faced the press together. Mugabe told us: 'We will be removing the war veterans from the farms we are not resettling.' He added that this would happen 'within the next month'.[4] Countless television news programmes showed Mugabe saying these crucial words. Even *The Herald*, his faithful propaganda broadsheet, chose to carry them on its front page, placed in bold type for emphasis. Mbeki left for South Africa satisfied with his handiwork. The summit had not only yielded a private guarantee, but Mugabe had followed this up with a public declaration. Mbeki could not have asked for more.

Yet on the very next day, Mugabe loftily contradicted himself. In a speech to the Zimbabwe Farmers' Union, he said: 'I didn't say the war veterans should be removed.'[5] As for the idea of the UNDP leading a donors' initiative to resolve the land question, Mugabe appeared infuriated by the very suggestion. 'We can never allow a return to racial oppression. Our land is to us first. The donors can stay with their money,' he declared. 'We will not give up our land because of what the donors say.'[6]

Mbeki had been casually humiliated. No undertaking from Mugabe could be relied upon, for the simple reason that if it proved inconvenient, he was capable of convincing himself that he had, in fact, said the very opposite. The stark lesson of the Harare summit was that talking with Mugabe was a waste of everyone's time. He appeared to inhabit a parallel universe, where words lacked any meaning and reality could always be denied.

Henwood had already learned this lesson the hard way and, even before the fruitless summit with the South Africans, he appeared to have been goaded beyond endurance. On 25 July he decided to place all the pressure he could on Mugabe. In a brief burst of decisiveness, Henwood made a series of announcements. The patently illegal, 'Fast Track' resettlement programme would be challenged in the courts. Henwood was taking the unprecedented step of personally petitioning Mugabe to restore law and order. And he went further by declaring that, for the first time in its history, the CFU would support a general strike.

Closing down every pillar of the economy was the sole weapon in the hands of Mugabe's opponents. Thrust together by their shared opposition to the government, white farmers and black workers had this one and only means of retaliation. Moreover, when the terror campaign outlasted the election and continued regardless, the MDC and what passed for civil society in Zimbabwe were confronted with a crucial test. Would they respond or lie down and take it? How much more could Mugabe get away with? Prompted by the MDC, the Zimbabwe Congress of Trade Unions (ZCTU) began discussing a general strike at the end of July. Back in 1997 and 1998, Tsvangirai had used his leadership of the ZCTU to paralyse the country and wring concessions from Mugabe. Many hoped that history would repeat itself.

Yet by mid-2000 everything had changed. The tension was so great that, put bluntly, many trade unionists were too afraid to challenge the government. You could get away with that in 1998, but no longer. The dangers of opposition had been demonstrated beyond any doubt. So the ZCTU decided to remain undecided. The General Council of union leaders held a series of inconclusive meetings before, finally, it resolved to call a general strike for three days, starting on 2 August. This decision was reported around the world and Henwood offered the CFU's full support.

But at the last minute, the ZCTU leadership developed cold feet and resolved to scale down the stoppage to a single day. Unfortunately, no one remembered to announce which day had been chosen. Many white farmers were still prepared for a three-day strike and never learned of the change of plan. The Confederation of Zimbabwe Industries, which had tacitly backed the strikes of 1997 and 1998, came out against the action. It was all a mess. Confronted with this huge challenge, the ZCTU succeeded in giving the impression that it couldn't even organize people to do nothing for a day. In the event, a half-hearted strike took place on 2 August, joined by most farms and businesses, and made no impact whatsoever.

But Mugabe seized the opportunity to punish his opponents for their impertinence. On 31 July, the state press announced that another 2,237 white-owned farms had been identified for seizure, bringing the total in Mugabe's sights to 3,041. This move was in direct retaliation for Henwood's decision to back a general strike and launch legal action against 'Fast Track' land seizures. What was the CFU's response? On 10 August, Henwood caved in, withdrew the court challenge and blandly assured farmers that he was seeking 'meaningful dialogue' with the government.[7] The new mood of defiance had lasted for precisely 16 days. Dialogue, meaningful or otherwise, never happened and the expanded list of farms earmarked for seizure remained in force.

Defiance invites retaliation and the CFU had a powerful case for doing nothing. Alternatively, Henwood's only option was to take firm action, exert pressure on Mugabe and hope for victory in the long run. There were arguments either for action or inaction. But there was no case for choosing both. Resistance followed by immediate retreat could only bring disaster. By adopting this uniquely pointless course, Henwood achieved the worst of both worlds. He soon came to admit this and demands from ordinary farmers eventually led him to execute yet another U-turn: on 6 September he restored the legal challenge.

Did the MDC perform any better? Tsvangirai made no secret of his frustration with the CFU and believed Henwood was letting Zimbabwe down by failing to make a stand against Mugabe. In private, Tsvangirai could scarcely contain his contempt for white farmers who complained endlessly about their lot but did nothing to change things. So his aides quietly assured me that something big was in the wind. All through July, August and September, senior MDC figures took me aside and said that a showdown was approaching. Mugabe's days on the throne were, apparently, numbered. Christmas 2000 was repeatedly mentioned as the deadline for ousting him. The MDC would bang heads together and force the CFU and the ZCTU to raise their game, so that Mugabe really felt the heat. 'Mass action', a dramatic phrase beloved of the opposition, was on the verge of being launched. I was eventually briefed that Tsvangirai would put his bold plan on the record and I interviewed him on 29 September.

As usual, he was energetic, articulate and impressive. He was also angrier than I had ever seen him. Tsvangirai banged his fist on the table as he told me: 'We cannot afford Mugabe for one day longer, let alone until 2002. The objective of our action is very clear. It is to say to Mugabe, "You have become a national liability, this country is suffering because of your reckless-ness. We are not going to sit by and watch Zimbabwe go down the drain. We are going to take action to get rid of you."'

Mass action, in the form of a general strike and round-the-clock demon-strations would therefore be launched. The idea was to shut down Zimbabwe for as long as it took. Only when Mugabe threw in the towel and resigned would Tsvangirai relent. 'It's going to be massive, it's going to be countrywide and, for the first time, it's going to be in the rural areas,' he assured me. 'This is the moment. If we miss this historic opportunity, we would betray the people. Mugabe must go by Christmas. This time there is no compromise, no going back. It's either him or us.'[8]

Nothing happened. Absolutely nothing. To coin a phrase, Tsvangirai missed this historic opportunity and betrayed the people. By my count, he promised in public no fewer than 16 times that 'mass action' would be launched. But it was all hot air. The MDC were not serious. In reality, no one had the will to challenge Mugabe in this uniquely risky fashion. Yet by raising expectations only for them to be dashed, Tsvangirai damaged his credibility. Why did he make pledges which he had no intention of keeping? Why exactly did he use such expansive language in his interview with me, earning the *Daily Telegraph* headline 'General Strikes call to Topple Mugabe'? I will never know. I am forced to the conclusion that he didn't mean a word of it and spoke only for effect. In other words, Tsvangirai was in the business of cheap posturing, while his country fell apart.

This tendency was on full display in Rufaro stadium on 30 September, when he addressed a rally marking the first anniversary of the founding of the MDC. Tsvangirai told a cheering crowd of 25,000 that 'the time for mass action is now'. Then he added: 'What we say to Mugabe is "Please go peacefully. If you don't want to go peacefully, we will remove you vio-lently."'[9] With these words, Tsvangirai handed Mugabe a propaganda gift. In one sentence, he called into question the MDC's commitment to peaceful, democratic change, dismayed many of his closest allies and gave the government an excuse to arrest him at any time. Within days, the authorities had announced that Tsvangirai would be charged with 'incite-ment to violence' and this accusation was kept hanging over his head, like the sword of Damocles. It was a self-inflicted wound, betraying Tsvangirai's faults as a politician.

By September 2000 the depressing and inescapable truth was that Mugabe's opponents had failed the test posed by his repression. The CFU had managed to display both defiance and cravenness, incurring the penalties of both and the advantages of neither. The ZCTU had demonstrated that it was incapable of organizing a strike, which is, in the last resort, the only function of a trade union movement. And Tsvangirai had shown that he would say almost anything for effect. By his actions since the election, Mugabe had effectively asked: 'Are you going to stand up to me or lie down and take it?' The unpalatable reply was, on balance: 'We will lie down and take it.'

★ ★ ★

Cries of outrage and howls of abuse rose from the green benches. Men in suits waved their fists and shouted threats while the Speaker, clad in flowing black robes, called unavailingly for order. The furious storm continued, with jeers and cheers merging into a single, thunderous sound. It was the noise of heated debate, something never heard before in Zimbabwe's parliament.

The presence of 57 MPs from the MDC had transformed the atmosphere of the small debating chamber and Zanu-PF heavyweights were finding it hard to adjust to the presence of a parliamentary opposition. Many found it impossible to discard the habit of occupying the benches reserved for the opposition, on the left of the Speaker's chair, as they had done in the years when Zanu-PF held all but two seats. Vice-President Joseph Msika would usually lumber over to the opposition front bench and plonk himself down amid the MDC leadership, in a vainglorious attempt to pretend that his opponents did not exist. Yet on the afternoon of 25 October, they made their presence felt. After months of inactivity and Tsvangirai's empty threats about 'mass action', the opposition finally came up with a challenge to Mugabe. They sought nothing less than his impeachment and removal from office by parliament.

The audacity of the MDC left Zanu-PF speechless with rage. Jonathan Moyo's voice rose an octave when I spoke to him about the impeachment motion. 'Why are you even asking me about that? We will treat this motion with the contempt it deserves,' he said, while my mobile phone vibrated with his anger. That an opposition could demand Mugabe's removal from office was something beyond Zimbabwe's experience. To Zanu-PF loyalists, it was little short of sacrilege. You could see that on the faces of the MPs packed on the government benches as the MDC introduced its motion. Gibson Sibanda, parliamentary leader of the opposition, handed the Speaker the motion demanding Mugabe's ejection from office for 'gross misconduct' and 'wilful violation of the constitution'. Sibanda demanded impeachment proceedings 'in terms of section 29 of the constitution which provides for the removal of the President of Zimbabwe'. Those words provoked the howl of outrage from his opponents.

When the Speaker called for order, he did so while clad in a wig and flowing, black robes. He looked upon a golden mace and glittering dispatch boxes, resting on a table between ranks of green benches. Near the entrance to the chamber was a vast portrait of Queen Elizabeth II, encased in a golden frame. After two decades of independence and fierce denunciations of the colonial era, Zimbabwe's parliament was, and remains, completely, utterly British. Everything about the place, from the portraits of bewigged Speakers lining the walls to the Serjeant-at-Arms clad in buckles and braces, was steeped in the atmosphere of Westminster. Now the chamber even had cat-calls and jeers to complete the effect.

After provoking uproar, Sibanda sat down and, in theory, impeachment proceedings against Mugabe began from that moment. Outside, a crowd of 300 Zanu-PF loyalists (many of them squatters brought from occupied farms) mounted a noisy demonstration. They carried professionally printed banners reading 'WE SUPPORT OUR PRESIDENT', 'NO TO THE MOVEMENT FOR DESTRUCTION AND CHAOS' and, bizarrely, 'NO MACROECONOMICS, YES MICROECONOMICS.' Quite why this last slogan was chosen remained a mystery. In the corridors of parliament, all of Mugabe's allies had been assembled. The entire cabinet was dragged along in a show of support. It suddenly struck me that the occasion made Zimbabwe look like a proper, functioning democracy.

This was, of course, an illusion. Under the constitution, one-third of MPs could begin impeachment proceedings and force the establishment of a committee to investigate charges against the President. Yet removing Mugabe required the votes of two-thirds of the house, something the MDC, with 57 members out of 150, would never achieve. Moreover, the Speaker wearing his wig and gown was none other than Emmerson Mnangagwa. The arch-Mugabe-loyalist, booted out of parliament after being defeated amid appalling violence in his constituency of Kwe Kwe, had made a remarkable comeback. Mugabe ensured that his loyal disciple became Speaker of the very parliament from which the electorate had expelled him. It required a certain ingenuity to get someone who was no longer even an MP elected to this position but, thanks to the docile herd on the Zanu-PF backbenches, this was achieved.

Mnangagwa duly repaid his master by ensuring that the MDC's impeach-ment motion went nowhere. He was quite open about his intentions. Barely five days after its introduction, he told state television: 'MDC is not going to succeed in removing Mugabe from power and they know that.'[10] In accor-dance with the rules, Mnangagwa appointed a committee of MPs to consider the MDC's charges against Mugabe. He then ensured that it never held a single meeting. The MDC's bid to remove the President was carefully sabotaged from the outset by the supposedly neutral umpire on the Speaker's throne.

Yet from the MDC's perspective, it served its purpose. The opposition showed they could hit back and turn the heat on Mugabe for a change. But the risk was that Mugabe would be goaded to even greater heights of repression. A few hours before the impeachment motion came before parliament, Mugabe addressed a rally of supporters at Zanu-PF headquarters. He was incandescent with rage. He decided that the bid to remove him from office had been inspired by the MDC's white MPs, notably David Coltart, and lashed out accordingly. In a few sentences, Mugabe repudiated the very foundation of independent Zimbabwe, namely the official policy of racial reconciliation. Waving his right arm for emphasis, Mugabe said:

> The national reconciliation policy we adopted in 1980 is threatened, gravely threatened, by the acts of the white settlers in this country and we shall revoke that national reconciliation, we shall revoke it. We will proceed to revoke it and Ian Smith and the whites who participated in the massacre and genocide of our people, those whites who fought against us will be brought to trial . . . we will look for all those who fought on the side of Ian Smith, wherever they are in this country they must be arrested . . . the MDC will never ever run this country because they are used by whites.[11]

Mugabe did not act on his furious words. Smith happened to be in Britain at the time and the old Rhodesian returned, unmolested, to Zimbabwe a fortnight later. The significance of this episode lies in the picture it gives of Mugabe's fevered mind. To him, any stirrings of opposition were the work of sinister, unreconstructed Rhodesians, aiming to reverse Zimbabwe's independence. There were two corollaries of this position – any means could be used to fight this threat and Mugabe would have to stay in office until it was defeated once and for all. Far from being the climax of the struggle for power, the parliamentary election had been nothing more than a stage in its escalation.

★   ★   ★

Inside the tiny, ornate courtroom, the row of judges listened attentively. They wore grey wigs and flowing, black robes, complete with winged collars, yet if they felt any discomfort in the stifling heat of the African summer, they did not show it. On the contrary, all five judges listened with rapt attentiveness, leaning forward, their eyes narrowed and brows creased with concentration. Occupying a throne at the centre of the row, flanked by two colleagues on each side, was Anthony Gubbay, the Chief Justice. Under his leadership, the Supreme Court was hearing the most wide-ranging case yet brought by Zimbabwe's white farmers.

An artist who wished to capture a single instant that illuminated the conflict between Mugabe and his white opponents would have done well to choose 10 a.m. on 6 November, the moment when Adrian de Bourbon rose in the Supreme Court to represent the Commercial Farmers' Union. A senior white lawyer stood before the white Chief Justice and pleaded the case for white farmers, speaking in legalistic English, in a setting suffused with colonial tradition. For Mugabe and his followers, this symbolized everything that was unacceptable in Zimbabwe.

After 20 years of independence, the ultimate fate of white farmers still appeared to rest in the hands of an elderly white man, wearing a wig and robes, who collected stamps in his spare time and held an honorary fellowship at Jesus College, Cambridge. Whenever I watched Gubbay preside over the Supreme Court, I was filled with admiration and wonder. Admiration because every softly spoken word he uttered and every movement of his wise, bewigged head, was redolent with integrity and good sense. Wonder because it seemed unbelievable that such a creature could still hold high office in Mugabe's Zimbabwe. Gubbay was a glorious, inexplicable anachronism.

Born in Manchester in 1932, Gubbay emigrated to Rhodesia in 1958, after leaving Jesus College, Cambridge. I was not surprised to learn that he was President of the Oxford and Cambridge Society of Zimbabwe. He first sat as a judge during the Rhodesian era, yet Gubbay earned a reputation for being liberal and compassionate and clearly made a favourable impression on Mugabe. He elevated Gubbay to the Supreme Court in 1983 and made him Chief Justice in 1990.

When the CFU brought its appeal before the court, it fell to Gubbay and his four colleagues to hear the case. In essence, the farmers wanted the entire 'Fast Track' resettlement programme declared illegal. They pointed out that farms were being seized in defiance of the procedures laid down in the Land Acquisition Act and the government did not trouble to contest this fact. On 10 November the Supreme Court issued a landmark ruling and gave the CFU everything it wanted. The judges declared that the 'Fast Track' land seizures were unlawful and 'contravened the fundamental rights of the owners'. This order was granted with the consent of the government, as represented by Bharat Patel, the deputy Attorney-General. Thus Mugabe's regime put its name to a document declaring its flagship land policy to be illegal.

Did this make any difference? Of course not. Mugabe was beyond the stage where the law could influence him. A steady drumbeat of official propaganda had already prepared the ground for the government to simply press ahead with the seizure of farms, in open defiance of the law, just as the High Court orders demanding an end to the land invasions had been contemptuously swept aside. 'CALLING ON ALL PATRIOTS!' began a full-page advertisement carried in the state press on the day before the Supreme Court hearing. 'Say enough is enough. Put a stop to the madness. Say no to their arrogant abuses. This land is your land. Don't let them use the courts and the constitution against the masses.'[12] Gubbay was singled out for vilification and banners reading 'IMPEACH THE CHIEF JUSTICE, NOT OUR PRESIDENT' began appearing at Zanu-PF rallies. All this was carefully organized and the fell hand of Jonathan Moyo, appointed Information Minister in July, was clearly at work.

Because Gubbay was white, Moyo's task was made far easier. Mugabe's chief propagandist began by insinuating in the official press that Gubbay was a fake Zimbabwean and a covert Briton. 'Is he a British (*sic*) or a Zimbabwean?' Moyo demanded to know of Gubbay. 'He certainly cannot be both. And so the question must be answered to the full satisfaction of the nation as a matter of urgency . . . if this is not done, the Zimbabwean body politic will remain with a clear and present danger, a legal cancer or virus.'[13] New banners were hastily printed for Zanu-PF loyalists to wave: 'GUBBAY IS A FOREIGNER' and 'SAY NO TO RHODESIAN JUDGES.'

Language like this called into question the legitimacy of the entire Supreme Court and, after the striking down of 'Fast Track' land seizures, it was portrayed as a central part of the great imperialist conspiracy working to overthrow Mugabe. That the offending ruling had been granted with the consent of the government was conveniently forgotten. Instead, the propaganda fed on the composition of the Supreme Court bench, which might have been tailored to fuel Mugabe's paranoia. Nicholas McNally, another white, and Ahmed Ebrahim, an Asian, sat on Gubbay's right and left respectively. Wilson Sandura and Simbarashe Muchechetere, the two black judges, occupied the outer edges of the bench. To Mugabe this symbolized the balance of power on the court. The two whites sat at the centre and obviously called the shots. All the other judges were their puppets. Thus another Zanu-PF banner soon appeared: 'SANDURA IS A PUPPET OF THE WHITES.'

This was, of course, insulting nonsense. All of the judges were eminent lawyers with independent minds and it was ludicrous to suppose that they were in Gubbay's pocket. But logical analysis had never been Mugabe's strong point and, in his mind, with its judgement on the land issue, the Supreme Court became his enemy.

Hence its ruling was not only ignored, the government revelled in defying the law. In the two days after the 'Fast Track' programme was struck down, another 50 farms were promptly 'Fast Tracked', including one belonging to Tim Henwood. Mugabe appeared on television and declared: 'Whatever the courts might say on the matter, the land is ours and we will take it.'[14] The Zanu-PF leadership clearly decided that a dramatic gesture was needed to show their utter contempt for Gubbay and they decided to treat his court like a white-owned farm.

On 24 November a mob of 200 'war veterans' massed outside the Supreme Court's tiny, colonial era building in central Harare. They were led by Joseph Chinotimba, the notorious, squinting, gap-toothed rabble rouser, who called himself 'commander in chief of white farm invasions'. By now, Chinotimba had added to his list of distinctions – he was awaiting trial for attempted murder, after allegedly shooting his next-door neighbour for being an MDC supporter. His gang was allowed to surge into the ornate courtroom, chanting 'Zimbabwe is for the blacks' and waving placards reading 'IMPEACH THE CHIEF JUSTICE'. Gubbay and his colleagues had been about to make their entrance and they were forced to retreat to their chambers while the mob danced on the bench, roaring: 'Kill the judges.' Their other cry was 'Mugabe makes the law, not the courts.' Journalists and lawyers inside the courtroom were jostled and abused and proceedings were delayed for more than an hour.

The Supreme Court is located inside a high security zone, surrounded by government ministries. Chinotimba's latest invasion had plainly been organized by the authorities, and it showed, in Gubbay's later words: 'Absolute contempt for the institution of the courts as the third essential organ of a democratic government'. With typical understatement, Gubbay added: 'Disappointingly, there was no official condemnation of the incident. Not a word was heard from the Minister of Justice.'[15] The invasion of the Supreme Court was the clearest possible demonstration that Mugabe would unleash his mobs on anyone foolish enough to stand in his way.

By contrast, those who supported him would be handsomely rewarded. I was not surprised to learn that Chakwana Mueri, alias Comrade Jesus, the warlord of Karoi, had been mysteriously released from custody in October. Those charges of murder and 'public violence' arising from his leadership of Zanu-PF's murderous sweep through Kariba in April had been quietly dropped. The short, stocky, cap-wearing ringleader was a free man and, doubtless, a comfortable and affluent one. For his part in Zanu-PF's election campaign, Comrade Jesus had been rewarded with a tobacco farm near Karoi. By early November he was in possession of Childerley farm, one of the first to be invaded by squatters. Slim Botha, its previous owner, had died of a heart attack after being forced to abandon his home in the face of constant threats. Comrade Jesus, the man responsible for eradicating the MDC in Kariba, controlled Childerley's 1,000 acres. I thought of the shattered bodies of his victims, lying in the hospital overlooking the lake, and shuddered.

It was not only Comrade Jesus who escaped justice for the pre-election terror campaign. On 10 October Mugabe issued an amnesty that pardoned everyone involved in political violence between January and July. None of his followers needed to fear any retribution for the litany of crimes they had committed. Although murder was excluded from the amnesty, this was irrelevant since few of the 37 political killings recorded before the election were being investigated anyway. Mugabe had put in place a clear calculus of risk and reward. If you opposed him, you risked being attacked by a mob, even if you happened to be Chief Justice. If you supported him and showed your dedication by assaulting his opponents, you would be rewarded with the white man's land and protected by an amnesty. Every Zimbabwean knew where they stood.

★   ★   ★

By the end of 2000, Mugabe seemed possessed by a compulsion to show, over and over again, that he would never relinquish power and stop at nothing to crush his opponents. Another white farmer was murdered on 12 December, the sixth since April. Henry Elsworth, 70, was killed in a carefully planned ambush that also left his son, Ian, critically wounded.

The two had been driving across their land on Kwekwe farm shortly after nightfall, when they found a gate unexpectedly closed across their path. When Ian Elsworth stepped out of the car to clear the obstacle, a storm of automatic gunfire began. He was hit in the left arm and right leg and fell to the ground. As the car was raked with bullets from three separate firing positions, Henry Elsworth pulled his wounded son inside the vehicle. Although hit in the wrist and chest, the old man managed to stagger around the car to the driver's side, with the aim of throwing it into reverse and escaping. Yet the rapid fire grew still more intense and Elsworth was hit repeatedly. He fell across the injured body of his son and died a few minutes later. Just before the fatal shots were fired, Elsworth shouted towards the attackers: 'Please, please stop. We will leave Zimbabwe tomorrow. We will leave Zimbabwe tomorrow.'

All this was recounted by Ian Elsworth, 20, as he writhed in agony in the Avenues Clinic in Harare. Swathed in bandages, he was covered with sweat and dried blood, his face wracked by the pain of nine bullet wounds. His weak, croaking voice returned to one point again and again. His father was 'a helpless old man and they shot him down'. Henry Elsworth walked on crutches and suffered from prostate cancer. Nothing was stolen during the attack and the ambush bore all the hallmarks of an official, carefully executed operation.

A band of 80 squatters had been present on Elsworth's farm since February. Why was he singled out for murder? He was a former ally of Ian Smith, who had served in parliament as a Rhodesian Front MP. Back in

1994, Mugabe had publicly attacked Elsworth after the farmer was accused of assaulting a group of blacks who were chopping down trees on his land. Although the Supreme Court later cleared him, this incident had not been forgotten. When the death of another white farmer was necessary, the lame old man was chosen.

Mugabe followed this up with a barrage of inflammatory rhetoric. While Ian Elsworth's life hung in the balance and he endured emergency surgery on 13 December, his President spoke of war. 'Let us make it clear to the Commercial Farmers' Union that they have declared war against the people of Zimbabwe who have every determination to win it,' Mugabe said.[16] Soon afterwards, Hitler Hunzvi, still revelling in his role as leader of the shock troops carrying out the farm invasions, publicly delighted in Elsworth's murder. 'We are now fighting for our land and whosoever is killed, it's tough luck,' he said. 'It is now going to be very hard for commercial farmers. They may not even reap or harvest the crops they have planted. We have finished negotiating with them and what is now left is confrontation.'[17]

Hunzvi was in Harare for Zanu-PF's annual Congress, alongside 6,000 other delegates, who appeared to share his fanaticism. To chants of 'Zimbabwe was won through blood' the occasion opened on 14 December and swiftly degenerated into a festival of racial hatred. As I moved among the crowd and listened to their cries, it occurred to me that Elsworth's murder might have been ordered simply to raise morale and give Zanu-PF something to celebrate.

When Mugabe rose to address the gathering, he was cheered to the echo as he said these words: 'Our party must continue to strike terror into the hearts of the white man, our real enemy.'[18] The crowd rose as one, and a sea of fists punched the air. I noticed that among those joining the frenzy were Stan Mudenge, the Foreign Minister, who strutted around the world claiming that Zimbabwe was a tolerant democracy, and Francis Nhema, the Tourism Minister, who maintained that his country was a welcoming place for visitors. Both wore expressions of delighted fanaticism. It was an odious occasion, rounding off possibly the most disastrous year in the history of independent Zimbabwe.

In a landmark ruling on 21 December, the Supreme Court provided the best epitaph for the Zimbabwe of 2000. The justices forlornly ordered Mugabe to restore the rule of law: 'Wicked things have been done and continue to be done. They must be stopped. Common law crimes have been, and are being, committed with impunity. The government has flouted laws made by Parliament. The activities of the past nine months must be condemned.'[19] Instead, Mugabe moved to ensure that worse would happen in 2001.

NOTES AND REFERENCES

1 Speech, Zanu-PF headquarters, 25 October 2000, also broadcast on ZBC news.
2 Interview with the author, 21 June 2000 (on the margins of a CFU seminar for stressed farmers).
3 CFU press statement, 25 July 2000.
4 Press conference, Sheraton hotel, Harare, 2 August 2000.
5 Speech to Zimbabwe Farmers' Union, 3 August 2000. Remarks carried by a Reuters report.
6 *Ibid.*
7 See CFU sitrep, 10 August 2000.
8 Interview with the author, 29 September 2000.
9 Speech, MDC rally, Rufaro stadium, 30 September 2000.
10 ZBC news, 30 October 2000.
11 Speech, Zanu-PF headquarters, 25 October 2000, also broadcast on ZBC news.
12 *Sunday Mail,* 5 November 2000.
13 *Ibid.,* 4 June 2000.
14 Speech in Nigeria, covered on ZBC news, 7 November 2000.
15 Speech opening the legal year, Harare, 8 January 2001.
16 Speech to Zanu-PF central committee, 13 December 2000.
17 *The Herald,* 14 December 2000.
18 Speech to Zanu-PF Congress, Harare, 14 December 2000.
19 Quoted in International Bar Association report on the rule of law in Zimbabwe, sec. 7.47.

Chapter 11

Repression

January–June 2001

It is now only a matter of time before Zimbabweans put a final stop to
this madness in defence of their cultural interest and national security.
(Professor Jonathan Moyo, Information Minister, on the *Daily News*,
36 hours before a bomb destroyed the paper's printing press.)[1]

His face was contorted and his eyes wild with hatred. As he leaned out of the
passenger window of the pick-up, travelling at 75 miles per hour, the wind
threatened to blow away his green, paramilitary cap and tugged at the
Mugabe T-shirts worn by the motley collection of thugs piled into the open
back of his vehicle.

When I caught sight of Hitler Hunzvi, waving and screaming as he drove
alongside me on a lonely road, weaving its way through the rocky kopjes of
southern Zimbabwe, I discovered an interesting fact. If you are the target of
a high-speed ambush and you happen to wear glasses, your heart-drumming
fear causes their lenses to mist up.

Swerving erratically, Hunzvi's driver accelerated and drew parallel with
the car I was travelling inside. For perhaps 30 seconds, the snarling, twisted
features of Mugabe's chief rabble-rouser hovered a few feet away. I watched,
transfixed, as Hunzvi waved insistently for us to stop, while a dozen of his
youthful followers, some wearing olive green paramilitary fatigues, stared
with gleeful, intense loathing. They seemed to relish their breakneck ride in
the gleaming, white Zanu-PF pick-up. This horrifying vision lurched alongside the car I was sharing with three colleagues, one of whom, Andy
Meldrum, was at the wheel.

Then Hunzvi stopped trying to force us off the road and sped ahead, dis-
appearing around the next bend. I breathed again, until we turned the
corner and saw that Hunzvi had thrown his stationary vehicle across the
road, blocking our path. A vivid memory flashed across my mind. I thought
of the smoking, burnt-out wreckage of the car occupied by Talent Mabika

and Tichaona Chiminya, after a Zanu-PF vehicle laden with thugs had pulled this trick on them nine months earlier.

Andy screeched to a halt well before the obstacle and executed a swift U-turn. We roared away from our pursuer and neatly avoided another Zanu-PF truck, which raced towards us, flashing its headlights and threatening to swerve across our path – a kamikaze manoeuvre which would have killed everyone, white journalist and Mugabe fanatic alike, in a head-on collision. Minutes later, we were out of danger and within the safety of a convoy of MDC vehicles, carrying Morgan Tsvangirai. All four of us dissolved into hysterical, slightly manic cackles of laughter. Grant Ferrett, the BBC correspondent, had switched on his microphone at the moment of maximum tension and, thanks to his presence of mind, all Britain awoke to my yelps of fear broadcast on the *Today* programme the following morning.

It was not as if we were covering an important event. This was a by-election, for heaven's sake, nothing worth dying for. But in the Zimbabwe of 2001, even by-elections took on the appearance of civil war. The unfortunate people of Bikita West had elected an MDC MP by a wafer-thin margin of 281 votes during the parliamentary poll of June 2000. This man had died of natural causes and, in January 2001, Zanu-PF mounted an all-out effort to recapture the seat. Hunzvi was deployed in the area alongside hundreds of thugs, and the terror campaign began once more.

It was a wearily familiar re-run of the last election. Following Zanu-PF's tried and tested manual of electioneering, Hunzvi established a network of base camps and led his mobs on one brutal foray after another. Hundreds of people suspected of backing the MDC were hunted down for beatings and torture. This time, Zanu-PF's main torture centre was found a stone's throw away from the local police station. Hunzvi chose the rural district council office, a shabby building with sinister, barred windows, located in the centre of the dilapidated town of Nyika. Hunzvi was given use of about 20 Zanu-PF vehicles, and his shock troops, the usual core of genuine war veterans, surrounded by hundreds of unemployed thugs and hangers-on, terrorized the tiny villages scattered amid the rugged kopjes of this impoverished rural constituency.

A few minutes before trying to ambush us, Hunzvi had led an attack on five MDC youths he found beside the road. I met one of them soon after my escape from his clutches. Blood was congealed around Godfrey Koster's head and he spoke with a stammer. He was in his teens and wore an MDC T-shirt, which had almost cost him his life. Hunzvi and the Zanu-PF mob had set upon Koster and his friends with whips, clubs and iron bars. 'I was punched to the ground,' he said. 'Then they hit me on the head with an iron bar. I saw Hunzvi. He was the commander of the whole incident.' While Koster rolled on the ground, trying to shield his head from the blows,

Hunzvi shouted encouragement to his assailant and screeched: 'Don't beat him like you are beating your brother. Kill him, torture him.' These were the words of a man who not only led the War Veterans' Association, but was an MP from the ruling party and walked in and out of Mugabe's office at will.

When the MDC youths were reduced to bloody heaps lying beside the ditch, Hunzvi and his gang returned to their vehicle and roared away. Moments later, they happened upon four white journalists and would, no doubt, have inflicted the same on us. I watched as Koster winced with pain while his head wound was bandaged. Vivid, purple bruises blossomed along his legs and arms. One thought ran through my mind: this was a by-election, it didn't matter a damn, no one would ever know or care which party held Bikita West, and yet in Zimbabwe, even a completely irrelevant contest was an excuse for mindless violence. How could you ever have normal, peaceful elections in this country?

This time, there was a more sinister aspect of the campaign. While Zanu-PF started the violence and was responsible for most offences, the MDC had been sucked into the cycle of retaliation and revenge. I watched as 30 of the party's youths danced and sang in the centre of Nyika. They repeated one word, over and over again – '*Hondo*', meaning 'war'.

Tsvangirai had brought his own collection of thugs to Bikita West and they were responsible for violence that compared with anything inflicted by Hunzvi and his mobs. I listened with mounting horror as an MDC security official, whom I knew well, described how his party had set up 'base camps', from which youths were dispatched across the constituency. It all sounded grimly familiar. The official smiled mirthlessly and said: 'We can use the same methods as Zanu-PF. We know how they campaign and we can do the same.' We both knew what he meant by the 'same methods'. I remembered watching those three men being beaten and kicked like animals during the MDC's final election rally in June 2000. Political violence was contagious. Once the ruling party elevated mayhem to the central method of winning elections, it was only a matter of time before the opposition joined in. Perhaps inevitably, the MDC was contracting the virus.

A few days earlier, this had been demonstrated beyond doubt. Bernard Gara, a Zanu-PF supporter, was stabbed to death in the aftermath of a ruling party rally. All the evidence suggested that MDC supporters had been responsible for his murder. Thus Zimbabwe could not even hold by-elections without lives being lost, and this time the blame lay with the opposition.

But when it came to political violence, no one was more skilled or experienced than Zanu-PF. Bikita West proved that taking them on at their own game was a futile tactic that could only bring defeat. Official repression would always be more effective than anything the MDC could try. On 15 January, Zanu-PF duly recaptured the seat by the convincing margin of 12,993 votes to 7,001. Hundreds of people were recovering from their wounds and the Gara family was bereaved, all for the sake of choosing one obscure, nonentity of a candidate over another.

★   ★   ★

Official repression won Bikita West and Mugabe was bent on using the same methods to subdue the whole country. In 2001 the targets singled out by his struggle for power widened to include the last vestiges of a free society. Despite all the pressures of 2000, Zimbabwe's judiciary had remained resolutely independent, delivering a string of rulings embarrassing to the regime, and the country's tiny independent press had been vociferously critical of Zanu-PF. Mugabe now sought to deal with these irritants.

Perhaps the most doggedly persistent nuisance was the *Daily News*, the only independent daily paper. It was relentlessly critical of Mugabe, and Geoffrey Nyarota, the paper's editor, had an uncanny knack of getting under his leader's skin. On Heroes' Day in 2000, the annual occasion when Zimbabweans remember the dead of the Second *Chimurenga,* Nyarota chose this solemn moment to launch a blistering attack on the President. 'Impeach Mugabe' screamed the front-page headline and the message was driven home by a leading article accusing Zanu-PF's mobs of 'betraying our true heroes'. The *Daily News* said: 'By turning against the people, maiming, raping, robbing and murdering them, they have become outlaws, hated and despised by most citizens.'[2] Even in a democracy, that's strong stuff. In Mugabe's Zimbabwe, it drove the powers-that-be apoplectic with rage.

Hence Mugabe decided to silence this criticism once and for all. On 23 January, a 400-strong mob of Zanu-PF supporters was marshalled outside the *Daily News* headquarters in central Harare. They hurled threats and abuse at the office windows, and journalists working at their desks typed their stories while chants of 'We will finish you' and 'You will walk in fear' echoed from outside. Needless to say, the mob was led by Hitler Hunzvi, and his thugs were equipped with professionally printed banners reading: 'THE DAILY NEWS IS TRASH.' Afterwards, they happened upon Julius Zava, the paper's news editor, and beat him up in the street, before trying to bundle him inside a Zanu-PF pick-up. Only the intervention of three policemen saved Zava from abduction.

Minutes later, the gang assembled outside the Office of the President and Cabinet and was thanked for its efforts by Joseph Msika. The Vice-President stood beside Hunzvi and told them that the government would 'take steps' to deal with the *Daily News*.

Just what the authorities had in mind was not yet apparent. The next attack came three days later, when Jonathan Moyo excoriated the *Daily News* in an article carried by *The Herald*. He seized on the paper's coverage of the assassination of President Laurent Kabila of the Democratic Republic of Congo on 16 January, and sought to turn it into a *cause célèbre*. Kabila had been the leading light in Mugabe's dwindling band of genuine allies and 11,000 Zimbabwean troops were supporting his regime against Congolese rebels. With its customary eagerness to stir the pot, the *Daily News* reported (perhaps rightly) that Kabila's death was greeted with 'joy and jubilation' by most Zimbabweans.

Moyo decided he was furious about this and took the opportunity to damn the newspaper and all its works. 'Nothing has exposed the moral and professional poverty of some sections of the so-called independent media and dramatized the impossibility that the MDC can ever govern this country than their morbid, if not barbaric attempts to use the assassination of President Laurent Kabila as an opportunity for cheap political gain,' he wrote.[3]

Moyo then accused the *Daily News* of every outrage he could think of. The paper was guilty of 'corrupting our moral values', compromising 'our national interest', putting 'our heroic troops at risk', making 'deplorable and nauseating claims', displaying 'rank madness' and denigrating 'anything and everything that is nationalistic, Zimbabwean or African'. Moyo's closing words were: 'It is now only a matter of time before Zimbabweans put a final stop to this madness in defence of their cultural interest and national security.'[4]

He did not have long to wait – about 36 hours, in fact. Moyo's article appeared on Friday, 26 January. In the early hours of 28 January, some Zimbabweans made a determined attempt to put a 'final stop' to the 'rank madness' of the *Daily News*. At 1.45 a.m., tens of thousands of people across Harare were woken by the resounding bang of a shattering explosion. As the frightened occupants of countless homes rubbed their eyes and wondered what had broken the night's silence, the heavy metal rollers of the *Daily News* printing press settled into a tangled heap of smoking wreckage, underneath a gaping hole where the roof of the plant had once been. A bomb had been detonated in a brutally straightforward effort to silence the paper. Its modern printing press was utterly destroyed.

Moyo immediately condemned the bombing and professed that the government knew nothing about it. The attack was, presumably, a normal criminal incident. Exactly why a bunch of criminals should wish to go to the trouble and expense of blowing up a printing press, of all things, was left unexplained. What they stood to gain, or how they would have obtained the high explosive needed for this crime, was also left unclear.

The devastation was so complete that a very powerful device had obviously been planted. An analysis conducted by Michael Quintana, editor of *Africa Defence Journal,* suggested the following: 'Up to three eastern-made anti-tank land mines, bolstered by a limpet type detonator was used.' As for who was equipped with these weapons, Quintana wrote that only 'the Zimbabwean army . . . has access to the type of explosives used in the blast or the professional acumen to so completely wreck the machinery'.[5]

The *Daily News* paid the price of defiance, yet the bombing failed in its aim. The paper was not silenced. Nyarota managed to conclude a deal with another printing press and not a single issue was missed. Instead, pictures of the destruction caused by the blast went around the world and did incalculable damage to Mugabe's reputation. It was not the first or the last occasion on which iron-fisted repression proved counter-productive.

If the local press were going to be harried and pounded into submission, it was only a matter of time before the same was tried on foreign journalists. I was often surprised by the degree to which we were shielded from the harassment routinely endured by our colleagues working for the *Daily News,* the *Zimbabwe Independent*, the *Standard* and the *Financial Gazette,* the local independent papers. Mugabe and his minions ranted venomously and incessantly about the 'blatant lies of the British press'. When we covered Zanu-PF rallies or encountered squatters on occupied farms, we took our lives in our hands and all of us collected our share of death threats and narrow escapes. But otherwise, Harare's tiny coterie of resident foreign journalists was left largely to its own devices. Only once did Mugabe's office contact me directly to complain about a story I had written, and then it was over a footling matter that they did not trouble to pursue.

All this was about to change, and the first of our number to feel the heat was Joe Winter of the BBC. On 17 February, he was abruptly summoned by the Information Ministry, informed that his residence permit had been cancelled and given 24 hours to pack up and leave. Moyo had attacked Joe on a few occasions, but his reports were no more or less controversial than anything filed by his colleagues. Ironically, their last contact had been after Kabila's assassination, when Moyo rang Joe to congratulate him on the 'sensitivity' of his coverage. Joe was vulnerable because of a bizarre case of bureaucratic bungling, for which he bore no responsibility whatever.

Three months earlier, he had managed to renew his residence permit by following the normal procedure that everyone thought was still in force. He approached the official responsible for journalists at the Information Ministry, who was distinguished by his efficiency and courtesy, and asked for a letter of clearance, as required by the Immigration department. This letter was provided and Joe's application duly approved.

Yet after Moyo's appointment as Mugabe's propaganda supremo in July 2000, the Information Ministry had been formally abolished and swallowed by the Office of the President. Moyo made no secret of his belief that all his predecessors had been too soft on the international press and he decided that any letters allowing foreign correspondents to stay in Zimbabwe would be issued by him personally. But it seems that Moyo or his minions neglected to tell the officials concerned. Perhaps they forgot. These hapless functionaries thought the old procedure was still valid, so Joe got his renewal.

Picture Moyo's fury when he discovered that the correspondent of the BBC, the news organization he despised more than any other, had been given permission to stay in Zimbabwe until 2002 – by mistake. In his anger, Moyo must have ordered Joe's expulsion. During the meeting on 17 February, the officials were polite and businesslike and agreed that Joe, his wife Anne Marie, and their one-year-old daughter Anenti, could have a few days to wind up their affairs, instead of 24 hours. When I spoke to Joe soon after the meeting, he was calm, collected and reassured by this promise.

That night, a car drew up outside the Winter family's home in central Harare at 1.40 a.m. Four men piled out and scaled the garden wall. Joe and his wife were woken by the sound of fists hammering on their front door and angry voices bellowing for them to come outside. The bell rang over and over again and shadowy figures moved behind the house and pounded on the back door, while rattling every window. As the bedlam continued and the shouts grew more insistent and threatening, Joe rang his lawyer, a British diplomat and three other journalists who lived nearby. All rushed to his aid. 'We were terrified and we thought they were going to kill us,' he told me later. 'We didn't know who these people were.'

When the rescue party arrived a few minutes later, the men leapt into their car and drove away at high speed. Shocked and terrified, the Winter family immediately fled their home. Baby Anenti remained mercifully asleep throughout the ordeal, but Anne Marie was tearful and traumatized. She had had a premonition that something like this would occur and insisted on packing a few cases as soon as her husband returned from the Information Ministry. Now the family grabbed whatever belongings were to hand and left. They would never return to their home again.

The Winter family were rushed to the safety of a house owned by the British High Commission. Meanwhile, the gang went back to their home and treated it like a white-owned farm – they broke in, occupied the living room and lay in wait for Joe to return. This operation carried all the hallmarks of the Central Intelligence Organisation and was a vivid illustration of the lengths to which Moyo would go. Later on 18 February, lawyers acting for Joe were granted a High Court ruling that gave his family five days to wind up their affairs and ordered the authorities to leave them in peace.

Although this judgement was issued with the consent of government lawyers, Moyo displayed the regime's familiar attitude to the rule of law by publicly repudiating it. Instead, he began a barrage of propaganda aimed squarely at Joe. This was clearly designed to obscure Moyo's mind-boggling ineptitude. Not only had his department managed to renew Joe's residency permit by mistake, but the clumsy bid to expel him by the simple expedient of sending a gang to raid his house had provoked an avalanche of international protest. Pictures of the Winter family leaving their home in the dead of night, with Anne Marie clutching their baby, her eyes red with tears, flew around the world and Mugabe's regime was universally condemned yet again.

Of all the own-goals Moyo scored for his master, this was among the most spectacular. So he tried to cover his embarrassment by claiming that Winter had renewed his permit 'fraudulently and irregularly' by bribing the officials concerned. Moyo told the BBC that 'criminal charges' would be brought against their correspondent.[6] Anyone who knew Joe knew these accusations were ludicrous smears, but presumably the CIO gang was occupying his house with the intention of arresting him.

The Winters were holed up inside the British diplomatic property, unable to return home and collect the rest of their possessions, until 20 February when the BBC placed them on an early morning flight to Johannesburg. Miraculously, they were not intercepted at Harare airport and allowed to leave, although officials stamped 'PROHIBITED IMMIGRANT' in their passports. It was a few days before the gang gave up and left Joe's house and several weeks before his friends were able to forward the family's belongings.

Joe's expulsion was a tangled web of pettiness, spite and bungling, but from that moment onwards, I knew my days in Zimbabwe were numbered. It would not be long before Moyo's hand descended on my collar. Grant Ferrett, the other BBC correspondent, had left of his own accord a fortnight earlier and Joe's departure made me the only British journalist in the country.[7] From that moment, every story I filed seemed a bonus, every complete and unmolested day in Harare was a source of quiet relief. Whenever I heard Mugabe or Moyo rail against British journalists, I felt a surge of grim satisfaction. From 20 February onwards, 'British journalists' meant me. Two days later, Mugabe delivered a furious speech and accused the British press of spreading 'completely false' reports of 'rampant violence and instability'. He said: 'We are still the subject of malicious propaganda by external forces opposed to our land reform programme. This is affecting our image abroad.'[8] He made me sound very important.

★ ★ ★

One man in Mugabe's sights who was genuinely important was Anthony Gubbay, the Chief Justice. The Supreme Court's rulings against the 'Fast Track' land seizures on 10 November and 21 December had been the last straws, and from then on a ruthless vendetta was waged against the judiciary. Superficially, these courageous judgements made no difference whatever – as we have seen, they were simply ignored and farms were taken illegally. But an unlawful resettlement programme was one that no donor country could possibly fund. If Mugabe's central diplomatic objective was still to persuade Britain to pay for land reform, the Supreme Court had finally destroyed whatever slender possibility of success remained. Gubbay's bench of judges had, in effect, told the whole world that Mugabe led a lawless regime.

So the President sought vengeance. The pressure on the Chief Justice was ratcheted up with the aim of hounding him from office. Under Zimbabwe's constitution, only an independent tribunal, specially convened to hear charges of misconduct, held the power to remove judges. No conceivable case could be brought against Gubbay, so more familiar tactics were employed. Patrick Chinamasa, newly promoted to Justice Minister, appeared to hold the novel view that his main function was vilifying white judges. Moyo, that proven master of vituperation, played an important supporting role. Complementing the verbal attacks were straightforward threats of violence from Hunzvi's thugs.

The invasion of his court on 24 November – and those accompanying cries of 'Kill the judges' – had left Gubbay deeply wounded, and his tormentors quickly seized the advantage. Four days later, Chinamasa made a keynote speech and failed to condemn the invasion. Instead, he pointed out that Gubbay had joined the bench during the Rhodesian era and asked: 'How can personnel so high up in the pecking order of a regime grounded in racist grundnorm (*sic*) faithfully serve a democratic state?' Chinamasa added: 'I belong to a generation which brought fundamental revolutionary changes not through the law or a legal process but through the barrel of a gun.'

Chinamasa demanded to know whether Gubbay and the five other white judges (four of whom served in the High Court) had black friends. 'What company they keep, who their friends are, is also our legitimate business,' he said. 'The justification is we want to know what influences the values and opinions of judges . . . in a country of 12 million black people, it is unacceptable to get people appointed to the bench who in a year cannot claim to have interacted socially with a single black person.'[9]

All this was open to an obvious rejoinder – if Gubbay and the other white judges were so terrible, why on earth had Mugabe appointed them? Chinamasa later offered a simple explanation. It was all a mistake. His hapless president was, apparently, in the habit of appointing Chief Justices by mistake and only discovering his error ten years later. 'It was foolish magnanimity on our part to have appointed them judges,'[10] Chinamasa said.

On 17 January he threw away all restraint and demanded the resignations of Gubbay and every white judge. Chinamasa said they 'must be told their continued stay on the bench is no longer at our invitation. Their continued stay is now an albatross around the necks of our population.' He claimed that Gubbay's presence as Chief Justice meant that Zimbabwe was a 'semi-colonial state, half free, half enslaved'.[11]

With open season declared on the Chief Justice, Gubbay had to put up with a public attack from a fellow judge. Godfrey Chidyausiku, the Judge President of the High Court, had served Mugabe as a Zanu-PF backbencher and Attorney-General and was the favourite to take over as Chief Justice. He chose to rubbish his boss on 8 January by digging up a speech Gubbay had made in 1991, when he criticized a constitutional amendment that removed the judiciary's right to decide the level of compensation payable for land seizures.

This, Chidyausiku claimed, was 'an open invitation by the judiciary to the commercial farmers to sue [the] government'. He argued that Gubbay's speech of nine years earlier showed why the farmers had been confident enough to bring their case before the Supreme Court, and added, for good measure, that his boss's rulings were 'hardly tenable' and 'boggling the mind [*sic*]'.[12]

This insubordination was a direct challenge to Gubbay's authority that he could hardly ignore. Accordingly, he issued a public reprimand to Chidyausiku on 17 January, pointing out that the rulings for which he was being attacked had actually been granted with the consent of the government, making his subordinate's aspersions 'frankly ridiculous'. Gubbay ordered him to 'avoid making inflammatory statements'.

Yet the most revealing sentence in Gubbay's statement came towards the end, when he said that his reprimand came 'after anxious consideration'.[13] The pressure was clearly showing. For his pains, Gubbay was immediately reprimanded for making the reprimand by Moyo, who took it upon himself to brand the Chief Justice 'hypocritical, dictatorial and undemocratic'.[14]

Meanwhile, Hunzvi had piled on the pressure in the most blatant way possible. On 22 December, he responded to the Supreme Court's ruling on the land issue by giving all the judges 14 days to resign or else. At the end of a year scarred by one political killing after another, no threat could be taken lightly, and this was, perhaps, the single most important factor weighing on Gubbay's mind. He was 68, his wife, Wilma, was seriously ill, and he found himself the target of a vilification campaign from one of Africa's most ruthless regimes. Gubbay was simply not cut out for this sort of thing. He was a skilled lawyer, not a robust politician.

And so, on 19 January he found himself writing to Simon Muzenda, the Vice-President, pleading with the government to protect judges. 'We are fearful of our safety and the safety of our families,' wrote Gubbay. 'We find it difficult to carry out our onerous judicial duties when placed under pressure of this nature.'[15]

The response was a meeting with Muzenda and two cabinet ministers on 22 January. They showed no sympathy; on the contrary, during this encounter Gubbay was subjected to yet another attack. Muzenda, famed for his inability to utter a coherent sentence in any language, read out a prepared statement accusing him of 'aiding and abetting racism' and saying that the government had lost all confidence in him. During the exchanges, described in one account as 'emotionally charged', Gubbay was driven to say that if that was their attitude, he should perhaps resign. At the time, no one took this as a firm offer and the meeting ended inconclusively.[16]

Almost two weeks later, on 2 February, Chinamasa walked into Gubbay's chambers, perhaps with a gleam of triumph in his eye. The minister brusquely informed the Chief Justice that his resignation had been accepted and an announcement would be made that very afternoon. Thank you and goodbye. One can imagine Gubbay's feelings of sadness, anger and sheer, overwhelming weariness. By this stage, he had clearly been worn down. He threw in the towel and agreed to go on leave on 1 March and formally retire on 30 June. It was game, set and match to Chinamasa.

But hounding the Chief Justice into resignation was not enough for him. A week later, Chinamasa went to see Nicholas McNally, the other white on the Supreme Court, and Ahmed Ebrahim, the Asian. Nothing was more obvious than that the vendetta was purely racial. Wilson Sandura and Simbarashe Muchechetere, the two blacks on the bench, were not approached, although both were as stubbornly independent as their colleagues and had bravely endorsed every ruling on the land issue.

Chinamasa's strategy could not have been more crude – he wanted to pick off the non-blacks and then flood the court with a majority he arrogantly assumed would be pliant. So he told McNally to go because: 'The President does not want you to come to any harm.'[17] Ebrahim was given a similarly blunt message. Yet both men called Chinamasa's bluff and insisted on staying in office, drawing a furious response.

Moyo stepped into the fray and recalled Ebrahim's past career as a public prosecutor during the Rhodesian era. He decided that the judge and his colleagues were, in fact, 'former Nazis'. Mugabe had, apparently, taken a bunch of ex-fascists and made them judges by mistake. '[Ebrahim] is unacceptable to a free and just Zimbabwe. He represents the kind of example of a mistake that was made in appointing him,' said Moyo. 'If they [judges] had a conscience they would think about the past and do the honourable thing without pushing others to the limit. It is unjust to expect as judges former Nazis and their collaborators.'[18]

These 'former Nazis' were not to be cowed, and that perhaps explained what happened next. Piqued by defeat at the hands of his latest quarries, Chinamasa turned back to Gubbay with renewed ferocity. This harassed, vanquished figure would not only be removed, but humiliated as well. Chinamasa went about the denouement by demanding that an Acting Chief Justice preside over the Supreme Court, even before Gubbay's formal departure. When Gubbay replied that this step was 'premature', as he was bound to do, Chinamasa wrote a letter on 26 February laden with arrogance and loathing.

The minister took it upon himself simply to sack the Chief Justice. He summarily gave Gubbay 24 hours to clear his desk and 13 days to move out of his official residence. To maximize his humiliation, the letter of dismissal – entirely illegal, of course – was given to *The Herald* and appeared on its front page before Gubbay's copy had even reached him.

Thus Zimbabwe's most senior judge woke on 27 February to find, out of the blue, the headline: 'Gubbay to leave office tomorrow'. *The Herald* carried extracts from a letter he had not yet seen, in which Chinamasa accused him of 'misconduct' for 'reneging' on an alleged agreement that an Acting Chief Justice would be appointed the moment he went on leave. 'Accordingly . . . your term of office as Chief Justice terminates on 28 February 2001, by which time you should have cleared your belongings from your chambers,' wrote Chinamasa. 'In the meantime, you should make appropriate arrangements to vacate your official residence by not later than Friday 9 March.'[19]

This was too much for Gubbay. He responded by withdrawing his resignation and insisting that he would hold office right up until his fixed retirement date in April 2002. Incidentally, he denied ever discussing the appointment of an Acting Chief Justice with Chinamasa, let alone agreeing to this. I never met a Zimbabwean lawyer who would take Chinamasa's word over Gubbay's. The minister's crude bid to humiliate his target had backfired completely.

So the fight was on – Gubbay versus everyone else. Moyo now took centre stage. Late on 27 February, he announced that the regime was sticking to its demand and 'come midnight tomorrow, the Chief Justice's term of office will terminate, his office will be vacant'. Asked what would happen if Gubbay turned up for work on 1 March, Moyo replied that he would be prevented from entering the court by 'officers with appropriate authority', otherwise 'it would be like someone sitting in the middle of the street'.[20]

At 8.15 a.m. on 1 March, a stooping, silver-haired man, wearing a smart grey suit, drew up outside the Supreme Court at the wheel of an official Mercedes. A police officer meekly opened the gates of the car park and the staid, impassive figure disappeared inside the small, ornate building. In Moyo's idiom, Gubbay was now 'sitting in the middle of the street'. He had called Moyo's bluff, ignored the threats and turned up for work as usual, with no one trying to stop him. I spent most of that day standing under Gubbay's office window, alongside my colleagues, wondering what would happen next. Would the court be stormed and the Chief Justice dragged out? Would the government appoint a rival Supreme Court? Meanwhile, a few feet above my head, the elderly man at the centre of the storm quietly worked on routine cases.

The response to his defiance was wearily predictable. Gubbay was subjected to an outpouring of vitriol. Joseph Made, the Agriculture Minister and architect of the illegal land seizures, declared him a 'liar' who was 'not fit to be Chief Justice of this country'. For good measure, Made claimed that Gubbay was 'biased against blacks'.[21] In parliament, Chinamasa called Gubbay 'disgraceful, despicable and not worthy of a man in his position'.[22]

Most outrageous of all was a vicious diatribe delivered to a packed House by Christopher Mushohwe, a Zanu-PF backbencher and former Director in the Office of the President. His speech succeeded in rolling all of Mugabe's favourite conspiracy theories into a single, defining testament of Zanu-PF paranoia, the last word in official fantasy. Mushohwe's opening shot was that Gubbay 'thinks and behaves as if he is the last British Governor of Zimbabwe'. He then decided that 'the Chief Justice was deliberately planted in the Zimbabwean body politic by Lord Carrington so as to defeat Zimbabwe's independence'. Moving on to anti-Semitic slurs, Mushohwe claimed that Gubbay was linked to 'very powerful Jewish financial interests'. The judge also found time to 'manipulate and contaminate the thinking of young law students at the University of Zimbabwe'.

Gubbay must have been immensely busy for he was 'commanding many NGOs and donor agencies which he uses for the purpose of radicalizing Zimbabweans against their own government'. Gubbay's propaganda skills were such that he had 'subverted the thinking capacity of Zimbabweans' and 'the current wave of criticism which the government is facing . . . is a direct result of a strategy put in place by the Chief Justice in collaboration with his Whitehall handlers'.

Mushohwe then allowed his deranged imagination to run riot. He decided that Gubbay was in the habit of sentencing innocent Africans to death out of 'blood lust', leading him 'to kill as a form of sexual gratification'. In Mushohwe's fevered mind, Gubbay had killed 'more blacks' than 'any single soldier in the Rhodesian army'.[23] This poisonous slander came from someone who was plainly unhinged, but was no less hurtful for that.

Physical thuggery followed verbal thuggery on 2 March. Once again, Gubbay showed up for work and I spent most of the day outside the

Supreme Court. Who should appear but Joseph Chinotimba, accompanied by seven henchmen wearing dark glasses. This infamous, gap-toothed thug, still awaiting trial for attempted murder, strode to the entrance of the court and was immediately admitted by the policeman standing guard. Over 40 minutes later, the 'commander in chief of white farm invasions' re-appeared, wearing an inane grin beneath his white baseball cap.

'I talked to Mr Gubbay personally and I told him to vacate office today,' said Chinotimba proudly, with blobs of spittle spraying in a wide arc from his jaw. 'We are big people, we war veterans will defend our country to the last breath.'

'What will you do if he stays in office?' shouted one of my colleagues.

'Declare war!' Chinotimba fired back.

Then he stared at the white faces around him and cried: 'Jentamen, jentamen, go back to Britain!' With that, Chinotimba turned on his heel and walked off, surrounded by his faithful henchmen, who had helped him invade the Supreme Court and shout 'Kill the judges' three months earlier. We later learned that Chinotimba had been prevented from confronting Gubbay face to face but allowed to berate him over an internal telephone.

So Gubbay was now under threat of 'war' from one of Zanu-PF's most notorious bruisers. Shortly afterwards, I saw him emerge from the court, a slender, soberly suited figure. Gubbay was not alone. Behind him hovered a burly bodyguard, so large and muscular that he dwarfed the judge. For the first time ever, Gubbay was compelled to take this extraordinary precaution. He could not leave his office in broad daylight without this protective shadow.

Behind the scenes, lawyers representing the Chief Justice were holding talks with Chinamasa. Gubbay was plainly cracking under the pressure and willing to reach a deal. Late on 2 March an agreement was signed. The Chief Justice surrendered and agreed to go on immediate leave, pending official retirement on 1 July, in return for a written pledge from Chinamasa that no more judges would be hounded out of office. So ended the saga. At the cost of yet more damage to its shredded international reputation, Mugabe's regime had ousted its Chief Justice. To no one's surprise, the loyal and reliable Chidyausiku, who was not even a member of the Supreme Court bench, leap-frogged his superiors and was named as Gubbay's successor.

It is worth dwelling briefly on the parallels between Gubbay's treatment and that of Joe Winter. When Joe was summoned on 17 February, he agreed to leave Zimbabwe, for he had no choice. Moyo had won. The raid on Joe's home and all the nonsense about fraud and bribery were unnecessary and incompetent acts of sadism that succeeded only in tarnishing Mugabe's image even more.

Equally, Gubbay had been induced to go on 2 February. Everything that followed was completely futile, spurred by nothing more than an obsessive desire to humiliate him. The only result was to drag Zimbabwe through the mud. Thus Moyo and Chinamasa were bunglers – and malignant bunglers at that. A unique blend of vindictiveness and incompetence was, perhaps, the defining feature of Mugabe's regime. After all this, Chinamasa was shameless enough to make the following excuse for his behaviour. He claimed that Gubbay 'resigned his position voluntarily'.[24]

★ ★ ★

The narrow streets between the ramshackle houses of Chitungwiza were filled with children playing. Brightly dressed women sat beside the road, selling fruit arranged on sheets of plastic. Clucking chickens scampered in the dust and small groups of men drank *chibuku,* the traditional brew, shaded from the warm sunlight by the shadows of their tiny homes. It was a reassuringly normal scene, a sign that in Africa life goes on, through thick and thin.

But as I soon discovered, this impression was misleading. After dark, heavily armed soldiers roamed these streets, beating up anyone they found. Hundreds had been assaulted. A brutal crackdown was being waged against a town that had dared oppose Mugabe. While attacks on judges and journalists drew most attention, the poorest were suffering the most from official repression. The 300,000 people of Chitungwiza, Zimbabwe's third-largest town, were almost all jobless and lived in overcrowded shacks. This made them natural opponents of Mugabe and they had duly elected MPs from the MDC by overwhelming majorities.

From February onwards, soldiers moving in convoys of armoured vehicles were exacting a heavy price for this defiance. I met Beaula Makoko inside her tiny home. She sat on the dusty floor, while insisting that I should have the only chair – a rickety, wooden construction that creaked beneath me. Her four children, all toddlers, played around her and clung to her legs. She was thin, haggard and visibly weary, yet I had to politely stop her from cooking me *sadza* in a large iron pot, balanced on a tiny fireplace, outside the shack.

In a quiet, fearful voice, Makoko told me about her encounter with the soldiers. At least 15 forced their way into a bar near Makoni shopping centre, where she occasionally worked as a cleaner. Toting AK-47 assault rifles, they wore camouflage uniforms and red berets. The troops ordered everyone to lie on the floor and then set upon them with clubs, whips and sticks. They shouted 'We are beating you because you are MDC' and poured beer over their victims. Two soldiers threw Makoko to the floor and one planted a boot on the small of her back, before hitting her with a club over and over again. This continued, on and off, for half an hour. 'I thought they wanted to kill all of us. I was in fear that they were going to do it,' said Makoko.

After systematically assaulting everyone, the soldiers ordered them to leave the bar and, for good measure, kicked and punched them as they fled through the door. Makoko walked with a limp and displayed vivid bruises over a week after her ordeal. 'I still think they might come for me. It will take time for me to recover,' she said, as her three-year-old son, dressed in rags, tugged at her hair. Neither she nor anyone living in the streets nearby went out after dark. An unofficial curfew had been imposed on Chitungwiza. This was the price of defiance. I left Makoko sitting with her children in the inky blackness of their home, her eyes wide with fear.

Nearby, I bought a copy of *The Herald*. It was 21 February, Mugabe's 77th birthday, and his loyal newspaper had marked the occasion with a 12-page pull-out special. 'The nation congratulates him for remaining an unswerving nationalist and freedom fighter until such a ripe age under extremely trying times,' the paper gushed. Around me, the freedom fighter's people were wondering whether his army would be prowling their streets that night.

★   ★   ★

The crowds gathered outside the Zanu-PF headquarters building were often a good barometer of the situation in Zimbabwe. From February 2000, squatters massed around this tower block and used their 14 storeys as a base for the farm invasions, eating and sleeping in the building while waiting to be taken in official vehicles to properties targeted for occupation. They hung their washing on the fence outside and I once passed a long row of white undergarments, swinging in the breeze.

As the election approached, the party's thugs predominated and young men wearing Mugabe T-shirts formed most of the heaving throng that seemed to permanently flood the courtyard. From March 2001 onwards, the crowd changed in a subtle yet significant manner that betrayed a completely new phase in the struggle against Mugabe's enemies. Instead of Zanu-PF T-shirts, blue overalls and even smart suits predominated. Workers were massing outside Zanu-PF headquarters. The party's mobs had opened another ambitious campaign – the urban equivalent of farm invasions. Zanu-PF gangs began seizing on labour disputes and using them as pretexts for storming any business with the faintest link, real or imagined, to a white person. Factories and offices were being invaded.

At first, it was almost impossible to find out what was going on. Fear prevented people from speaking out. But the pieces soon fell into place.

Predictably enough, Hitler Hunzvi was leading the charge, with his faithful sidekick Chinotimba in tow. Fresh from his triumphant dispatch of Anthony Gubbay, Chinotimba was shooting to new prominence. In March he became Zanu-PF's 'political commissar' in the capital and supremo of the Harare War Veterans' Association.

The new offensive had two aims – white-owned businesses would be wrecked (worthwhile in itself) and money extorted from their owners. The spoils would be handed out to any workers who supported Zanu-PF, those who didn't would be beaten up. Simple, really. Just as black labourers had been pounded into submission on occupied farms, so urban workers would be treated the same way. Thus Zanu-PF hoped to break the MDC's stronghold in the cities. By late March, dozens of businesses were being stormed every week.

Dezign Inc. was among the first to be singled out. Chanting '*Pamberi ne Comrade Mugabe*,' a gang of 30 burst through its gates and then surged into the office of Danisa Mandoa, the General Manager. They demanded that he reinstate 88 workers, who were sacked several months earlier. I spoke to him on 6 April, one day later, and his voice wavered with suppressed fear. 'They kicked and punched me in my office. Then they dragged me through the factory,' he said.

After being hit on the head with an iron bar, Mandoa was frog-marched to Zanu-PF headquarters, a distance of three miles. During the journey he was abused, kicked, punched, spat upon and pelted with stones. He was dragged to the ninth floor of the building (immediately below a row of offices occupied by politburo members) and interrogated for three hours. Hunzvi appeared and accused Mandoa of supporting the MDC. 'They were saying that Dezign was owned by the whites, that I was sacking Zanu-PF supporters and hiring MDC people,' said Mandoa. In fact, a white family had a 30 per cent stake in the firm, while the workers held 40 per cent of the shares. Facts had never been Hunzvi's strong point and he was not satisfied with this explanation.

With blood streaming down his face, Mandoa was dragged outside and forced to address a baying mob of 100 in the courtyard. Only after he had chanted obedience to Mugabe and promised to reinstate the sacked workers was he allowed to go. When I spoke to him on a mobile phone, Mandoa was in a car, heading for Harare airport. He was leaving for South Africa and had no intention of ever returning to Zimbabwe. The textile firm had suspended operations, jeopardizing 120 jobs, in a country where unemployment exceeded 50 per cent. Hunzvi was doubtless proud of his handiwork.

This incident was typical of many. Usually a threatening letter from Chinotimba or Hunzvi was the first warning of trouble. One business received the following missive:

Do you know J CHINOTIMBA I am me now. My friend you are on fire. It's a serious case this one. What happen this guy tell me I am a war vet do you know me. You are going to suffocate okay. I am serious to talk about that. Why don't you give him a notice before that I am going to shut you. I am coming there on Wednesday to see which is taking place OK . . . you are in trouble now okay. I am me J CHINOTIMBA who saying that to you.'

In case this is not entirely clear, Chinotimba wanted £5,000 – or else. The business on the receiving end of this diatribe (which continued in the same vein at great length) was busted two days later. Chinotimba led the pack and perhaps used the negotiating skills perfected during his dealings with Gubbay.

Zanu-PF's new offensive was distinguished by its ever-widening list of targets. Not content with raiding factories and offices, the mobs soon began gunning for shops, hotels, hospitals and even aid agencies – anything with the faintest connection to a white person. On 25 April, no fewer than 20 organizations were raided in Harare in the space of about eight hours.

The most serious incident occurred in the Avenues Clinic, Zimbabwe's largest private hospital and one of the best in Africa. Mugabe had chosen its spotless, well-equipped facilities for his wife when she gave birth to their children, yet this appeared to offer no protection. A mob of 20 burst into the hospital's reception while 140 patients were receiving treatment and 15 operations were under way. Another truckload of thugs was on stand-by outside. The Avenues later described them as: 'Young, well built, impatient, aggressive and insolent. Some of them were high on illegal substances.'

Malcolm Boyland, the British managing director, was summoned and ordered to pay £70,000 to 35 workers sacked after an illegal strike in 1995. No ifs, no buts, just pay up. To rub in the message, one of the Zanu-PF ringleaders stabbed his finger at Boyland and shouted: 'I know where you are, I will come and deal with you.' Another threatened to drag him to Zanu-PF headquarters and put him in 'a room with no doors' – Zimbabwean slang for a coffin.

The hospital rang the police, whose national headquarters is a three-minute drive away, and asked whether the forces of law and order might possibly consider offering protection. The answer, on balance, was 'No'. Left alone to handle the situation and facing a stream of threats, Boyland agreed to make the payment. In Mugabe's Zimbabwe even hospitals were not safe from his mobs.

One hour later, the Friedrich Ebert Foundation, a German development organization, was raided. A gang of 20 stormed its office in Harare's quiet suburb of Belgravia. This time they demanded £8,000 for two workers sacked in 1999. Worried about the safety of the staff, the German ambassador went to negotiate with the mob in person. For over three hours Fritz Flimm talked with them and he was eventually forced to make the payment, in return for a promise that the Foundation would be left in peace. Flimm rang two cabinet ministers and asked for help. The only response was three sheepish policemen, who explained apologetically that they had 'no mandate' to deal with the situation.

Next on the hit-list was Meikles Department Store on Robert Mugabe Street, the oldest shop in Zimbabwe. A gang of ten rounded up its employees and marched them to a rally at Zanu-PF headquarters. Then they burst into the head office of Meikles Stores on Speke Avenue and seized two managers. They were held prisoner at Zanu-PF headquarters for several hours and cajoled into making payments to sacked workers. For good measure, Barbours and Greatermans, two other department stores in central Harare, were also invaded.

Even by Zimbabwean standards, this was getting ridiculous. The Ministry of Labour was responsible for mediating the disputes that usually provided the excuse for attacks. Its officials were now handing out files to the mobs and telling them which companies to invade. When walking through central Harare, it became perfectly normal to see gangs clustered outside offices. Could there be any clearer demonstration of a breakdown of law and order than the spectacle of thugs raiding a hospital in the heart of the capital with absolute impunity? Of businesses being stormed in broad daylight, under the noses of the police? Of the headquarters of the ruling party being used, quite openly, as a combined torture centre, armed camp and prison?

I often wondered whether the most powerful men in the country were ever concerned by the fact that people were being tortured and imprisoned on the floors beneath their offices. Every politburo member worked in Zanu-PF headquarters and arrived at the tower block aboard gleaming Mercedes. Did they hear the cries of the victims? Did they see the mobs thronging the courtyard? Did they glimpse the blood that must have spattered the walls? Or did they close their eyes and ears and continue telling the world that violence in Zimbabwe was an invention by British journalists?

Needless to say, they did the latter. When Zed Rusike, leader of the Confederation of Zimbabwe Industries, sought help from four cabinet ministers, they agreed to a meeting and then failed to show up.[25] Meanwhile, Moyo chose to declare that 'instead of seeking President Robert Mugabe's intervention, the CZI leadership should seek to meet the workers who have genuine grievances and try to address them'.[26] Zimbabweans could not expect help from their government. The mobs were in control and they were, of course, indistinguishable from the government.

And so the list of targets widened. A drunken gang stormed the Harare

Children's Home, which cared for 92 orphans, on 23 March. They were looking for Maria Sithole, the home's director, because they suspected her of supporting the MDC. When they failed to find her, the bearded thugs vented their frustration by beating up a security guard. 'The children were just returning from school and many of them saw what happened,' Sithole told me. 'These are already children who are traumatized and I'm sure it brought back some of their memories. The ones who saw what happened were quite shaken. It was chaotic while the men were here.' Over the next few weeks, Sithole was forced to evade two further visits from the gang.

The Harare headquarters of CARE International, the American aid agency, was stormed on 5 May, and Dennis O'Brien, its Canadian director, abducted in the presence of the police. He was held for several hours at Zanu-PF headquarters and when James Wall, the Canadian High Commissioner, went to the building to secure his release, the envoy was jostled and abused. Mobs made two more visits to the Avenues Clinic, and Boyland was forced into hiding by death threats. He soon decided to leave Zimbabwe for good. SOS Kinderdorf, one of the largest children's charities in the world, saw its office in central Harare raided on 11 May and was forced to close for several days.

Having moved from businesses to hospitals to orphanages to charities helping destitute kids, the Zanu-PF gangs then turned to foreign embassies. In Mugabe's fevered mind, most Western diplomatic missions were covertly supporting the MDC, with the British High Commission being most prominent in his pantheon of infamy. So Hunzvi declared that embassies were next. 'We will be visiting them soon to express our displeasure and to warn them to stop interfering with our internal matters,' he said.[27]

How did the Ministry of Foreign Affairs respond? Willard Chiwewe, its permanent secretary, duly gave the green light to the mobs. In a statement on 27 April, he began by piously asserting that diplomats would 'continue to receive the full protection of the law as well as assistance from the Ministry of Foreign Affairs'. But there was a catch: 'However, those diplomats who, for whatever reason or background, seek to further the interests of one political party against another, or to act as an agent of one political party against another, may not hope to receive assistance from the Ministry of Foreign Affairs.' Chiwewe added that 'such diplomats would have set aside the relevance and usefulness of this Ministry' and 'chosen to live with the fortunes of the party they would have chosen to support'.[28]

As all diplomats from Europe or America were suspected of backing the MDC, this remarkable statement was tantamount to the withdrawal of protection from every mission representing the Western world. Even by Mugabe's standards, this was an extraordinary step and it caused a storm of protest. International criticism was, of course, nothing new and the regime revelled in ignoring it. But this time, the protests came from close to home.

Simon Khaya Moyo, Zimbabwe's High Commissioner in Pretoria, was summoned to receive a formal dressing-down from the South African government. Mugabe's most powerful neighbour was displeased that his gangs had not only threatened embassies but raided 18 South African companies as well. This pressure began to have an effect. Chiwewe quietly retreated on 2 May by circulating a message to all missions, asserting that his ministry had 'the honour to reaffirm its protection'. Nonetheless, the British Council library was closed indefinitely on 10 May because of the risk of attack. Located a few streets away from Zanu-PF headquarters, it was more vulnerable than the British High Commission, which occupied the top floors of a modern tower block.

The mayhem went on for another week before it was finally curbed. John Nkomo, the Home Affairs Minister, announced on 16 May that the raids should 'cease forthwith' and police made 28 arrests. Yet the anarchy had served its purpose. Terror had been sown in the capital, perhaps 300 businesses, charities and other organizations attacked, and the dangers of supporting the MDC made clearer still. Chinotimba and Hunzvi had served their master well.

★   ★   ★

A few days later, the principal architect of Mugabe's terror campaign suffered a misfortune. On 21 May, Hunzvi collapsed in Matabeleland and was rushed to hospital in Bulawayo. Stricken, he lay in an intensive care bed, surrounded by mournful visitors clad in paramilitary uniform. All that effort on behalf of his master had imposed a hectic schedule. Many long months of raiding farms, busting factories, running torture centres, whipping mobs into frenzies, issuing death threats, storming charities, beating people with iron bars and chasing journalists had taken their toll. It must have been exhausting. And think of the personal inconvenience. After Hunzvi generously donated his surgery for use as a torture chamber, the new occupants probably failed to clean up the mess. The 51-year-old stormtrooper was on his last legs.

On 1 June, Hunzvi was transferred to Parirenyatwa hospital in Harare where he lay in ward B6, clad in his beloved, olive-green paramilitary cap. A solemn Chinotimba paid a visit and fought back a manly tear when he was filmed by state television. Other dejected figures, carrying axes and wearing Mugabe T-shirts, filed into his ward. In the end, poor Hunzvi decided that his visitors were bewitching him and chose to suffer alone. The bell was tolling. On 4 June, I rang Parirenyatwa hospital to check on his condition. 'He is feeling much better,' a friendly matron assured me: then I knew the worst had happened. Comrade Hunzvi had passed on. Never again would a journalist see his inimitable features from a speeding car.

And so it proved. On the lunchtime news, state radio announced that Comrade Hunzvi was no more. A eulogy was offered: 'Comrade Hunzvi led landless Zimbabweans in land occupations and also helped workers in disputes with their employers.' That was one way of summarizing his career. More notable was the absence of any announcement on the cause of his death. Hunzvi had, of course, succumbed to an AIDS-related condition and this was, as usual, being hushed up. AIDS was devastating Zimbabwe but the stigma attached to the syndrome was such that no one would ever admit to dying of it.

On the following day, Mugabe issued a heartfelt tribute. Comrade Hunzvi was a 'man of immense revolutionary commitment and dedication to patriotic duty'. Mugabe singled out his 'selflessness' for praise and said: 'Predictably, Comrade Hunzvi was demonised and disparaged by a hostile and vicious local and international campaign that sought, as it still does, to preserve the iniquitous colonial land ownership imbalance in Zimbabwe.'[29] That was my fault.

Mugabe announced that Hunzvi would be declared a National Hero and laid to rest in Heroes' Acre, alongside Joshua Nkomo and all the other titans of Zimbabwean history. The state funeral in Zimbabwe's equivalent of Westminster Abbey took place on 8 June and was attended by 7,000 mourners. Hunzvi's body was borne on a gun carriage, accompanied by a crowd carrying banners reading: 'The struggle continues'. Cabinet ministers, MPs, generals and air marshals gathered at the graveside. Strangely enough, no judges were present. 'You indeed deserve the halo of a national hero. Go well, son of the soil,' said Mugabe, delivering the eulogy.

Around him, the hillside was thronged with Hunzvi's followers and, curiously, there were no outbreaks of murderous violence on occupied farms or among the heaving streets of Harare's townships on that day. The President and the mobs who kept him in power were united in grief. But the terror campaign would outlive its leader.

Notes and References

1 *The Herald*, 26 January 2001.
2 *Daily News*, 11 August 2000.
3 *The Herald*, 26 January 2001.
4 *Ibid*.
5 *Africa Defence Journal*, Newsflash no. 2, 28 January 2001.
6 Interview on BBC World Service, *Newshour*, 18 February 2001.
7 All the other British papers had Zimbabwean correspondents, except for the *Guardian* which used an American.

8 *The Herald,* 22 February 2001.
9 *Ibid.,* 29 November 2000.
10 *Ibid.,* 8 December 2000.
11 *Ibid.,* 19 January 2001.
12 Speech opening the legal year, Bulawayo, 8 January 2001.
13 Statement from Chief Justice Gubbay, 17 January 2001.
14 *The Herald,* 18 January 2001.
15 Extracts from the letter were carried in *The Herald,* 19 January 2001.
16 See account given in the International Bar Association report into the rule of law in Zimbabwe, sec. 10.5.
17 McNally's account, given to the International Bar Association and journalists.
18 *The Herald,* 23 February 2001.
19 *Ibid.,* 27 February 2001.
20 Press conference, 27 February 2001.
21 Conversation with journalists outside Supreme Court, 1 March 2001.
22 *Hansard,* 28 February 2001, col. 4616.
23 *Ibid.,* cols 4654–68.
24 International Bar Association report into the rule of law in Zimbabwe, sec. 10.2. After hearing this excuse from Chinamasa, the IBA delegation wrote: '[We are] satisfied that this is not the case and that Chief Justice Gubbay was forced into early retirement by relentless pressure . . . and threats of violence which the government appear at the least to have condoned.'
25 See Zed Rusike's interview in *Financial Gazette,* 10 May 2001.
26 *Financial Gazette,* 10 May 2001.
27 *Ibid.,* 26 April 2001.
28 Statement from Ministry of Foreign Affairs, 27 April 2001.
29 *The Herald,* 5 June 2001.

Chapter 12

The Wheels Come Off

June–December 2001

The wheels have come off there. The situation has become untenable when it is seen that the highest office in the land seems to support illegal means of land reform, land invasions, the occupation of land, beating up of people, blood flowing everywhere. (Tito Mboweni, Governor of the South African Reserve Bank, on Zimbabwe, 22 August 2001)[1]

A vast portrait of Mugabe, enclosed in an ornate, golden frame, glowered over the government office. I sat under the President's steely gaze and listened as Jonathan Moyo explained in calm and polite tones that I was no longer welcome in Zimbabwe. The long-expected moment had finally arrived on the evening of 26 June.

I confess that Moyo had always unnerved me, and visiting him to discover whether I was about to make a hasty exit was not an experience I enjoyed. One moment he could be a model of reasonableness, the next spitting with rage. This unpredictability, the sense that he was on a hair trigger, formed a carefully contrived part of his persona. As I reclined in one of his armchairs, I had no idea whether I would see Moyo the emollient university professor of political science, or Moyo the raging propagandist.

In the weeks before this meeting, his attacks on the British media had verged on the hysterical. 'Merchants of violence' was the latest epithet that he had hurled at us. On the last occasion when I asked him a question at a press conference, my reward had been an eight-minute tirade that closed with the phrase: 'You've gone too far this time.'

Yet during most of my encounters with Moyo, he was polite, businesslike, occasionally humorous and careful to inject a sense of menace. So it was on this occasion. My residence permit was due to expire on 16 July and the *Daily Telegraph* had written to Moyo's office asking for an extension. Now he politely delivered a message that was brief and to the point. Permission had been refused. I must leave the country before the expiry of my current permit. It was 'purely an administrative matter'. I repeatedly asked for a reason, and was repeatedly rebuffed with the mantra 'It was an administrative decision'. The furthest Moyo would go was: 'We took into account several factors.'

Arrayed beside me were George Charamba, once Mugabe's spokesman, now Moyo's permanent secretary, and two other officials, both of whom took notes ostentatiously. It was quite a gathering for a 'routine' matter. As for the hint of menace that Moyo usually brought to proceedings, this time he casually let slip a detail about my future plans that he could only have learnt from a tapped telephone conversation, an intercepted e-mail or an informant. 'We have been watching you' was the not-so-subliminal message.

After this, Moyo had almost nothing to say, while Charamba remained silent and the officials did nothing but scribble. I wondered why he had bothered agreeing to a meeting. I left after half an hour, amid fake *bonhomie* and a joking invitation from Moyo to visit Zimbabwe for the solar eclipse in 2002. The point of all this was pretty clear. Moyo would claim that what amounted to my expulsion was a routine matter, of no importance whatever. If my departure drew criticism, he would put on a show of pained innocence while dispatching the last British correspondent in the country.

Less than an hour after the conclusion of this meeting, the *Daily Telegraph* faxed a letter to Moyo, urging him to reconsider his decision and pointing out that my enforced departure would attract 'widespread international coverage' and 'reflect badly on President Robert Mugabe's government'. The letter added: 'The last *Daily Telegraph* correspondent to be expelled by an African government was in 1972 by Idi Amin. Such odious comparisons would surely not serve to promote Zimbabwe's interests.'

With no doubt that Moyo would stick to his guns, I drove home immediately after leaving his office and began packing. At 6.30 the following morning the insistent ring of my mobile phone roused me. It was Firle Davies, a BBC producer in Harare and a good friend. 'Have you seen *The Herald* yet?' she asked.

'Erm no.'

'I think you should have a look. I'm afraid you've made the front page.' As I rubbed sleep from my eyes, Firle read out the story planted by Moyo:

The Tory-owned *Daily Telegraph* last night threatened the government with a tirade of bad publicity from the international media unless it renewed its resident correspondent David Blair's work permit . . . Prof. Moyo received a threatening letter from the *Daily Telegraph* . . . a situation Prof Moyo said was highly unacceptable and arrogant . . . 'this is one example where people are demanding that they must be allowed to stay in the country for as long as they like and give themselves permits'.[2]

The story continued at monotonous length and Firle and I laughed over the image of Moyo as a brave, plucky figure, standing firm against bullying by the international media and nasty journalists who presumed to award themselves *carte blanche* to stay in Zimbabwe for ever. But I could not help remembering the raid on Joe Winter's house and the propaganda blitz that he was forced to endure. Was the same in store for me? How would Moyo respond when the *Daily Telegraph,* which had scrupulously refrained from printing a word until he had been given a chance to respond to the letter, delivered a riposte to this tendentious story?

A few minutes after speaking to Firle, I decided to leave my home later that day, move somewhere safe and depart from Zimbabwe within 72 hours. In theory, I could stay for over a fortnight, until my residence permit expired, yet I had no doubt that if I tried, my departure would be hastened by the sudden arrival of four men in a high-speed car in the dead of night. Either that, or I would be stuffed into jail for a while before being put on a plane. So 27 June was the day I had long dreaded. A day filled with packing belongings, saying goodbye and enduring the faint apprehension that comes from being slated on the front page of a propaganda broadsheet in a dictatorship.

The *Daily Telegraph* was generous enough to treat my effective expulsion as the main story of the day and I was able to write a full account of my meeting with Moyo. I was made the subject of the paper's first leader, which pointed out that my enforced departure was entirely self-defeating. 'No country in a world of proliferating communications can any longer cordon itself off and make censorship effective . . . Zimbabwe will be able to suppress more of the truth, but it will fail to improve its reputation as a result.'[3] Not for the first time, Moyo was scoring an own goal on behalf of his master.

Friends around the world were kind enough to call with their good wishes and it was reassuring to know that I was not alone. Jack Straw, the British Foreign Secretary, issued a statement of concern. The International Press Institute in Vienna wrote to Mugabe, asking him to overrule Moyo and allow me to stay. Basildon Peta, Secretary-General of the Zimbabwe Union of Journalists and one of the most courageous people I have ever met, condemned 'in the strongest possible terms' the decision to get rid of me. In Johannesburg the South African National Editors' Forum said it was 'appalled'.

As darkness fell, I moved out of my home in the suburb of Borrowdale and drove to York Lodge, a quiet and secluded refuge several miles away, where I hoped I would be safe from anything Moyo had in mind. That night I dined with what remained of the Harare press corps, who joked about the likelihood of my next meal being in Chikurubi maximum security prison.

Nothing happened that night and on the morning of 28 June, there were no calls at dawn, meaning that Moyo's counterblast in *The Herald* could not have been too serious. It took the form of a gloriously witless cartoon, portraying me with an enormous nose, wearing a vast panama hat and ragged trousers that barely covered my knees. 'The Zimbabwe immigration department has refused to renew my work permit. What shall I do?' I was shown asking plaintively. Beside me was a large newspaper with spindly legs and arms, carrying the label: 'DAILY TELEGRAPH'. Brandishing a pen in a threatening fashion, the paper was saying: 'Don't worry, we will BOMB Zimbabwe with bad publicity until it gives in.' If that was the best they could do, there seemed little to worry about, but I was still advised not to risk spending a night at home.

It took Moyo's propaganda machine a while to get into gear. When it did, *The Herald* carried the headline 'David Blair had different agenda' and described me as: 'A rabid racist who should never have been allowed to enter Zimbabwe in the first place' and a 'vile character'. My articles had been: 'Insulting to the government and their supporters, provocative in the extreme, designed to create divisions among the people of Zimbabwe and cause black-on-black violence, blatantly one-sided and a complete distortion of the current realities.' I was, apparently, 'an agent of a ruling class which is known for its contempt for poor people'.[4] The piece hinted darkly that I had some involvement in the murder of Patrice Lumumba, the Congolese leader, in 1961.

I left Harare on 30 June, seen off at the airport by my colleagues, who had lived through the turbulent fortunes of the press in Zimbabwe. Jan Raath, the veteran correspondent of *The Times*, had been chucked out in 1986, despite being a Zimbabwean citizen, although the government relented and allowed him back after a few months. Other seasoned hands like Angus Shaw of Associated Press had seen off the many journalists expelled by Ian Smith.

In accordance with what my colleagues called 'a long-standing tradition', allegedly observed by all journalists (or 'agents of the ruling class') leaving Harare compulsorily, a solar topee was plonked on my head, an Arsenal scarf draped around my shoulders and a picture taken of me underneath a portrait of Mugabe. This tradition, probably designed to cause 'black-on-black violence', failed to get me arrested on departure. I was in Johannesburg a few hours later. I have no hope of returning to Zimbabwe while Mugabe's government remains in power. But while that country may be out of sight, it is never out of mind.

★   ★   ★

Barely five weeks later, pillars of smoke were rising into the clear winter skies over the lush, agricultural heartland of Zimbabwe. The verdant fields of Mashonaland, north of the town of Chinhoyi, a beautiful area of green plains and rocky kopjes that I had come to know well, were the scene of carefully organized attacks on white-owned farms, on a scale unequalled in the peacetime history of the country. Almost 50 farms were looted and wrecked, forcing the evacuation of at least 350 people from their homes. Women and children fled as Zanu-PF mobs were turned loose, with the open collusion of the police. In short, a corner of Zimbabwe was ethnically cleansed, spreading yet more terror. It was a vivid reminder that over 900 white farms were still occupied by invaders, and landowners were among Mugabe's principal targets.

The pretext for the operation came on 6 August, when a mob of squatters massed at the gates of Liston Shields farm near Chinhoyi. As they broke through the security fence and tried to smash down the door of the home-stead, Tony Barkley, the farmer, decided he could not face this emergency alone. He sent out an emergency call on the radio and 15 of his neighbours responded. What happened next remains in dispute to this day. Zanu-PF leaders claim that when these landowners rushed to Barkley's rescue, they launched a vicious attack on the squatters. Philip Chiyangwa, the local MP and Zanu-PF provincial chairman, told me: 'White farmers ganged up. They went haywire. They attacked innocent people who were settling on their land. Some of them lost their limbs in the process. The result was that they incensed the settlers.'[5]

Furious farmers described this version of events as a travesty of the truth. When they drove towards Barkley's home, they said squatters stoned their cars and launched yet another attack on them. Police were quickly on the scene – a suspicious departure from normal behaviour – and clearly decided that only one side of the story was worth listening to. All 15 farmers were rounded up and dumped in the cells at Chinhoyi police station. When six of their friends visited them to deliver food and blankets, they were promptly arrested as well and thrust behind bars.

This was the signal for a renewed bout of mob violence. On the follow-ing day, 7 August, gangs rampaged through the centre of Chinhoyi, assaulting any white people they found, including elderly women. Mag-dalina Hartmann, 72, was beaten as she queued in a post office by an assailant who screeched 'white bitch' over and over again. Another woman in her sixties was attacked in a supermarket. Hendrik Spreeth, a local man, was stabbed in the street and needed 20 stitches for two wounds. In all, ten people were injured and the entire white population of Chinhoyi – about 150 strong – fled the town.

I was not surprised to learn that all this had unfolded in Chinhoyi, a town I had visited often. The provincial capital of Mashonaland West was one of those places which Zanu-PF controlled from top to bottom – the policemen were all party loyalists, most of the nearby farms had been invaded and the occupying mobs provided the muscle for any dirty work that needed to be done. Zanu-PF's local headquarters – a shabby building just off the town's main street – was already notorious as a torture centre and armed camp. Shortly before the election, I had met three men who were imprisoned and beaten in one of its backrooms. Not surprisingly, all the evidence suggested that the attacks were carefully organized and targeted on any whites visiting the farmers held behind bars. Police openly colluded with the marauding gangs and refused to accept reports of assaults.

Worse was to follow as a major operation swung into gear. At 5.50 a.m. on 9 August, a mob gathered at the gates of the homestead on Two Tree Hill farm near Lion's Den, 30 miles north of Chinhoyi. The gang confronted Charl Geldenhuys, the farm's manager, alongside his wife Tertia, their daughter Resje, 11, and ten-month-old baby boy, Charl-Emil. As the family cowered inside their home, the thugs shouted: 'We want you out, we want you out here. We want to see your blood flow.' Meanwhile, the gang felled trees across the access roads, sealing off the farm and preventing neighbours from rushing to the family's aid.

Then they set about looting the place. Trapped inside the homestead, the family watched as the farm's workshop and sheds were pulled to pieces by the gang of 70, who loaded their booty on to Geldenhuys's nine tractors and trailers, driving the vehicles away in relays. Many of the looters were drunk and they hurled threats at the terrified family. Tertia Geldenhuys remembered that her daughter 'saw one man with mad eyes trying to climb the fence. She was convinced he was going to kill her father and mother. Then, she thought, she would be alone in the house with the baby. Every now and then she started sobbing and screaming uncontrollably. I then had to try and calm her.' Charl Geldenhuys called the police time and again, but no help arrived.

Eventually, the gang tired of looting and massed around the security fence surrounding the homestead, while one man broke through the gate by smashing its lock with an axe. When a guard dog ran towards him, he casually drew a handgun and shot the animal dead. In panic, Charl Geldenhuys ran outside, shouting for the mob to leave his family alone. The looter took a shot at him but missed. His wife and children huddled inside and listened to the firing, assuming the worst. 'I thought 70 war vets were going to rush in and kill us all,' Tertia wrote. 'I called Resje and explained to her that the reason why we live is to die one day, and that day was today. In a short while, we would all be together in heaven with God.'

But the mob did not storm the farmhouse. Instead, they returned to looting everything around it, while the family packed their belongings and prepared to abandon their home to the gang. At 3 p.m., after over nine hours of terror, the police finally arrived. They were not alone. With the officers were three of the most powerful men in the area – Peter Chanetsa, the Provincial Governor, Ignatius Chombo, the Local Government Minister, and Chiyangwa, revelling in his role as party supremo. A camera crew from state television was on hand and it soon became clear that the Geldenhuys family would not only be terrified, but publicly humiliated into the bargain.

Chombo, a burly man wearing a suit and tie, confronted them outside their home and, as Tertia cradled her baby, accused them of being responsible for everything. 'So you shot at this innocent man and missed him and killed your own dog today,' said the minister. Speechless with shock, the family listened as he berated them, while the cameras recorded every minute of their discomfort. While the mob hovered around the homestead and Charl-Emil alternately sobbed or sucked his thumb, Chombo accused his parents of colluding with other farmers to attack 'innocent black settlers' on their land. 'Government is not quite amused by that,' was his curious way of explaining that events on Two Tree Hill farm were, in some way, justified retribution. Then the minister and his delegation left, while the Geldenhuys family packed everything they could carry and fled their home.[6]

All around them, similar scenes were being repeated. Gangs up to 300 strong were systematically looting farms around Doma, Mhangura and Lion's Den. In response, the farming community ordered a general evacuation and every family fled the area. By nightfall on 9 August, 19 farms had been wrecked and abandoned and the mayhem continued unabated. On 10 August another nine properties were stormed and looted, while small convoys took farming families to safety. Black workers were too numerous to be evacuated and they were left at the mercy of the gangs. Scores were assaulted and hundreds driven from their homes. Not content with wanton destruction, by 11 August the mobs were blocking roads and preventing overland evacuation, so three light aircraft were brought in by farmers and used to rescue families trapped by the gangs. Some farmers began painting radio call signs on the roofs of homesteads, helping the planes to communicate with them – a tactic last used during the bush war of the 1970s.

The looting went beyond simple theft. Light fittings were torn from walls, taps left running, windows shattered and gaping holes smashed through roofs. Two farms were set alight and razed to the ground, while everywhere else, anything that could not be carried – a grand piano in one case, washing machines on many occasions – was vandalized and destroyed. The clear intention was to make these farms uninhabitable and prevent their owners from ever returning. This was ethnic cleansing with a vengeance, and as many as 4,000 thugs were involved.[7]

The looting only subsided on 15 August, after six days of mayhem, and by then almost every farm in the selected area had been abandoned and destroyed. The authorities had, quite clearly, mounted the whole operation. Police made some belated arrests, but earlier, they had stood by and watched while their vehicles were actually used to transport stolen goods. One eye-witness after another testified to this and the *Daily News* carried a detailed account on 14 August.

By their visit to Two Tree Hill Farm, Chanetsa, Chombo and Chiyangwa had shown that they were, at the very least, co-operating with the mobs. Without the approval of these local supremos, the latter two being blood relatives of Mugabe, how could the looting have continued for so long? Chiyangwa was later caught on camera ordering a Zanu-PF gang to hunt down MDC supporters: 'I don't want to see any MDC people campaigning in my area. Look for him, thrash him within an inch of his life. By the time you catch him, beat him so hard that when he reports it, he can't blame anyone. It's his problem.'[8] These were the words of a rising star of Zanu-PF.

The 21 white farmers whose imprisonment had begun all the trouble were, incidentally, held in freezing cells for 17 days before being granted bail. They were repeatedly paraded on state television, handcuffed, shackled, wearing prison uniform and with their heads shaved. John Nkomo, the Home Affairs Minister, declared them guilty of causing the violence before they had even appeared in court. 'The farmers have been attacking people,' he said. 'No war veterans have been causing any violence.'[9] When Nkomo spoke those words, the entire white community of Chinhoyi had already fled this non-existent violence.

How did the regime seek to explain away this series of outrages? By common consent, the cover story they eventually arrived at excelled even their own renowned standards of absurdity. The official line was as follows. The white farmers had looted their own farms because the British told them to. I am not making this up. *The Herald* broke this feat of investigative journalism beneath the headline 'EXPOSED'. Peter Chanetsa seized on the presence of the light aircraft evacuating families and favoured the world with the following statement on 22 August:

> Investigations into the forces behind the mass looting have established that the farmers instructed their farmworkers to randomly loot their

properties whilst two fixed wing aircraft and a helicopter equipped with powerful photographic and transmitting gadgets hoovered (*sic*) above recording all the activities . . . That the said aircraft were transmitting to those on the ground coincided with an approach by the British High Commissioner Brian Donnelly who insisted on proceeding to the Doma/Mhangura area to assess the situation. These developments would therefore indicate that . . . the stage-managed looting was a preplanned (*sic*) move specifically designed to give the false impression of mass victimisation of whites and lawlessness.[10]

Such were the fiendish powers of British diplomats that they were even capable of persuading white farmers to wreck their own homes and, presumably, terrify their own children. This nonsense was, and remains, the official explanation for six days of rural anarchy during which scores of blacks were assaulted, hundreds rendered homeless and about £10 million worth of property destroyed.

This wanton destruction may well have served its purpose by sowing general terror, but it was also another giant step towards the ruination of commercial agriculture and, by extension, of the economy as a whole. On 29 June, 18 pages of *The Herald* were filled with a list of another 2,030 farms identified for seizure. By this time, 4,593 white-owned farms, about 90 per cent of the total, were in the process of being acquired. Over the next few months, mob violence forced about 25 per cent of them to close down altogether and most had faced disruption over the previous year. When farmers cannot grow food, people go hungry. That unavoidable truth was beginning to strike home. Thanks to the Mugabe model of land reform, Zimbabwe was on the brink of famine.

In April the Famine Early Warning System Network projected a 42 per cent fall in the maize crop for 2001 and forecast a shortage of 458,000 tons. By July the best estimates for the maize deficit had risen substantially. A report by the Food and Agricultural Association put the figure at 579,000 tons. To prevent a famine in the early months of 2002, Zimbabwe would have to import this amount. Yet because of the economic crisis, no foreign currency was available to cover the cost, so Mugabe would be reduced to calling for food aid. Thanks to his land policies, it was unmistakably clear that Zimbabwe, once the bread-basket of southern Africa, would suffer a self-inflicted famine in early 2002 unless the world came to its rescue. Simba Makoni, the reforming, respected and powerless Finance Minister, publicly admitted as much and sought help from the United Nations Development Programme. Joseph Made, the loyalist Agriculture Minister, blithely denied that there was any cause for alarm. 'There is no need for the government to import maize . . . I have flown around the country and seen that there is plenty of maize in the communal and resettlement areas,' he said.[11] Thankfully, no one believed him.

Zimbabwe's relentless descent baffled and appalled all of its neighbours. Prompted by the continued decline of the Rand, Tito Mboweni, Governor of the South African Reserve Bank, pulled no punches on 22 August when he said 'the wheels have come off' Zimbabwe. For his pains, he was called 'flippant, ill-considered and ill-informed',[12] by Moyo. Yet on 7 September some thought that Mugabe had, at last, been hauled back from the brink. Seven foreign ministers from Commonwealth countries, including Britain and Zimbabwe, met in Abuja, the Nigerian capital, and signed a 'breakthrough' agreement. Under this deal, Mugabe agreed 'to restore the rule of law to the process of land reform' and 'take firm action against violence and intimidation'. He gave a 'commitment to freedom of expression' and agreed that 'there will be no further occupation of farm lands'. In return, Jack Straw, signing for Britain, held out the carrot of £36 million for land reform if these conditions were met.

★   ★   ★

Did this 'breakthrough' make any difference? None whatever. Over the years, almost everyone had discovered that assurances from Mugabe were not worth the paper they were written on. It was now Straw's turn to learn this lesson the hard way after barely three months as Foreign Secretary. In the six weeks after the signing of the Abuja agreement, over 800 violent incidents were recorded on occupied farms and police remained equally unwilling to act. Despite Mugabe's 'commitment to freedom of expression', the BBC remained banned from Zimbabwe, as they had been since July, and foreign correspondents still found it impossible to get permission to visit the country. Routine harassment of the MDC continued unabated. Abuja was dead before the ink was dry.

It could not have been otherwise. Had Mugabe observed the agreement, he might as well have handed over power to Tsvangirai immediately. Without violence and intimidation he stood as much chance in the coming presidential election as Jack Straw. Observing the law would have dramatically restricted Mugabe's ability to reward his followers with white-owned land. After all, about 1,000 farms had been officially resettled under the 'Fast Track' scheme declared illegal by the Supreme Court. What was he going to do – give them all back?

True to form, Mugabe spent the last weeks of 2001 preparing the ground for his re-election with systematic thoroughness. He signalled his intention to dispossess almost every white farmer before the presidential poll by issuing a decree on 9 November. This amended the Land Acquisition Act to mean that any farmer in receipt of a 'Section 8 occupation order' now had three months to pack up and leave. In the meantime, he was confined to his home, barred from working the farm, and the resettlement of his land could begin immediately. There was no avenue for appeal. That piece of paper was the end of the line. Perhaps 1,000 farmers had already received it and Mugabe's decree was cleverly worded to apply retrospectively. Colin Cloete, who had succeeded Henwood as leader of the CFU, was reduced to saying: 'Never has our nation fallen so low.'[13]

Mugabe had, of course, been seizing farms anyway, regardless of the law, but this decree afforded a veneer of legal legitimacy to what was already happening. All that remained was for those awkward Supreme Court judgements made under Gubbay's tenure – the ones declaring the entire land resettlement programme illegal – to be somehow reversed. Having installed a reliable Chief Justice, Mugabe took the next logical step: on 28 July he packed the court with his supporters. At a stroke, the Supreme Court bench was enlarged from five members to eight and three new judges appointed – all with links to Zanu-PF. Mugabe had specifically promised not to make this move. In a meeting with seven senior lawyers from the International Bar Association back in March, he smoothly averred that he had 'no intention' of expanding the court. The delegation reported: 'We were very pleased to receive that assurance.'[14] Pleased they may have been, but it was utterly worthless.

The new appointees justified their existence on 4 December, when the Supreme Court duly ruled that Mugabe's land seizures were completely legal. All the judgements made under Gubbay were summarily reversed and the government given full authority to proceed with dispossessing white farmers. Five justices heard the case – four of them new arrivals. The one dissenting judgement came from Ahmed Ebrahim, the survivor from the Gubbay era. Chief Justice Chidyausiku used the ruling to declare that land reform was a matter of 'social justice and not, strictly speaking, a legal issue'.[15] Those were the precise words Mugabe had employed all along.

With the land problem finally solved, the President sought to do away with every last vestige of fairness in the electoral system and remove all possibility of defeat. Mugabe brought forward an entirely new set of rules for the presidential election, carefully framed to maximize his advantage. Amendments to the Electoral Act published on 7 November stripped all Zimbabweans living abroad of the right to vote – except soldiers and diplomats, who were assumed to back Mugabe. Everyone else faced unprecedented requirements for voter registration. City dwellers were ordered to produce proof of residence, in the form of title deeds, rental agreements or utility bills. When you live in a shack in a heaving township, this is quite a challenge, and hundreds of thousands of people in Tsvangirai's heartland faced being disenfranchised.

In the rural areas, the new regulations ordered village chiefs to vouch for everyone registering to vote. As each headman is paid a grant by the government and almost all support Mugabe, none would be likely to vouch for anyone suspected of backing Tsvangirai. Any chief foolish enough to do so would, doubtless, be severely dealt with. Other rules were designed to give Mugabe a free hand to run the election with one outcome in mind. The amendments banned independent observers and outlawed voter education programmes run by civic groups. At a stroke, the likes of Pierre Schori, and all those other troublesome observers who had exposed the brutality of the parliamentary election, were banished from Zimbabwe. That contest had been too close for comfort and Mugabe was clearly determined that no risks would be taken in the climactic struggle ahead.

He was also anxious to deal with the irritating press criticism that inexplicably dogged his every move. A new media law was announced on 30 November, giving the government, acting through a 'media and information commission', the right to bar journalists from working and close down newspapers. Foreigners would be prevented from entering Zimbabwe to serve overseas newspapers, while any citizen wishing to report for the international media would need special permission from the government. This proposed law sounded the death knell for the embattled *Daily News* and the other last redoubts of the free press.

Only one thing remained – an excuse for suppressing the MDC altogether. That seemed to arrive on 5 November, when Cain Nkala, an obscure official of the War Veterans' Association, was murdered in Bulawayo. His death was immediately blamed on the MDC, and a Zanu-PF mob rampaged through the city and burned down the opposition party's regional headquarters. Dozens of MDC activists were rounded up and placed behind bars on the flimsiest of charges and, by late November, the party in Matabeleland had been effectively shut down.

With the world's attention focused on the war in Afghanistan, Mugabe decided that Zimbabwe was also waging a struggle against terrorism. The dangerous terrorist group was, of course, the MDC, with Tsvangirai presumably cast as Zimbabwe's Osama bin Laden. In a grotesque parody of CNN's coverage of the American campaign in Asia, state television news in Harare was soon shown with a logo in the corner of the screen reading: 'FIGHTING TERRORISM'. In case anyone didn't get the message, Vice-President Joseph Msika gave the MDC a specific threat: 'If they are looking for a bloodbath, they will certainly get it.'[16] *The Herald* went further. It decided that the MDC was 'reliving the Nazi era' and compared Tsvangirai with Hitler.[17]

Somewhat to his own family's surprise, the wretched Nkala was declared a National Hero and buried alongside such luminaries as Hitler Hunzvi.

Mugabe, who had probably never met Nkala, delivered the eulogy at his state funeral on 18 November and chose to call the MDC and white farmers 'terrorists' no fewer than 20 times. 'The MDC perpetrators of violence and crimes against humanity and their international sponsors should also know their days are numbered. The time is now up for the MDC terrorists,' he said.[18] Mugabe took the opportunity to expand his ambitious range of conspiracy theories. He decided that the MDC was being funded not only by the British government, but also the 'British Labour party, the Conservative party and the Liberal Democratic party.'[19] Now everyone in Britain was part of the great conspiracy, except possibly the Green party.

The cast of 'terrorists' grew still further on 23 November to include my former colleagues. Jan Raath, Angus Shaw, Andy Meldrum, Basildon Peta and two other journalists serving the foreign press were slandered by an anonymous 'government spokesman' in *The Herald*. They were accused of 'assisting terrorists', and the 'spokesman' added: 'We would like them to know that we agree with President Bush that anyone who in any way finances, harbours or defends terrorists is himself a terrorist. We too will not make any difference (*sic*) between terrorists and their friends or supporters.'[20]

While the regime swirled in its own fantasies, dreaming of terrorists and conspiracies, inflation soared to 97.9 per cent, unemployment rose to 60 per cent and the economy contracted by a further 8 per cent, making it the fastest shrinking in the world. At that dizzying rate of decline, Zimbabwe would be completely de-industrialized within three years. The toll of political killings for 2001 stood at 41, bringing the total to 88 since the referendum in 2000. To this must be added 39 black farmworkers murdered by squatters.[21] On 14 December the United Nations World Food Programme announced that 558,000 Zimbabweans were in need of immediate food aid. 'We need to start delivering food to thousands of hungry people as fast as possible,' said Judith Lewis, the WFP's regional director. 'People are really struggling to survive and they're resorting to selling off meagre belongings as a last option to buy food.'[22]

On the same day, Mugabe addressed the faithful at Zanu-PF's annual Congress, held in Victoria Falls. Fear of 'terrorists' among the Harare press corps and the MDC caused a no-fly zone to be imposed over Zimbabwe's premier tourist attraction and the skies were patrolled by helicopter gunships. Beneath this impenetrable screen, Mugabe rallied his troops for the coming election. He did not talk about the half-million Zimbabweans facing starvation, the countless people eking out impoverished lives in the townships, nor the wasteland that had once been the best farming land in Africa. No, Mugabe talked about the British and the MDC. He decided that Tony Blair had been 'a very troublesome little boy at school' and readied his supporters for a 'fight' with the opposition. 'This is a real physical fight and we have to prepare for it,' he declared.[23] With his fist clenched firmly in the air, Mugabe promised to stay where he was, into an indefinite future.

★   ★   ★

Zimbabwe was a thoroughly baffling place for any outsider. As I covered one disaster after another, I often found it impossible to make sense of events and fell into believing that this was a country where people simply behaved inexplicably. That was just the way of things. Yet this was intellectually lazy. To understand Mugabe's behaviour required an appreciation of the history and political culture of his country, and here the continuity between Zimbabwe and Rhodesia was astonishing. Furthermore, the personal parallels between him and Ian Smith increasingly struck me. These two bitter foes, revelling in their hatred for one another, were so alike in method and outlook that they almost formed an unholy partnership.

To start with the cultural continuities, it is quite evident that Mugabe and his followers lived in a fantasy world, beset by wild conspiracy theories. But Smith and his gang had at least equalled their feats of imagination. In fact, conspiracy theories were the very basis of Rhodesia, and the leading lights of this extraordinary rebel state inhabited what Lord Blake called a 'strange world of fantasy'. In his magisterial *History of Rhodesia,* Blake summarized the curious beliefs entertained by Smith's followers in the Rhodesian Front:

> Theories were propounded about the hopeless and inherent inferiority of the African and the danger of a world-wide conspiracy against Rhodesia consisting not only of Communists, independent African states and international financiers, but also comprising the Fabian Society, the London School of Economics, the BBC, the American Peace Corps, the State Department, the World Council of Churches, the World Bank, UNESCO and 'other offshoots of the greatest communistic and devilish institution in the world knows as the UN' – to quote J. R. Ryan, the RF member for Salisbury Central. It was against this unholy and, one might think, somewhat improbable alliance, that the RF was doing battle on behalf of 'civilised, responsible, Christian standards'.[24]

By propounding this rubbish, Smith introduced paranoia into his country's politics. He embedded this corrosive culture in its government. Mugabe simply picked up where his old foe had left off. In fact, he even inherited the cast list of evil conspirators. The very same forces that had sought to do down Rhodesia were, it seemed, massing against Zimbabwe. The BBC, international financiers, the State Department and the World Bank were, in

Mugabe's view, seeking his overthrow as well. Moreover, the American Peace Corps was barred from working in Zimbabwe in 2001 and the World Council of Churches prevented from sending observers to cover the parliamentary polls of 2000. Same conspiracy, same conspirators.

As for the propensity of Zimbabwean politicians to take wild decisions based on nothing but delusion, they had also learned this from Rhodesia. Historians wring their hands when asked to explain Smith's decision to commit treason and transform his country into a rebel state with the Unilateral Declaration of Independence in 1965. Having interviewed every leading figure in Smith's government and the man himself, Blake was reduced to writing:

> I found it almost impossible to extract any logical reasons for UDI from the many members of the RF or its sympathisers who were kind enough to listen to my questions . . . UDI becomes a piece of madness, a sort of collective rush of blood to the head that cannot be explained by rational means at all.[25]

Mugabe's Zimbabwe was run by several people who, not to mince words, were a few apples short of a picnic. So was Smith's Rhodesia. His crew included the likes of the Duke of Montrose, who served as Agriculture Minister. When Harold Wilson visited Salisbury in October 1965 and was given a banquet by the Rhodesian élite, His Grace's idea of entertaining their guest was to mount the table and dance a jig, while keeping a penny clenched between his buttocks. At the conclusion of this performance, the Duke proudly demonstrated to the Prime Minister that the penny had indeed remained in place. Montrose was, at least, a harmless lunatic. That could not be said of some in Smith's cabinet. P. K. van der Byl, the grisly character who served variously at the Information, Defence and Foreign Ministries, would reportedly fill his spare hours by clattering over the plains in a helicopter, taking pot shots at blacks below.[26] Compared with this, Hunzvi and company seem pretty normal.

Rhodesia was a rebel state, standing alone against the rest of the world, in pursuit of an ideal that Smith clung to with blinding fervour. Equally, by the close of 2001, Mugabe was totally isolated, not only from the developed world, but increasingly from his African neighbours as well. He revelled in this sense of embattlement and struggle and justified it by reference to his own ideal. For in his own terms, Mugabe's actions were entirely rational. He was, emphatically, not deranged. He had a vision of an independent, self-sufficient country, where the indigenous black people would till all the land and reward their leader by keeping him in power for ever. To achieve this goal, he was willing to bear isolation, while seeking to rationalize it by reference to an imaginative array of conspiracy theories, just as Smith had done.

As for the personal parallels between the two men, perhaps the most obvious is their limitless capacity for self-delusion. Both are serial fantasists. As we have seen, Mugabe could convince himself that the British were intercepting his oil supplies on the high seas, massing an invasion force in Botswana and sending hit squads to assassinate his cabinet. Perhaps most dangerously, he was also in the habit of deciding that solemn assurances given by him at public occasions had not, in fact, taken place at all.

Equally, Smith's turgid, unreadable memoirs are notable only for being packed with fantasy. He is capable of claiming that he was in favour of black majority rule all along and, by the way, every African had the vote in Rhodesia. Thus Smith writes:

> At no time in the history of our country was there any attempt to interfere with free access to the voters' roll and the principle of unimpeded progress to majority rule. But right up to the present day one still comes across articles accusing Rhodesians of trying to perpetuate white minority rule – such is the power of the Communist propaganda machine![27]

Coming from a man who passed a new constitution in 1969 that made majority rule impossible for centuries and then declared: 'I don't believe in black majority rule ever in Rhodesia, not in a thousand years,'[28] this striking statement can only be explained by a propensity for self-serving delusion on a truly Mugabe-esque scale.

Yet the most tragic parallel between the two men is also the most crucial. Everything that Smith did was completely futile and self-defeating. Because of UDI, the black opposition was radicalized and took to the bush for an armed struggle. In a country where the white minority was 4 per cent of the population and falling year on year, it should have been obvious that the guerrilla war was un-winnable. Moreover, the problem with brutal conflicts is that they produce leaders like Mugabe. With almost uncanny incompetence, Smith waited until Mugabe had achieved dominance over the liberation movement and then waited a little more, until Rhodesia had effectively lost the war and the moment of maximum weakness had arrived, before choosing to negotiate a settlement. The result was Lancaster House, and the rest we know. The final outcome of UDI was that white Rhodesia dealt with its most dangerous enemy at the point when its hand was weakest. The endgame was a transfer of power after a pointless war, on terms far worse than could have been achieved 15 years earlier. In a bitter irony, Smith did more than anyone else to bring Mugabe to power, and the old

Rhodesian must therefore take his share of the blame for all that followed.

The law of unintended consequences will also destroy the last tattered shreds of Mugabe's reputation, even among his most ardent followers. Zimbabwe will not emerge from his rule as a proud, self-sufficient nation, with prosperous black people owning all of their land. As is already evident, Mugabe will soon be dependent on the Western world to feed his people. Thanks to an officially inflicted disaster, Zimbabwe will be reduced to proffering a permanent begging bowl to the World Food Programme. When Mugabe finally takes his leave, nothing is more obvious than that Britain, the IMF, the World Bank and every donor country will assemble an international rescue package to help clear up the damage he wrought on his country. Because of Mugabe, Zimbabweans will be more dependent on the goodwill of the Western world and less in control of their own destiny than at any time in their country's history. Coupled with his disastrous management of the economy, Mugabe's land grab will prove just as futile and counter-productive for him as UDI was for Smith. The only difference is that Mugabe may not live to see the consequences and we might be spared his memoirs.

Between them, Mugabe and Smith have dominated their country since 1964. For 37 years these two proud, brave, stubborn, charismatic, deluded fantasists have held the reins of power. Looking at their respective records, I suggest that only one further point needs to be made. Neither should have been allowed anywhere near running a country. Smith's true station in life was, perhaps, treasurer of a provincial rugby club. Mugabe would have made an excellent junior lecturer at the Revolutionary University of Havana. It was their country's enduring tragedy that these men were given such power.

If Morgan Tsvangirai becomes their President, most Zimbabweans will be euphoric and this emotion will, for once, be entirely justified. Unlike his predecessors, he is not a fantasist, nor does he have their cold indifference to human life, developed by all leaders who have fought wars. On the contrary, he is warm, gregarious, likeable and, above all, refreshingly normal. It is impossible to imagine Tsvangirai heaping vitriol on an ethnic minority or inciting his followers to violence. His two most striking qualities are courage and charisma. Challenging Mugabe has required extraordinary amounts of clear-eyed, steely bravery. Tsvangirai has proved equal to the task and, among many Zimbabweans, particularly the urban poor, he is nothing less than a folk hero.

But there are two areas where Tsvangirai is untested. He would take over a bankrupt, devastated country and he has yet to show that he has the grasp of policy detail and the imagination needed to turn the situation around. His own ideological journey has been an erratic one. He first attacked Mugabe from the left, after the government's acceptance of an IMF Structural

Adjustment Programme in 1991. Now he leads a party committed to engagement with the rest of the world. Like its leader, the MDC is steeped in Zimbabwe's trade union movement. Tension between this faction in the party and their rivals from what remains of the country's commercial and industrial base is already evident. Tsvangirai will have to resolve this tension quickly. I have no doubt that the realist in him will push his government to throw in its lot with the IMF, however much his heart may harbour doubts.

This brings us to his second possible weakness. If Tsvangirai takes power, he will find himself in the centre of a political minefield. The MDC is a disparate coalition, stretching from urban workers to poor township dwellers to employees of shambolic state industries to white landowners to black farmworkers to well-heeled businessmen. The one thing that unites all these people is opposition to Mugabe. Take him out of the equation and put the MDC in power and the party could fragment. Keeping it together will require political cunning of an order that Tsvangirai has not yet shown.

Furthermore, restoring order in Zimbabwe may prove extraordinarily difficult. Mugabe has politicized the highest echelons of the police, army and civil service. His placemen hold all of the key positions. Will they be willing to take orders from Tsvangirai? One of the first things the new government will have to do is restore order on commercial farms – the *sine qua non* for economic recovery – and this will require the eviction of thousands of people from white-owned land. Will soldiers and policemen, effectively members of the uniformed wing of Zanu-PF, obey orders to carry out an operation of this sort? Even if they do, could chaos then result? The famous 'war veterans' would like nothing better than for Tsvangirai's early days in power to be scarred by a bloodbath that could take on the appearance of civil war.

Tsvangirai's government should, I suggest, have three immediate priorities. The first must be economic recovery, without which nothing else can be achieved. The best analysis suggests that the damage done to Zimbabwe's economy is so profound that no revival will be possible without a large injection of capital from outside. Perhaps $1 billion will be needed. Within days, Tsvangirai will have to hammer out a deal with the donors and the IMF and begin economic reform.

Second, he will have to tackle the catastrophic AIDS epidemic. This book has neglected the hideous damage this disease is inflicting on every level of Zimbabwean society. Let me offer one illustration – in the ten weeks I have spent writing this book, 0.001 per cent of all Zimbabweans have died of AIDS.[29] At least 25 per cent of the adult population is infected with HIV and, if nothing is done, life expectancy will plummet to 27 within ten years. Mugabe has lamentably failed to get to grips with this growing disaster, and if Zimbabwe is to survive as a country, it must be tackled. This can only be done with outside help and, here again, Tsvangirai will have to act within days.

Third, no Zimbabwean government will have any peace until the land issue is settled once and for all. Tsvangirai has said as much to me on many occasions. The MDC has sensibly proposed handing over the matter to an independent commission, on which everyone will be represented, and giving it the freedom to hammer out a solution, balancing the needs of the landless poor with the interests of commercial farmers. There is universal consensus behind the need for land reform and it should not take long for a plan to be worked out, once Mugabe's corrosive fingertips are removed from the issue.

Those will be the immediate priorities, but Tsvangirai will face many daunting tasks: taking the endemic violence out of Zimbabwean politics, framing a new, home-grown constitution that allows for genuine democracy, and withdrawing his troops from the Congo, to name but three. But he will have one key advantage. Tsvangirai will be buoyed by the wave of relief and euphoria that will accompany Mugabe's departure. People will cheer him in the streets, while donors queue up to throw money at him. He must use that honeymoon period to the full.

But all this is to run ahead of ourselves – he will have to take office first. What are Tsvangirai's chances of coming to power in the election that must come before 1 April 2002? As we have seen, Mugabe is busily tilting the electoral playing field in his favour to the point where it threatens to become vertical. Combine the one-sided electoral arrangements with the incessant political violence still sweeping the country, and it is difficult to see how Tsvangirai can prevail. Thanks to almost two years of repression, the MDC barely functions in Midlands, Masvingo or the three provinces of Mashonaland. It was once dominant in Matabeleland, but the post-Nkala crackdown has dealt it a major blow. That only leaves the cities, and here the new rules could disenfranchise many of its voters. Revulsion with Mugabe is such that the election will still be an open contest, and a Tsvangirai victory cannot be discounted, but the chances are not great. In all likelihood, Mugabe will, somehow, win through.

Yet if Mugabe is re-elected at the age of 78, supposedly to serve another six-year term over a devastated country, it is hard to see him surviving for long. His era is, quite plainly, drawing to a close. All that remains to be seen is how much damage will be done before he finally departs. I fail to understand how he can possibly survive the looming whirlwind of 2002 – economic collapse, famine, international isolation. At some stage the patience of his people will crack and a popular revolt will sweep him away, Milosevic-style. Or nature may suddenly intervene and remove him from the scene.

Whatever fate has in store for Mugabe, political change will come in 2002, and not before time. For only new leadership will allow Zimbabwe to recover from its vicious spiral of decline – nothing could be clearer than that. This tantalizing vision of change is all that Zimbabweans have left to cling on to. Every last hope is vested in this one final chance for a country that was – and could yet be – the jewel of Africa.

NOTES AND REFERENCES

1 Speech, African investment seminar, Stellenbosch, 22 August 2001, reported on News24 (SA).
2 *The Herald,* 27 June 2001.
3 *Daily Telegraph,* 28 June 2001.
4 *The Herald,* 19 July 2001.
5 Interview with the author, 7 August 2001 (by telephone, obviously).
6 Extracts from Chombo's confrontation with the Geldenhuys family were shown on ZBC, SABC and Channel 4 News.
7 CFU estimate, statement by Colin Cloete, 15 August 2001.
8 Shown on Channel 4 News, 3 September 2001.
9 ZBC, 8 August 2001.
10 Statement by Governor Chanetsa, 22 August 2001.
11 *The Herald,* 7 May 2001.
12 News24 (SA), 28 August 2001.
13 CFU statement, 15 November 2001.
14 International Bar Association report, sec. 12.34.
15 Quoted in SAPA (South African Press Association Newsagency) report, 5 December 2001.
16 *The Chronicle* (Bulawayo), 12 November 2001.
17 *The Herald,* 14 November 2001. This piece by Phillip Magwaza ranks with Christopher Mushohwe's attack on Gubbay in parliament as the last word in Zanu-PF paranoia. I found both very funny. They would make a Zimbabwean weep.
18 Speech, Nkala's funeral, 18 November 2001.
19 *Ibid.*
20 *The Herald,* 23 November 2001.
21 Figures from Zimbabwe Human Rights Forum and CFU. In total, eight white farmers were murdered between April 2000 and December 2001. A figure of nine is sometimes given. This includes Willem Botha, who was not a farmer and whose killing had no political motive.
22 BBC news online, 14 December 2001.
23 *Ibid.*
24 Robert Blake, *History of Rhodesia,* Methuen, London, 1977, p. 374.
25 *Ibid.,* pp. 382–3.

26 See Max Hastings, *Going to the Wars*, Macmillan, London, 2000, p. 187.
27 Ian Smith, *The Great Betrayal*, Blake, London, 1997, p. 103.
28 Televised statement, RBC, 20 March 1976, shown on BBC TV, *Rebellion*.
29 Based on Ministry of Health estimate of 1,200 deaths per week and a population of 12 million. The 1,200 figure is probably conservative.

Index

The index covers names of all people and places mentioned in this account as well as the main events and organizations.